Reasoning

Reasoning

A Social Picture

Anthony Simon Laden

OXFORD
UNIVERSITY PRESS

OXFORD
UNIVERSITY PRESS

Great Clarendon Street, Oxford, OX2 6DP,
United Kingdom

Oxford University Press is a department of the University of Oxford.
It furthers the University's objective of excellence in research, scholarship,
and education by publishing worldwide. Oxford is a registered trade mark of
Oxford University Press in the UK and in certain other countries

© Anthony Simon Laden 2012

The moral rights of the author[s] have been asserted

First Edition published in 2012
First published in paperback 2014

Published in the United States of America by Oxford University Press
198 Madison Avenue, New York, NY 10016, United States of America

British Library Cataloguing in Publication Data
Data available

Library of Congress Cataloguing in Publication Data
Data available

ISBN 978-0-19-960619-1 (Hbk)

ISBN 978-0-49-870641-0 (Pbk)

For Jacob, Raphaël, and Clara

Preface and Acknowledgements

I used to want to be a game theorist. Not just any kind of game theorist, mind you, but a game theorist who would analyze the rules and norms of reasonable interaction. I thought I might develop a formal theory to describe the norms that govern the give and take of people who are concerned to be responsive to one another rather than to each maximally satisfy their ends. And even when I drifted away from game theory, I still harbored an ambition to develop a formal theory of reasonableness.

This book was born from that ambition, and finally lays it to rest. But not in the manner I expected when I began. In the course of writing it, I came to see that while we need a clear and detailed picture of the interactive activities that call for reasonableness, such a picture will not yield the kind of formal theory I once aimed for. I have become increasingly convinced that our extant ways of thinking about reasoning distort our understanding of the responsive, reciprocal interaction that calls for reasonableness. There are, I have come to see, two very different kinds of activities that we routinely call "reasoning." We reason to figure things out, solve problems, and reach judgments. This is the activity philosophers and social scientists, as well as game-theorists, generally have in mind when they think about reasoning. But we also reason in the course of living together, when we are responsive to those with whom we live and neither commanding nor deferring to them. The reasoning that goes into responsive living together is the subject of this book. When philosophers and social scientists analyze this second kind of activity, they tend to use the tools and frameworks developed to make sense of the first kind of activity. It is my contention that that approach has been a mistake. If we are to truly see and appreciate the requirements and values of the activities that call for reasonableness, we need to learn to approach them differently. Doing so turns out to require not a new formal theory of the reasonable, but a more thoroughgoing reorientation in our thinking: what I call a social picture of reasoning.

According to this social picture, reasoning is an activity that is social and ongoing. It consists of inviting others to accept that our words can speak for them as well. Reasoning, so understood, is a species of conversation, not a genus that includes more specific paths to judgment such as deduction, induction, and abduction. It is a form of relating to others that can be contrasted with non-reciprocal forms of interaction such as commanding and obeying, ignoring or manipulating. It is governed by a set of characteristic norms. But it turns out not to be susceptible to description by the kind of formalism that rational choice theory provides.

Although this book does not achieve my early ambition, it does, in important senses, go beyond it. More than offering a novel theory, it invites the reader to think differently. Thinking differently requires making a kind of leap. You can't get there by building out from your accustomed ways of thinking in small, manageable steps. This book is an attempt to say what things look like on the other side of that leap, because that is the only way I know how to entice others to take it. But you should be warned that if you are unwilling at some point to make such a leap into a different way of thinking about reasoning and what kind of activity at least some forms of reasoning are, then the sum total of arguments in this book are likely to leave you unsatisfied.

Because I am concerned here to bring into view a different way of thinking about what reasoning is and does, and because this is a work of philosophy, and thus takes itself to be an instance of reasoning, the book has certain features that call for comment. First, if reasoning is a matter of inviting others to see what you see rather than compelling them to agree with you, then philosophy, or at least some forms of it, has to adopt the voice and idiom of invitation. I try to do this here. In part, that means that I focus on showing the attractions of thinking about reasoning as the social picture describes it rather than showing conclusively why we must think this way if certain other premises are true. I don't think we must, of necessity, be reasonable, but I do think we lose a great deal if we fail to be. And if we cannot even get the activities that call for reasonableness clearly into view, we may not even be aware of what we are missing.

Second, in trying to describe an activity that I take to be central to human living together, I have tried to do so in a way that avoids the technicalities and the internecine debates that characterize much contemporary philosophy. I have relegated most discussions of and comparisons with the work of other philosophers to the footnotes. My hope is that this strategy allows an uncluttered presentation of the main line of argument while nevertheless offering guideposts by which those readers who wish to can situate this project among better-known ones.

Third, throughout the book I make use of examples from Jane Austen's *Pride and Prejudice*. In fact, more words are spent discussing passages from Austen's novel than are spent discussing the details of other philosophical views. I did not start out to write so much commentary on the novel or make it as central as it has become to the writing of the book. I began looking to Austen for some diverting examples of conversation, and with the thought of inserting some elegant wit into the tedious prose of philosophy. But I found that the more time I spent with it, the more I realized that *Pride and Prejudice* explores a picture of reasoning very similar to my own. Of course, the time and social structures of Austen's novel are very different from our own and the conventions governing the kinds of conversations and interactions that make up her novels do not hold sway over our own conversations. And yet, I don't think that unfits them as examples here. For one thing, what counts as reasonable in *Pride and Prejudice* is, as in this book, a kind of responsiveness to others, rather than a deference to a social order of reason and value. Though such responsiveness can be shaped by the conventions of one's time and place, it is not determined by them, and so we should be able to recognize such reasonableness and its absence, even across the divide of centuries.

Finally, there is a feature of this book that is essential to its genesis and aspiration but is almost entirely absent from its pages. In thinking about reasoning, I have been deeply influenced by the work of feminists, critical race theorists, and others who have been critical of the work of philosophy for its reliance on what might be called false universalizations, and an associated attitude of arrogance towards ways of thinking and living that do not fit into its theories. I do not think that contemporary analytic philosophy has taken these criticisms sufficiently to heart. One of my hopes for this book is that it does better. Though it is not a work of feminism, post-colonialism, or race theory in the traditional sense, it can be read as providing resources for such projects. At the very least, I would be remiss in not here expressing my gratitude for all that this critical work has done to shape my own.

I have been fortunate in trying to think through these matters in the many people who have been willing to think with me. I learned early on the value and joys of non-combative philosophy from James Tully and the late

John Rawls, how to think clearly and well about reasons and rationality from Amartya Sen and Chris Korsgaard, and how to think about the social with Hegel from Fred Neuhouser. Though the roots of this book lie in ambitions that date to my earliest days studying philosophy, it first came to seem like a real project during a semester-long leave at the Institute for the Humanities at the University of Illinois at Chicago in the spring of 2005. During that semester, I gave a talk there entitled "How to Derive the Rational from the Reasonable (a Sketch)," part of which lives again in Chapter 7. In the following years, I wrote three other papers, parts of and ideas from which find their way, in one form or another, into the current book. "Evaluating Social Reasons: Hobbes vs. Hegel" was published in the *Journal of Philosophy* in 2005 and now makes up parts of Chapters 7 and 8. "Negotiation, Deliberation and the Claims of Politics" appeared in *Multiculturalism and Political Theory* (2007), a book I co-edited with David Owen, and many of its arguments are now to be found in Chapter 6. Finally, "The Trouble with Prudence" was published in *Philosophical Explorations* in 2009, and some of its ideas find their way into Chapter 8.

The remaining pieces that went into making up the social picture came together during 2007–8, a year of research leave generously supported by UIC and a Research Fellowship from the Alexander von Humboldt Stiftung, hosted by Christoph Menkein Potsdam and Axel Honneth in Frankfurt. Beyond Axel and Christoph, I am grateful to the following conversation partners for making that year such a stimulating and productive one: Stefan Gosepath, Robin Cellikates, Candace Vogler, Ciaran Cronin, and Paul Patton in Berlin, and Rainer Forst, Marcus Willaschek, Martin Saar, Jörg Schaub, and the members of Axel's colloquium in Frankfurt. The book took form as a book for the first time during a sabbatical semester in the spring of 2009 granted by the Philosophy Department at the University of Illinois at Chicago. I taught an earlier version of it to my seminar in Social and Political Philosophy at UIC in the fall of 2009 and benefitted enormously from those discussions and the members of the seminar's probing questions, many of which I fear still remain unanswered. A later version was the subject of two very helpful meetings of a Chicago area Ethics reading group, and I am grateful for the participation of Richard Kraut, Kyla Ebels Duggan, Jon Garthoff, Andy Koppelman, Charles Mills, Anne Eaton, and Sam Fleischacker in those conversations. The last round of major and minor revisions were completed during the summer of 2011, and were supported in part by a grant from the Spencer Foundation, which also supported work on earlier revisions.

Throughout this entire process I have been fortunate to have the best colleagues in philosophy, colleagues who regard both the work of philosophy and of a philosophy department as a collective endeavor, done together and not merely side-by-side, and I have especially benefitted in the development of the ideas in this book from discussions with and feedback from Anne Eaton, Sam Fleischacker, Marya Schechtman, Charles Mills, Sally Sedgwick, and Peter Hylton.

David Owen, Jim Tully, Talbot Brewer, Tamar Schapiro, Elizabeth Anderson, Patchen Markell, and Tamar Szabo Gendler have all read parts of this project at various points and given me valuable feedback. David, and especially Jim, deserve special mention for having read multiple versions of the whole manuscript. My friend Mike Friedman (not the philosopher) kindly read Chapter 1 to tell me if it made any sense to a non-philosopher. It is hoped that the current version does. I have presented parts of it under various titles to the Philosophy Departments at Indiana University, the University of Southampton, the University of Utrecht, Monica Betzler's colloquium in Berne, Axel Honneth's colloquium in Frankfurt, members of the Excellence Cluster on the Formation of Normative Orders in Frankfurt, the philosophy and social sciences conference in Prague (2008), the Political Science Department of the Catholic University of Lublin, Poland, a meeting of the Dewey Seminar on Education, Justice and Democracy at the Institute of Advanced Studies in Princeton, and a conference on Reason and Power in Frankfurt. I am grateful for all those opportunities and the discussions they afforded.

Peter Momtchiloff expressed interest in and enthusiasm for this project when it was still a vague aspiration, and has been patient, wise, helpful, and all things one would want in an editor since. The three anonymous readers he found gave me much to think about, and what more could an author ask for from his readers? To all those who have read versions of this project, I have done what I could to respond to your responses. I have not answered or silenced all your criticisms and concerns. But I hope to have moved our conversations forward. If I am right here about the value of the activity of reasoning, perhaps that is enough. Turning the words of a manuscript into the object you are holding in your hands (or reading on your screen) required the help of several other people, and I am grateful to my copy-editor Martin Barr, and to Eleanor Collins, Daniel Bourner, and the rest of the production team at Oxford for their help.

No acknowledgements to a work on living and reasoning together would be complete without much heartfelt thanks to and love for those with whom I live, and who teach me every day how to live well: to Caroline Guindon, who makes me laugh and helps me think, and who always has good reasons, and to our children, Clara, Raphaël, and Jacob Laden-Guindon, who fill me with wonder and ever-increasing awe. Can we read a book now?

Chicago, September 1, 2011

Contents

PART I
An Alternative Picture

The terminology of philosophical art is coercive: arguments are *powerful* and best when they are *knockdown*, arguments *force* you to a conclusion, if you believe the premises you *have to* or *must* believe the conclusion, some arguments do not carry much *punch*, and so forth. A philosophical argument is an attempt to get someone to believe something, whether he wants to believe it or not. A successful philosophical argument, a strong argument, *forces* someone to a belief . . .

Why are philosophers intent on forcing others to believe things? Is that a nice way to behave towards someone?

Robert Nozick, *Philosophical Explanations*

A *picture* held us captive. And we couldn't get outside of it, for it lay in our language, and language seemed only to repeat it to us inexorably.

Ludwig Wittgenstein, *Philosophical Investigations*

Prologue

It is, I imagine, the rare reader of *Pride and Prejudice* who identifies with Mr. Collins, the Bennets' obsequious, rather stupid, vicar cousin and heir to their estate. And yet.

And yet, his proposal of marriage to Elizabeth Bennet should sound painfully familiar to anyone used to the rituals and rhetoric of the lecture hall.

Listen for a minute:

"Almost as soon as I entered the house I singled you out as the companion of my future life. But before I am run away with by my feelings on this subject, perhaps it will be advisable for me to state my reasons for marrying—and moreover for coming into Hertfordshire with the design of selecting a wife, as I certainly did . . . "

"My reasons for marrying are, first, that I think it a right thing for every clergyman in easy circumstances (like myself) to set the example of matrimony in his parish. Secondly, that I am convinced it will add very greatly to my happiness; and thirdly—which perhaps I ought to have mentioned earlier, that it is the particular advice and recommendation of the very noble lady whom I have the honour of calling patroness . . . "

"Thus much for my general intention in favour of matrimony; it remains to be told why my views were directed to Longbourn instead of my own neighbourhood, where I assure you there are many amiable young women. But the fact is, that being, as I am, to inherit this estate after the death of your honoured father . . . I could not satisfy myself without resolving to chuse a wife from among his daughters, that the loss to them might be as little as possible, when the melancholy event takes place . . . This has been my motive, my fair cousin, and I flatter myself it will not sink me in your esteem. And now nothing remains for me but to assure you in the most animated language of the violence of my affection. To fortune, I am perfectly indifferent, and will make no demand of that nature on your father, since I am well aware that it could not be complied with."[1]

---

[1] This and subsequent passages in this section are from Jane Austen, *Pride and Prejudice*, Oxford World Classics, ed. James Kinsley (Oxford: Oxford University Press, 2008), vol. I, XIX, 80–4.

Mr. Collins makes a proposal, and like anyone trained in the rhetorical arts of professing and preaching, his proposal amounts to a proposition, an assertion, which is then backed up by reasons. Moreover, despite the fun that Austen here pokes at Mr. Collins, it is worth noting that his reasons, as absurd as they are in the context, have the form that someone schooled in philosophical work on reasoning or even the more mundane art of middle school essay writing might recognize: they start with the general reasons for undertaking the kind of action he is doing, and then work to more particular aspects of it. Moreover, they rest on the sorts of considerations that philosophers have generally counted as reasons: his duties, his own happiness, the authoritative commands of his superior in rank, wisdom, and character, and his own position to reduce the suffering of others. All good reasons when we don't encounter them in the mouth of Mr. Collins. But Austen is not finished with Mr. Collins or with us, for Elizabeth, the object of all this proposing and reasoning has been sitting quietly by, and, as with all good talks, there is now time for discussion:

"You are too hasty, Sir," she cried. "You forget that I have made no answer. Let me do it without farther loss of time. Accept my thanks for the compliment you are paying me, I am very sensible of the honour of your proposals, but it is impossible for me to do otherwise than decline them."

"I am not now to learn," replied Mr. Collins, with a formal wave of the hand, "that it is usual with young ladies to reject the addresses of the man whom they secretly mean to accept, when he first applies for their favour; and that sometimes the refusal is repeated a second or even a third time. I am therefore by no means discouraged by what you have just said, and shall hope to lead you to the altar ere long."

The proposal is rejected. The talk meets with objections. But Mr. Collins expects no less. This kind of coquettish give-and-take is all part of the game. No one wants his talk to be met with mute acceptance. The sign of a good talk is the energy of the ensuing discussion. Of course, the discussion period is not over:

"Upon my word, Sir," cried Elizabeth, "your hope is rather an extraordinary one after my declaration. I do assure you that I am not one of those young ladies (if such young ladies there are) who are so daring as to risk their happiness on the chance of being asked a second time. I am perfectly serious in my refusal.—You could not make me happy, and I am convinced that I am the last woman in the world who

would make you so,—Nay, were your friend Lady Catherine to know me, I am
persuaded she would find me in every respect ill qualified for the situation."
"Were it certain that Lady Catherine would think so," said Mr. Collins very
gravely—"but I cannot imagine that her ladyship would at all disapprove of
you. And you may be certain that when I have the honour of seeing her again
I shall speak in the highest terms of your modesty, economy, and other amiable
qualifications."

Elizabeth now backs her refusal to accept Mr. Collins's proposal by trying to
rebut his reasons. And while one of these objections starts to hit home, and
our speaker begins by taking it seriously, he soon finds his feet again and
offers a defense. But Elizabeth also begins a different line of criticism here.
By raising the matter of her own happiness, which had not figured into his
reasons, she begins to insist that all his words have somehow not been
directed at her, in particular, but only at her insofar as she is a representative
of a type, a type which she also doubts actually exists. When her direct
rebuttal of his reasons fails to make a difference, it is this second kind of
objection that she pursues:

"Indeed, Mr. Collins, all praise of me will be unnecessary. You must give me leave
to judge for myself, and pay me the compliment of believing what I say. I wish you
very happy and very rich, and by refusing your hand, do all in my power to prevent
your being otherwise. In making me the offer, you must have satisfied the delicacy
of your feelings with regard to my family, and may take possession of Longbourn
estate whenever it falls, without any self-reproach. This matter may be considered,
therefore, as finally settled." And rising as she thus spoke, she would have quitted
the room, had not Mr. Collins thus addressed her,

"When I do myself the honour of speaking to you next on this subject I shall
hope to receive a more favourable answer than you have now given me; though
I am far from accusing you of cruelty at present, because I know it to be the
established custom of your sex to reject a man on the first application, and perhaps
you have even now said as much to encourage my suit as would be consistent with
the true delicacy of the female character."

Although in this exchange, Elizabeth offers a counter to yet another of
Mr. Collins's initial reasons, her objection shifts gears in an important way.
She now begins to question the rules of the game Mr. Collins is playing
directly. If his proposal was an *offer* of marriage, then there must have been
space for her to refuse it. And yet it is becoming clear to her that he has not

left such space, that her objections are not having an effect on him precisely because his offer was not an offer at all but rather an assertion and his replies merely defenses of his original position. He is, she and we may be realizing, despite being obtuse, well trained in the art of professing. And the problem with this exchange may lie there. So it is time to bring out the big guns and begin to question his presuppositions:

"Really, Mr. Collins," cried Elizabeth with some warmth, "you puzzle me exceedingly. If what I have hitherto said can appear to you in the form of encouragement, I know not how to express my refusal in such a way as may convince you of its being one."

"You must give me leave to flatter myself, my dear cousin, that your refusal of my addresses is merely words of course. My reasons for believing it are briefly these:—It does not appear to me that my hand is unworthy your acceptance, or that the establishment I can offer would be any other than highly desirable. My situation in life, my connections with the family of De Bourgh, and my relationship to your own, are circumstances highly in its favor; and you should take it into farther consideration that in spite of your manifold attractions, it is by no means certain that another offer of marriage may ever be made you. Your portion is unhappily so small that it will in all likelihood undo the effects of your loveliness and amiable qualifications. As I must therefore conclude that you are not serious in your rejection of me, I shall chuse to attribute it to your wish of increasing my love by suspense, according to the usual practice of elegant females."

Elizabeth presses her objection yet again, this time moving to the meta-level. His mode of address has left her no way to be heard as refusing, and so she has raised this as the source of his problem: the talk was fine as far as it went, but we now see that its presuppositions are not so easily defensible. He claims to be offering something, but it would seem that he is really doing something else: imposing himself on her, and, as such, his reasons for action are wanting.

But Mr. Collins is ready once again: if there is a problem here, it is not his, but his audience's. From his vantage point, what she says is "merely words," a fact supported by her lack of good reasons that could counter his. Since they are merely words, their meaning might be anything, and, moreover, they might, as he has heard the words of "elegant females" sometimes do, mean just their opposite. He is, he concludes, still entitled to his original claim. But there is time for one more question:

"I do assure you, Sir, that I have no pretension whatever to that kind of elegance which consists in tormenting a respectable man. I would rather be paid the compliment of being believed sincere. I thank you again and again for the honour you have done me in your proposals, but to accept them is absolutely impossible. My feelings in every respect forbid it. Can I speak plainer? Do not consider me now as an elegant female intending to plague you, but as a rational creature speaking the truth from her heart."

"You are uniformly charming!" cried he, with an air of awkward gallantry; "and I am persuaded that when sanctioned by the express authority of both your excellent parents, my proposals will not fail of being acceptable."

Although Elizabeth brings us back to the question of rationality, and suggests Mr. Collins is failing to respect hers, our speaker has hit his groove, and is undeterred: his audience has been charming, and thus he need not withdraw or alter his proposal. It has survived on this occasion. It is time to thank our speaker, and adjourn for a reception and a friendly dinner.

Works of philosophy are generally understood to be in the business of making proposals to rational creatures, but their authors too often wind up assuming the attitude of Mr. Collins: their proposals are assertions; their reasons serve as foot soldiers whose job is to defeat opposition and defend the author's position; and their final sense of authority often comes from a failure to take wholehearted rejection of their assertions as anything more than "mere words." Whole books could no doubt be written on this attitude and how it entered philosophical thinking and writing. In this book, I will suggest that one of the problems results from our standard way of thinking about reasoning, and that if we want to make genuine proposals to rational creatures, we need to think differently about these matters. In particular, we need to understand the activity of reasoning and thus also of philosophy as like making a genuine and heartfelt proposal rather than a caricature of one; as inviting rather than professing.

1

The Initial Sketch

1.1 Living Together

Consider two people who live together. If they are of the "happily ever after" variety found in fairy tales and romantic novels, then they have probably reached their current state through a proposal and an engagement. As they move into the realm of ever after, where the real living together goes on, they must not only make joint decisions, but also participate together in what John Milton described as "a meet and happy conversation:" an ongoing interaction through which they continually attune themselves to one another.[1] In living together, they share, build, and renovate various spaces beyond their physical dwelling: spaces of meaning and spaces of reasons. This book explores how we might, and perhaps they do, live together. It does so by proposing a particular picture of the activity of reasoning. According to this picture, the central components of the activity of reasoning include proposing, engaging, conversing, and other activities of mutual attunement, rather than calculating, deducing, problem-solving, and judging. The activity of reasoning pictured here brings into view possibilities for living together that are often hard to see clearly from within our standard ways of picturing and talking about reason. The value of adopting the picture of reasoning proposed is that, like a new pair of glasses, it helps us see these possibilities more clearly.

The social picture developed in this book describes reasoning as the responsive engagement with others as we attune ourselves to one another and the world around us. Thus, I am reasoning in this sense when I am

---

[1] This is Milton's description of marriage from his treatise *The Doctrine and Discipline of Divorce*. It is frequently quoted by Stanley Cavell in his discussions of both marriage and conversation. See, for instance, Stanley Cavell, *Conditions Handsome and Unhandsome* (Chicago: University of Chicago Press, 1991), 104.

listening to your response to what I have said and taking it seriously as itself calling for an appropriate response, or when I am telling a story in response to something you have said or done that is meant to situate me vis-à-vis you in some normative space. In contrast, our standard picture of reasoning describes reasoning as the activity of reflectively arriving at judgments through the alignment of the progress of our thoughts with certain formal structures in order to better navigate the world, to solve particular problems and, perhaps, seek out the truth or the good. I am reasoning according to this picture when I am working out the implications of a moral commitment, or figuring out whether the evidence in front of me is sufficient to justify my belief in the truth of a proposition, or figuring out how best to accomplish my aims given the obstacles I face. Though these are contrasting pictures in all sorts of ways, they need not be mutually exclusive. Both are important human activities and there is value in understanding both of them more clearly. On many occasions, we engage in both of them. Part of figuring out what an appropriate response to you is may require me to evaluate the evidence you have presented to me, or how what you have said affects my evaluation of evidence I already have. The point of working out the details of a social picture of reasoning as a distinct picture is to insist on these two points: (1) that these two activities are different, and it need not be the case that the only way to do one of them is to do the other. Beginning from the standard picture turns out not to be the best route to understanding the activities captured by the social picture. (2) The activity of responsive engagement and attunement is also properly described as reasoning, both in virtue of the features discussed below and in virtue of ordinary language. In other words, just because the kind of responsive and reciprocal interactions discussed here are forms of reasoning does not mean that they must be or are best described using the conceptual framework developed by our standard picture of reason, and just because many of these activities are not described as reasoning by our standard picture of what reasoning is doesn't mean they are not reasoning.

We often fail to appreciate, or misdescribe, the activities of reasoning discussed in what follows because we regard them as merely a variety of the activity of reasoning as the standard picture describes it. Such a failure to appreciate interpretive alternatives and the concomitant possibilities for action can place obstacles in the way of our living together as we might. It is common, for example, to think that the only fair alternative to violent conflict in the face of disagreement is a kind of bargaining, where each side tries to get as much as it can and give as little as possible on the way to a compromise. This shapes how we approach such disagreements and the search for solutions. With the aid of the social picture, it turns out that we can imagine a range of other alternatives, where those who disagree come to see each other not as opponents and obstacles, but as partners from whom they might learn and with whom they might search for truly shared modalities of living together. Another consequence of thinking differently about reasoning is that it helps to avoid a certain arrogance on the part of those who think they have reason on their side, whether these be academic experts, politicians, or garden variety know-it-alls. Such figures are all too quick to think of those who disagree with them as somehow lacking in reason, and thus not to be fruitfully engaged in the search for shared ways of living together but to be maneuvered around and manipulated. There may be times when such a judgment is correct. But it is important not to move too quickly to such a conclusion. One reason not to is that a rush to such judgment contributes to a certain distrust of reason as being merely the velvet glove on the fist of power, whether bureaucratic, imperial, Western, male, or white. The result of this reaction is a belief that the path to justice or to forms of reciprocal living together is one that leads away from reason. The impression that our choice is between the arrogance of reason and the rejection of reason is also a consequence of only having the standard picture in mind when we think about reasoning. It is part of the wisdom of Austen's *Pride and Prejudice* that it not only so incisively portrays and mocks the arrogant voice of reason in the figure of Mr. Collins, but also imagines a heroine whose reaction to such arrogance is not a rejection of reason in favor of unbridled passion, but rather a search for a different kind of reasoning partner. To fully understand what Elizabeth Bennet looks for (and ultimately finds), we need to unpack the further features of this activity I am calling reasoning.

Much of the rest of this chapter lays out five central features of a social picture of reasoning, and contrasts them with a more standard picture of reason. Reasoning is, according to the social picture this book paints, (1) an activity or practice that is (2) social, and (3) ongoing and largely consists of (4) the issuing of invitations (5) to take what we say as speaking for our interlocutors as well.[2] With this sketch in place, I offer some reflections on the kind of argument offered here. The chapter ends with a look ahead to the rest of the book.

1.2 Reasoning Is an Activity

The first distinctive feature of the picture of reasoning drawn here is that it is a picture of *reasoning* (the activity) rather than of *reason* (the faculty or set of principles). In other words, the social picture characterizes a set of activities as reasoning in virtue of their having a certain shape or point or characteristic norms rather than their being the product of certain mental machinery or being guided by certain abstract principles. Reasons, then, will be characterized as those things that get offered and exchanged in reasoning. Reason, the faculty, if there is such a thing, will involve those mental capacities that make it possible for us to engage in this activity.[3] Contrast this with a standard way of proceeding through these terms: starting with reason as

---

[2] In drawing a contrast between the social picture painted here and "the standard picture" I do not mean to suggest that no one else has described or conceived of reasoning as I do here, or that all or even most other philosophers who have thought about reason have adopted all the aspects of the standard picture. Although I engage at various points throughout the book with various philosophical conversations about reason, my aim here and in the book is to clearly lay out a possibility for thinking, not survey the state of an academic discipline. Nevertheless, it may be helpful here to drop some names by way of broadly situating this project within contemporary philosophy. Here, then, is a list of heroes and fellow travelers. Heroes are those who strike me as having both articulated the essential aspects of the social picture of reasoning and who have also been influential in my own coming to see its features, and they include: Ludwig Wittgenstein, John Rawls, Stanley Cavell, Onora O'Neill, and James Tully. Fellow travelers are those whose work departs from the standard picture in some but not all relevant respects (for instance, by picturing reasoning as social but not ongoing) or who, though rather closer to the social picture developed here, were not as influential in my own formulation of it. They include Rousseau, Kant, and Hegel, as well as Steven Darwall, Jürgen Habermas, T. M. Scanlon, Christine Korsgaard, Axel Honneth, Robert Pippin, and Robert Brandom. The list of fellow travelers is more heterogeneous with some, notably Brandom and Pippin, articulating views that are rather close to the social picture painted here. Neither list is exhaustive and the distinction between them not always hard and fast.

[3] In this sense, I am engaged in a project very much like the one T. M. Scanlon describes himself as taking on in the first chapter of his *What We Owe to Others*, describing the contours of the concept of reasons in part by locating them "as the central element in a familiar form of reflection" ((Cambridge, MA: Harvard University Press, 1998), 17–18). Beginning one's reflection about reason from the activity of reasoning is the hallmark of what are known as social–pragmatic theories of reason, found, for instance, in the work of Brandom and Habermas. Robert Brandom, *Making It Explicit* (Cambridge, MA: Harvard University Press, 1998). Jürgen Habermas, "What Is Universal Pragmatics?," in *Communication and the Evolution of Society*, trans. Thomas McCarthy (Boston: Beacon Press, 1979). To the extent I offer a different description of the contours of reasoning than these authors, it is because I locate reasoning within somewhat different activities. These differences will become clearer as the chapter proceeds.

either a faculty or a set of transcendent principles, one defines reasons in terms of the deliverances of reason, and reasoning as the activity of exchanging or offering reasons.

Those who start their accounts of reasoning from this standard picture of reason make a distinction between practical and theoretical reason, where practical reason is concerned with what to do and theoretical reason is concerned with what to believe. This distinction plays a less central role on a picture that begins with the activity of reasoning. For one, what distinguishes the activity of reasoning that the social picture describes from its closer cousins is not its subject matter but the level and kind of responsiveness it calls for. Sometimes, as I argue in later chapters, the subject of our reflection shapes our interaction, and this leads to some distinctions between theoretical and practical reasoning. But when it comes to the overall picture presented here, it would be a mistake to ask right off the bat whether it is a picture of practical or theoretical reasoning. A more apt description might be that it is a practical picture of reasoning: a picture that takes reasoning to be something we do.[4]

The importance of starting from reasoning rather than reason becomes clearer as the book unfolds, but note here a difference between the respective contrasts that occupy the ground floor of the two pictures. Starting with a characterization of reason, and then defining reasoning as the activity of or according to reason, leads to a picture of reasoning as an activity of rational or logical calculation and determination, a norm-governed engagement with forms or structures or according to principles of reason. So pictured, reasoning stands in contrast to thinking that is emotional or intuitive or arbitrary. Mr. Collins, concerned to not let his passions run away with him as he proposes marriage, may be a caricature, but he is a caricature of this picture of reasoning.

On the other hand, if reasoning is pictured as a particular way of relating to and interacting with others, then reasoning is a (perhaps the) central activity of living together because in reasoning we are relating to one another in ways that are reciprocal and responsive to each other. Since not every way of interacting with others is properly reciprocal and

[4] Brandom and Habermas offer pragmatist pictures of reasoning, focusing on speech acts rather than language per se. Habermas nevertheless stresses a strong distinction between practical and theoretical reason.

responsive, not every form of interaction involves reasoning. Reasoning in this sense requires that we are not commanding or ordering, ignoring or manipulating, blindly obeying or deferring. This kind of reasoning can be characterized in terms of a set of characteristic norms that derive from the type of activity it is rather than from an independent account of the faculty of reason or the rational order. From this starting point, reasons can be defined as what we offer and exchange when reasoning, and so determined via the characteristic norms of the activity, not the characteristic features of a faculty or a set of formal structures. Elizabeth Bennet accuses Mr. Collins of not reasoning with her, not treating her as a rational creature, precisely because by closing off possibilities for response he violates the norms of this activity. Although the propositional content of what he says shows proper responsiveness to a set of relevant considerations in favor of acting as he does, he does not show proper responsiveness to her.

One consequence of this change in the generation of the category of reasons is that it blurs the boundary between reason and various standard contrastive terms like emotion, feeling, sentiment, or affect. What we say to one another counts as the offering of a reason on this picture only when it is an appropriate move in the activity of reasoning. The status of various claims and assertions as reasons is thus highly context dependent. The same words or different words with the same meaning may count as reasons if offered in one tone or with a certain affect, or when offered to a certain person in a certain situation, and not in others. Part of the content of a reason I offer someone can be bound up with my affect in offering it, insofar as that communicates something about my emotional or sentimental relationship to what I am saying or to whom I am saying it. Within the activity of reasoning this book depicts, reason's essential characteristics have little or nothing to do with being cold, hard, or calculating, attributes called to most minds by the term "rational." Characterizing reason from this picture of reasoning as the capacities that allow us to offer and respond to reasons in this broader sense means that reason so understood includes our emotional capacities and various attitudes like care, concern, or love in addition to our ability to calculate, infer, and judge.

Philosophers have long disagreed about whether there is any connection between being moral and being rational. The primary focus of their attention when such disagreements are joined is the figure of the highly articulate, clever, and thoroughly immoral person, whether the evil tyrant of ancient nightmares or the psychopaths and serial killers of our own. Such figures can calculate and judge, and effectively direct and organize their actions. Their immorality lies in their being unresponsive to others, unwilling to enter into reciprocal relations with them. From the perspective of the picture I draw here, however, the very features that make them immoral are what makes it the case that they do not reason. I do not mean to suggest that adopting the picture of reasoning on offer here settles the debate about the relation of rationality and morality. For one, those who dispute the connection between reason and morality think of the debate as turning on whether there are non-moral foundations for morality. The picture of reasoning on offer here can't answer that question, because it sidesteps it. Reasoning, as it is described here, is already a value-rich activity. So even if this form of reasoning is closely tied to being moral, that does not show that morality has non-moral foundations, only that reasoning so pictured is not a morally neutral activity.[5]

1.3 Reasoning Is Social

The particular activity that I wish to call "reasoning" in what follows has four central features. All of them can be found in a famous characterization of reason by Immanuel Kant. It is a characterization that I return to throughout the book. In the *Critique of Pure Reason,* Kant writes that:

Reason must in all its undertakings subject itself to criticism; should it limit freedom of criticism by any prohibitions, it must harm itself, drawing upon itself a damaging suspicion. Nothing is so important through its usefulness, nothing so sacred, that it may be exempted from this searching examination, which knows no respect for persons. Reason depends on this freedom for its very existence. For reason has no

---

[5] That reasoning is not a value-neutral activity has been a common theme of both Kantian and Aristotelian rejoinders to those who oppose the question about the rationality of morality above. See, for instance, John McDowell, "Virtue and Reason," *Monist* 62, no. 3 (July 1979): 331–50, Christine Korsgaard, "Skepticism about Practical Reason," in *Constructing the Kingdom of Ends,* 311–34 (Cambridge: Cambridge University Press, 1996). As will become clear, my approach to this conclusion takes a different path: it is not because values are one of the things that reason either detects or constructs, or that reasoned investigation presupposes a value orientation to begin with, but because the activity of reasoning is, being a form of reciprocal responsive interaction with others, a form of moral interaction: reasoning with others is one way of treating them morally.

dictatorial authority; its verdict is always simply the agreement of free citizens, of whom each one must be permitted to express, without let or hindrance, his objection or even his veto.[6]

Kant here insists that reason's authority rests in its constant and ongoing openness to criticism. Once we close off avenues of criticism, whether in the name of usefulness or respect for the sacred, including persons and their particular positions, we have thereby ceased to reason and begun to issue or obey commands. One way to avoid closing off criticism is to always leave open the possibility of further challenges to what we say, and thus to never draw final conclusions. This suggests that reasoning, since it cannot reach once-and-for-all conclusions, must be an ongoing process. If, in addition, we reject the thought that anyone is all-knowing, then being always open to criticism inevitably means being open to criticism from others. So Kant's claim here implies, though it does not explicitly require, that reasoning must be something we do with others: a social activity. But if reasoning is social and ongoing, this further suggests that in giving someone a reason, we cannot be drawing a final and unimpeachable conclusion. Rather, the offer of a reason must be a genuine offer, an invitation: open, as Kant does say, to being vetoed by others. And finally, what that invitation amounts to is an invitation to regard what was said as a genuine reason, which is to say a request to regard this corner of the space of reason as the speaker has laid it out. Acceptance of a reason, then, involves an acknowledgement that we share some, perhaps small, space of reasons.[7] Sharing such a space, however, makes it possible for either of us to speak for both of us, and so we can describe the invitation the reason proffers as an invitation to take another's

[6] *Critique of Pure Reason*, trans. Norman Kemp Smith (New York: St. Martin's Press, 1933), 593 (A738/B766). Kant here is talking of reason (*Vernunft*) and not reasons (*Gründe*) or reasoning, but I take it that for Kant, what makes the considerations we offer one another reasons (*Gründe*) is that they have something like the backing of reason (*Vernunft*) a backing, the passage brings out, that requires an open-ended engagement in something like reasoning. In other words, purported reasons are really reasons when they carry the authority of reason as this is realized by reasoning.

[7] Here I follow Onora O'Neill's discussion of Kant, and in particular the passage cited above in Onora O'Neill, "Reason and Politics in the Kantian Enterprise," in *Constructions of Reason*, 3–27 (Cambridge: Cambridge University Press, 1989). Thinking of reasoning in terms of a social space of reasons will perhaps be most familiar from the work of Wilfrid Sellars and, following him, Robert Brandom, who takes himself to be engaged in a basically Hegelian project. Wilfrid Sellars, *In the Space of Reasons*, ed. Kevin Sharp and Robert Brandom (Cambridge, MA: Harvard University Press, 2007), Brandom, *Making It Explicit*. One can find variants of this picture in the work of Stanley Cavell, who takes himself to be articulating thoughts he finds in Wittgenstein and sometimes Emerson and sometimes Kant. Stanley Cavell, *The Claim of Reason* (Oxford: Oxford University Press, 1979).

words as speaking for us as well.[8] Thus, from this claim of Kant's, we can extract the four central features of a social picture of the activity of reasoning.[9] I unfold each in turn in what follows.

To describe reasoning as social is, in some sense, hardly controversial. No one that I know of explicitly denies that we can reason with one another, or even that we reason better when we do so. But in describing the picture of reasoning developed here as a social picture, I mean to make a stronger claim: reasoning is fundamentally something we do together. This claim does not deny that I can reflect on and think through problems on my own, but to insist that insofar as what I do in so reflecting is to count as considering reasons, it has to make reference to and thus be answerable to whether I can intelligibly offer these reasons to others, and, in many cases, to whether my invitations are likely to be accepted. This means that all reasons are what might be called "we"-reasons or social reasons.[10] Many people who have discussed social reasons in recent years have taken them to be a special subset of reasons, a subset that might need to be treated differently than individual reasons, but nevertheless not the whole class of reasons.[11] If,

---

[8] That reasons might be analyzed in terms of speaking for others is one way to understand Kant's connection between reasoning and universalization. For an explicit analysis of Kant in these terms, see David Velleman, *Self to Self* (Cambridge: Cambridge University Press, 2006), though on Velleman's reading, the process of universalization gives us a way to bring reasoning to an end, by reaching conclusions that are good once and for all.

[9] Although I have cited a passage from Kant to illustrate this position, unpacking Kant's remark in this way requires following suggestions rather than merely reading what it explicitly says, and this explains both why some who accept the claims in this passage and cite it as a touchstone of their own work, do not approach reasoning as I attempt to do here, and why many people will see the position outlined here as more in line with Hegel than Kant. For examples of Kantian positions that differ from the one offered here, see Christine Korsgaard, *The Sources of Normativity* (Cambridge: Cambridge University Press, 1996), and Rainer Forst, *The Right to Justification*, trans. Jeffrey Flynn (New York: Columbia University Press, 2011). For examples of Hegelian philosophers tracing views resembling the one offered here back to Hegel, see Robert Pippin, *Hegel's Practical Philosophy: Rational Agency as Ethical Life* (Cambridge: Cambridge University Press, 2008) and Robert Brandom, *Reason in Philosophy: Animating Ideas* (Cambridge, MA: Harvard University Press, 2009).

[10] I discuss the importance of "we"-reasons and their place in reasoning together in my "Outline of a Theory of Reasonable Deliberation," *Canadian Journal of Philosophy* 30 (December 2000): 551–80; "Evaluating Social Reasons: Hobbes vs. Hegel," *Journal of Philosophy* 102, no. 7 (July 2005): 327–56; and "Negotiation, Deliberation and the Claims of Politics," in *Multiculturalism and Political Theory*, ed. Anthony Simon Laden and David Owen, 198–217 (Cambridge: Cambridge University Press, 2007).

[11] See, for instance, Samuel Freeman, "Reason and Agreement in Social Contract Views," *Philosophy and Public Affairs* 19, no. 2 (spring 1990): 122–57, who calls such reasons "public," and uses them to distinguish Hobbesian from Rousseauvian social contract theories; Christine Korsgaard, *The Sources of Normativity* (Cambridge: Cambridge University Press, 1996), and "The Reasons We Can Share," in *Constructing the Kingdom of Ends*, 275–310 (Cambridge: Cambridge University Press, 1996), where she refers to reasons as intersubjective and finds their original articulation in Kant; Charles Taylor, "Exlana-

however, we conceive of reasons as invitations to speak for others, then "we"-reasons are not some special case, but the whole field.

To see why, it helps to unpack the metaphor of a space of reasons. First, reasons form a space in the mathematical sense: they are not merely a set of discrete points but are connected to one another by sets of inferential relations.[12] On the social picture of reasoning, these relations are the product of the norms governing the activity of reasoning. Second, reasons form a space in the geographic sense: they constitute a realm that we can occupy. That is, a full mapping of a space of reasons would not only have to describe sets of inferential relations between reasons but would have to situate each of us within that space, saying in effect, which reasons are reasons for each of us. Third, a space of reasons is essentially public, social, and shareable, and thus neither the product of individual mental structures nor merely the result of the structure of the natural world. As with other public spaces (both physical ones such as parks, and social ones created by forms of political action), sharing a space of reasons does not require that we stand at exactly the same point. Whether we share a space of reasons is not only a matter of where each of us stands, but how we relate to one another through the mediation of the space in question, and how we understand our joint responsibility for its upkeep and renovation.[13] We can thus unpack what is distinctive about the spaces of reasons we (re)construct by reasoning

tion and Practical Reason," "Irreducibly Social Goods," and "To Follow a Rule," in *Philosophical Arguments*, 34–60, 127–45, 165–80 (Cambridge, MA: Harvard University Press, 1995), where he talks of "common understandings" and traces their importance in practical reasoning to Hegel and Wittgenstein; and Onora O'Neill, "Four Models of Practical Reasoning," in *Bounds of Justice*, 11–28 (Cambridge: Cambridge University Press, 2000), where she contrasts "action-based" accounts of practical reason with "teleological" ones, tracing the former back to Hegel, Wittgenstein, and Kant, and the latter to Plato and Hume.

[12] Brandom, *Making It Explicit*. The characterization of reasons as structured by inferential relations is central to Brandom's picture of reasoning, which has many affinities with the picture I present here. Acknowledging that the space of reasons is structured by such relations may seem to dissolve the difference between a social and a standard picture of reasoning insofar as it seems to admit that what is essential to a space being a space of reasons is its formal structure and not its shared construction. The difference lies, however, not in the existence of a connection between formal structure and publicity, but in terms of how that connection is understood, and which way the order of explanation goes. According to the standard picture, it is because the space of reasons has a fixed, objective structure that we can all enter it and it is thus public. According to the social picture, it is the public nature of the activity of reasoning that gives rise to a stable and formally structured space that we can inhabit together. It is a feature of Brandom's pragmatism that he takes the latter position, as do I.

[13] I am grateful to Patchen Markell for pushing me to be clearer about the imagery of a shared space, and in particular its mediating function that allows us to stand together without standing at the same place.

together by thinking about how certain kinds of interaction construct certain spaces. Doing so will also develop a vocabulary for describing the social picture of reasoning in more detail.

Let's say, then, that I share a space of meaning with you when what we say to one another is mutually intelligible, not merely in the sense that I know what all the words you say mean, but I can understand what you mean when you say them, which requires also that I can see your point in saying them, here and now, to me.[14] Sharing such a space already includes sharing normative standards, in particular about the intelligibility and thus the appropriateness of saying things in certain contexts, what Ludwig Wittgenstein calls a "form of life."[15] We might put the point this way, also borrowing from Wittgenstein: sharing a space of meaning in this sense means not only not having a private language, but not using language privately. In other words, if I am interested in making myself intelligible to you, I not only have to use a language you know, but use it in a way that you recognize.

Finding what you say intelligible, however, does not require that I am moved to say the same thing under the circumstances or to give the same importance or weight to what you say that you do. It thus does not require either that I take what you say as an invitation to share a space with you or that I accept your invitation. There are thus ways of communicating intelligibly with one another that do not count as reasoning on the social picture. Of course, that you have said it and that I understand what you have said and why can serve me as reasons to believe certain things, especially about you. But your point in so speaking to me may not have anything to do with instilling or grounding such a belief. You may have merely been bearing witness or trying to work out your own thoughts (which, interestingly enough, is often done better in the presence of others). Alternatively, you may be providing me with information about yourself or some feature of the world. As presented, the information is not part of the activity of reasoning, though it may play a role in constituting reasons. So I can understand what you say in this full-blooded sense without thereby taking you to be reasoning with me, and thus without

[14] This is a point I take from Stanley Cavell's reading of Wittgenstein and to which I return in Chapter 3.

[15] Ludwig Wittgenstein, *Philosophical Investigations*, trans. G. E. M. Anscombe (Oxford: Wiley-Blackwell, 1991), §§23, 241.

taking your words to be offering me reasons or even potential reasons.[16] And, yet, understanding what you say even at this level does require that we share some normative space, a space of meaning, and so we can say that we need to share such a space if we are going to speak to one another and not merely at or past one another. If, beyond saying things that are intelligible to one another, we interact through what we say in ways that make our activity a shared one, then we engage in a conversation, and thus speak with and not merely to each other. Idle conversation can include reasoning, but it need not. It does, however, require that we do not merely lecture each other.

Two people share a space of reasons (or at least part of one) if each not only understands what the other says but can affirm it. In such a case, they inhabit at least this corner of this normative space together or at least take themselves to be similarly oriented within the same space. When we wish to share a normative space in this fuller sense, we must not only speak with one another but attempt to speak for one another. Attempting to speak for you rather than merely to or with you invites your responsiveness to what I say in a different manner. When I merely speak to you, it may be a matter of indifference to me whether you respond at all, and your response can even be the last thing I want. Think here of wanting to get something off your chest by ranting about it and being met with a set of solutions to your problem.[17] Merely registering that you understand what I am saying can be enough. When we speak with one another, however, we each expect a heightened level of responsiveness and reaction to what each of us says, even if we are not trying to find common ground or even staking out positions. What counts as an appropriate response, and what an appropriate response to that response, can thus still be loosely defined.

When, however, I try to speak for you in the sense that I do when reasoning, I call for your response, not only to what I have said, but to my

---

[16] Note here a crucial difference between the activity pictured on Brandom's account of the game of giving and asking for reasons as he develops it in *Making It Explicit*, and the activity pictured as reasoning here. For Brandom, any assertion with propositional content enters one into the game of giving and asking for reasons, as it commits the speaker to certain other claims and licenses others to certain inferences about the speaker. On my account, the making of assertions is part (but only part) of the wider activity of conversation, which has its own norms. I reserve the term reasoning for forms of conversation that exhibit a heightened level of responsiveness among the participants.

[17] Deborah Tannen, *You Just Don't Understand: Women and Men in Conversation* (New York: William Morrow and Co., 1990).

invitation to take it as something you would say as well.[18] Replying to an invitation does not require accepting it: you can (re)affirm that my words speak for you, too, but you can also mark your distance or your different understanding of what you would say and thus what we could say together. It is ultimately our sharing a world to the point where we can each speak for one another as well as ourselves, say what the other would say, that marks our sharing reasons, and thus in an important sense, having reasons that are reasons for us. Being able to speak for one another involves sharing a space of reasons, not merging into a single self, or occupying a single point of view, just as sharing an apartment involves living together in a physical space, not occupying the same point within it.[19] Since sharing such a space of reasons is both the basis and the result of reasoning together, it turns out that reasoning is an activity that requires and reconstructs a shared world, and this is the sense in which it is a deeply social activity.

That reasoning is a matter of figuring out where and how we can speak for others, and thus the shape and content of the "we"s we form together means that it is at least one way that we determine, in the sense both of discovering and of constructing, the contours of our relationships with others, and thus, inter alia, the contours of our own identities. On this social picture of reasoning, the value of reasoning is that it allows us to build truly reciprocal and thus shared relationships to one another, to live together and not merely side-by-side.

Let me explain. To undertake an activity such as reasoning *together* is to share in that activity, to see it as governed by a shared set of norms or rules that mediates and constructs our actions as interactions in part by making them intelligible to each of us as moves within this shared framework. It is not enough to engage in an activity together that each of us is performing that activity with an eye to what the other is doing and how each of our actions intertwines with the other. Although we might be able to isolate each of our individual movements or speech acts from one another and analyze our interaction in this way, if it is truly an activity we do together, then something is missing from such an analysis. When we are acting

---

[18] The idea of a reason as involving a call is introduced by Fichte and further developed in contemporary idioms by Steven Darwall, *The Second-Person Standpoint: Morality, Respect, and Accountability* (Cambridge, MA: Harvard University Press, 2006).

[19] For further elaboration of this point, see the discussions of attunement in Chapter 4.2–3.

side-by-side, in contrast, each of us is acting as an independent agent, even if each of us is in various ways attentive to what the other does, perhaps merely to avoid colliding, or perhaps because what I say or do figures as an input into your reflections and decisions about what to say or do. If we begin to think about reasoning as something that individuals do on their own, and then try to picture the activity of reasoning together, we are likely to wind up describing people reasoning side-by-side, perhaps in complexly interrelated fashion, but side-by-side nonetheless.[20] To picture reasoning as an essentially social activity, however, is to picture an interaction that is not reducible to individual actions, and whose agents do not think of themselves as merely reacting to and predicting what others do. Clear cases of acting together include playing a game as a team, or engaging in a lively conversation where no one has an agenda other than the liveliness of the conversation itself. At this stage, these remarks can only be suggestive, as someone committed to something like the standard picture of reason will insist that all of these activities can be analyzed in terms of individual actions that intertwine and mesh together, and so will not accept or see that there might be a fundamental difference between acting or reasoning together and side-by-side.

Like the two pictures of reasoning, the activities of reasoning together and reasoning side-by-side need not be mutually exclusive, and some relationships might require skill at both. Consider, for instance, a married couple. Among their tasks is the performance of various basic activities of household and life management. Someone needs to cook meals, go shopping, help the kids with their homework or take them to school. They need to work out rules of bathroom etiquette, and adjust their standards of cleanliness to one another. All of this can be done by reasoning side-by-side, and a marriage can fail despite both parties truly loving the other, if they are unable to arrange the coordination of their common lives. If and when we fail to live side-by-side, we bump into one another, and do harm and find it more difficult to each pursue our individual goals. At some point, life becomes nasty, brutish, and short.

---

[20] For an example of this kind of approach that nevertheless takes seriously the distinctiveness of the phenomenon of collective action as different from individual action, see Michael Bratman, "Shared Cooperative Activity," *Philosophical Review* 101, no. 2 (April 1992): 327–41, and "Shared Intentions," *Ethics* 104 (October 1993): 97–113. I discuss these matters further in Chapters 5 and 6.

But a couple that was perfectly skilled at such reasoning, but nevertheless had forged no truly shared life together would also be missing something. Part of forging such a shared life is inhabiting shared spaces of meaning and reason together. Such sharing allows them to truly understand each other, complete each other's sentences, and answer each other's questions before they have been fully asked. It allows them not only to reason side-by-side and coordinate their lives, but to reason and thus live together. When we fail to live together, we find ourselves alone, unable to reach out to others around us, to make ourselves intelligible to them, to interact with them as fellow subjects. The isolation that failure to reason together creates is not a matter of a failure of coordination. It is the sense that no one understands what you say or do, or who you are. Such isolation can be the result or the cause of madness, even a kind of death.[21] There is I think, no better guide to the value and perils of living together, and the pain of failing to do so than Jean-Jacques Rousseau. And while unraveling all his insights into this matter is a project for a whole other book, it is helpful to make some brief remarks here. First of all, Rousseau thinks that the capacity to live together is, in a sense, what makes us fully human. The creatures he describes as inhabiting the state of nature in the *Discourse on Inequality* are remarkable, chiefly, for the fact that they live merely side-by-side and that they have not yet taken the first steps on the road to humanity.[22] Because they live side-by-side, however, they are basically satisfied and free. They are not subject to the pains of misrecognition and insult, and so the deepest forms of human suffering are not open to them.[23] Conversely, they are not capable of the deepest forms of human joy, whether love or the ecstasy that comes from uniting into a political society.[24] As Rousseau snidely says in a note to the *Discourse*, the solution for our own unhappiness and dependence cannot be to go

---

[21] These connections help explain Stanley Cavell's insistence on the link between skepticism and tragedy in *The Claim of Reason* (Oxford: Oxford University Press, 1979) and throughout his writing.

[22] Jean-Jacques Rousseau, "Discourse on the Origin of Inequality," in *"The Discourses" and Other Early Political Writings*, ed. and trans. Victor Gourevitch (Cambridge: Cambridge University Press, 1997). For a discussion of Rousseau's *Discourse* that takes this line, see my *Reasonably Radical: Deliberative Liberalism and the Politics of Identity* (Ithaca, NY: Cornell University Press, 2001), ch. 2.

[23] Rousseau, "Discourse on Inequality," 166.

[24] On love, see ibid. 164. On ecstasy of political union, see Jean-Jacques Rousseau, *Politics and the Arts: Letter to M. d'Alembert on the Theatre*, ed. and trans. Allan Bloom (Glencoe, IL: Free Press, 1960), 125–7. On the suffering of being alone, see Jean-Jacques Rousseau, *Reveries of a Solitary Walker*, trans. Peter France (New York: Penguin, 1979), 27 (First Walk, par. 1).

back to the forests to live with the bears. Once we have begun to relate to others, we must either command and be commanded or learn to reason together.[25] Merely aiming to coordinate our actions to allow us to live side-by-side is no longer enough.

Reasoning together allows us to bridge these gaps of isolation because it involves not only saying things that are intelligible to others, but others hearing what we say as intelligible. Certain forms of violent trauma leave their victims isolated and alone in part because of the unintelligible (the unspeakable) nature of what has happened to them. Survivors of trauma thus talk about the importance, for their recovery and re-entry into human relationships, of having someone hear and accept their stories, and the difficulty and isolation they feel when no one listens to them this way.

> It is not sufficient for mastering the trauma to construct a narrative of it: one must (physically, publicly) say or write (or paint or film) the narrative and others must see or hear it in order for one's survival as an autonomous self to be complete. This reveals the extent to which the self is created and sustained by others and, thus, is able to be destroyed by them. The boundaries of the will are limited, or enlarged, not only by the stories others tell, but also by the extent of their ability and willingness to listen to ours.[26]

Note here that what is lost through such trauma and is regained in mastering it is not the ability to live alongside others, but the ability to live together with them.

As these examples suggest, living together is not something that comes automatically for us. We do not come by a shared order either by instinct (like ants) or by virtue of some metaphysical fact or supernatural command (like soldiers in God's army). Rather, if we are to share a world, we must build it together. To describe reasoning as a social activity is thus to describe it as the activity of making, maintaining, and inhabiting such a world in the form of a shared space of reasons.

---

[25] See Rousseau, "Discourse on Inequality," 182–83, and *Émile*, trans. Allan Bloom (New York: Basic Books, 1979), 48.
[26] Susan Brison, *Aftermath: Violence and the Remaking of the Self* (Princeton, NJ: Princeton University Press, 2001), 62.

1.4 Reasoning Is Ongoing

Philosophical work on reasoning is full of descriptions of people encountering reasons, whether by invoking or confronting or considering them.
And in most of that work, the descriptions of those encounters paint them as
episodic, as occurring in finite, basically self-contained chunks with a more
or less clear beginning and a more or less clear end. The thought that we
encounter reasons episodically is built into much thinking about reasons and
the place they hold in our lives, although it is not so frequently stated or
used as a means of characterizing sets of positions about reasons.[27] Even
many people who hold that reasoning is a deeply social activity in the way
described above think of reasoning as episodic, and thus depart from the
picture presented here. To picture reasoning as an ongoing activity is to
deny that we can adequately understand it as episodic.

To understand why, it helps to have some examples of episodes of
reasoning in place:

1 I need to meet a colleague for lunch and also run an errand, and need to
    figure out how to do both of these given the available time, means of
    transportation, and a variety of other constraints. I devote some time to
    thinking about it, see a path that satisfies my aims while obeying the
    constraints, and either take the path now or decide that it is the path
    I will take at the appointed moment.[28]

2 I take up a difficult theoretical problem in philosophy or mathematics,
    and, over a period of years, in both concentrated moments at my desk
    and idle moments in the course of my life, turn my attention to the
    problem, try out various approaches to a solution, and, ultimately, if

---

[27] Candace Vogler comes as close as anyone to explicitly making use of the episodic nature of
reasoning in arguing for a particular conception of practical reason, one that holds that practical reasoning
is, as she puts it, calculative in form (that is, has something like a means–end structure to it). See Candace
Vogler, *Reasonably Vicious* (Cambridge, MA: Harvard University Press, 2002), esp. 168–70.

[28] I mean here to be purposely vague and ambiguous about an issue that many regard as of central
importance to any account of at least practical reason: namely, whether such reasoning merely leads up to
or also involves either decision or action. I think that what is at stake in answering it one way or another
depends in part on what picture we have of reasoning, and so I don't want to prejudge the matter here.
(Of course, one could turn this approach on its head and insist that we are compelled to answer this
question of the relation of at least practical reason to action in a certain manner, and then use this as
grounds for opting for one picture of reasoning over the other (Vogler's argument in *Reasonably Vicious*
can be read this way).)

I am fortunate enough, work out a solution or at least make progress in that direction.

3 We must come to an agreement about how to spend the afternoon. We deliberate together, find common ground, and from that ground, work out a plan for the afternoon that we can all support.

4 I have some time on my hands as I sit on the train, so I turn my mind to trying to understand Swiss politics or the nature of practical reason.

What makes the reasoning in all of these cases episodic is that it takes place in a clearly bounded region of space and time and is internally directed at its own termination.[29] That is, whether or not the reasoning is started up as a result of outside forces setting a problem, or the play of idle thoughts and time focusing one's attention, and whether or not the reasoning is all done in a single sitting, or proceeds in bits and pieces over a long span, and whether or not it is successful and does in fact come to an end, in each of these cases, the reasoning is directed towards reaching a conclusion, a solution or a decision that, *inter alia*, brings the episode of reasoning to an end. This is even true of the final case, where I idly turn my attention to a topic. I am not merely attending to a topic, but trying to figure it out or understand it, and this attempt has its own internal standards of success. If, after reflecting for a while, I come to feel that I have adequately or satisfactorily understood what I was thinking about, then I have succeeded. If the success is clear enough or the topic limited enough, I may take my reaching such a conclusion as grounds for bringing this episode of reflection to a close, and turning my attention elsewhere. To see that the standard of success is, in this case, internal to the activity of reasoning about a given topic, contrast it with the case where I turn my mind to something not to figure it out or better understand it, but as a form of distraction, to better endure a boring train ride or a painful dental procedure. In such a case, success is measured and the episode of reasoning bounded by the external events I am trying to endure. When the dentist finishes drilling, I can stop reasoning regardless of what progress I have made.

---

[29] Realists about reasons may hold that the reasons themselves and perhaps the inferential structures of their relationships to one another are not so easily located. But, even then, the reasoning that adverts to these structures is temporally located.

To say that reasoning is episodic is to make a claim about the activity of reasoning and not the structure of the space of reasons.[30] It means that we imagine the paradigmatic cases of reasoning as limited in time and subject, and measure their success in terms of progress towards an end. This picture of where and how we reason then brings with it certain other features. Since episodes of reasoning are directed at something which is not itself an episode of reasoning, but a decision or conclusion or greater understanding, the point of reasoning is to bring us to (or closer to) that goal. The aim of reasoning is, we might say, to be able to stop reasoning.[31] If we are deliberating together about what to do in order to make a joint decision, we have failed if we just keep on deliberating. Moreover, if we do reach a conclusion, then it will be odd for someone to keep discussing the matter merely in order to prolong the activity of reasoning. Of course, our bouts of reasoning may follow one another without a gap, overlap, or may lead directly to their successors, as when reaching a decision about ends leads to reasoning about how to bring them about, which in turn leads to reasoning about implementing the plan decided upon. But, even then, each bout of reasoning is a bounded, episodic activity.

Thinking of reasoning as taking place in bounded episodes that do not merely stop but arrive at an end fits well with a standard view about the point of reasoning: to make conclusive judgments in the form of beliefs or decisions: to make up our minds. We can make up our minds in bounded episodes of reasoning if reasoning is directed at conclusions, and thus at a kind of end, and reasoning can be so directed if reasons play some role in contributing to or bringing us closer to such an end. In fact, it may be hard to imagine within this picture in what sense one would be reasoning if one was not trying to reach a conclusion or deploying claims or information that

---

[30] Picturing reasoning as episodic is thus independent of questions that are hotly debated in epistemology between foundationalists, contextualists, and coherentists about the status of claims to knowledge.

[31] Those of an Aristotelian bent might wonder where the activity of contemplation that Aristotle regards as making up the best form of life fits in to this characterization. The value of contemplation, after all, is in large part that it has no end beyond itself and thus no internally directed termination point. It may be that contemplation is a form of reasoning that best fits within the social picture. Here I merely note that the difficulty of explaining (and of understanding) what Aristotle has in mind in these sections of the *Nicomachean Ethics* that discuss contemplation may be a sign of the hold that the standard picture has on us insofar as it makes it seem paradoxical for an activity to be both a form of reasoning and non-episodic.

were in some sense thought to advance towards such a conclusion. As Candace Vogler expresses this position:

If what "comes to mind" or "goes through one's head" between setting out to figure out, for example, what to plant and deciding what to plant has the sort of relevance to the garden project that it must if we are to describe [it] as the content of garden-directed practical reasoning—rather than, say, idle speculation or the inward rehearsal of a song that is stuck in one's head,—then this will be because the process was a means to, or part of, deciding what to do . . . [R]easoning must be a means to or part of decision-making; otherwise, what's taking place isn't *practical deliberation* at all.[32]

And, for many situations, this seems exactly right: we offer reasons in order to end our (perhaps internal) conversations. If we are reasoning together about how to spend the afternoon, it is natural to assume that each of us offers the other reasons in the hope that we can bring the deliberation to an end and get on with the business at hand.[33]

But notice that if we take reasons to aspire to a kind of decisiveness in this sense, it is hard to also hold onto Kant's insistence that it is definitive of reason, and thus presumably reasoning, that it remain open to criticism. That is, if reason must harm itself if it does not continually open itself to criticism, then it looks as if reason harms itself if it comes to an end. One common way to square this circle is to say that reasoned conclusions are always subject to revision and review, so that once a bout of reasoning has come to an end, there is the implicit possibility of reopening it in the face of new information or attitudes. But there is a way to give a more robust reading to Kant's insistence by picturing reasoning not as an episodic and end-driven activity but an ongoing one.

To start to imagine how reasoning could be reasoning and yet ongoing, it helps to think of other species of interaction that are both responsive and ongoing, such as casual conversation, and then ask about the possible place

---

[32] Vogler, *Reasonably Vicious*, 166.

[33] The assumption that reasoning is end-directed can just as easily shape a social theory of reasoning, such as Habermas's. Though Habermas makes a strong distinction between strategic and communicative reasoning, he analyzes communicative reasoning in terms of its aim of finding rationally motivated agreement. See, among others, Jürgen Habermas, *The Theory of Communicative Action*, trans. Thomas McCarthy, 2 vols. (Boston: Beacon Press, 1984), "What Is Universal Pragmatics?" and "Discourse Ethics: Notes on a Program of Philosophical Justification," in *Moral Consciousness and Communicative Action*, trans. Christian Lenhardt and Shierry Weber Nicholsen (Cambridge, MA: MIT Press, 1990). This marks a major difference between his view and the one developed here.

of reasoning within them. In other words, if reasoning is a species of conversation, then, like casual conversation, it may not need to be directed at an end or aimed at its own termination. It turns out that characterizing the activity of reasoning in terms of the responsiveness it demands also leads to a way of picturing reasoning as an ongoing activity. On the social picture being sketched here, offering someone a reason lies between ordering her to do as the reason directs and merely making noise in her general vicinity. When I order you to act, I remove space for you to determine what you do. When you hear my words as mere noise or a plea rather than a reason, you leave no space for me to determine what you do. Taking my words as potential reasons means you leave some space for them to make a difference in what you do. Likewise, offering you what I take to be a reason, and not a command, means that I leave space for you to rebut or criticize it.

I think we should spend the afternoon cleaning up the house, because, well, it's a mess. I offer its messiness as a reason to you for spending the afternoon so. Even though I do so in the hope that you will agree and we can get to it, by offering you a *reason*, I am implicitly giving you space to reject it, and thus to keep on talking. Were I in a position to command you, there would be nothing to discuss. Note that this would also be true if you take what I say as offering something less than a reason because, for instance, you can only hear it as noise or because you treat it that way. One thing that distinguishes commands and noise from reasons, then, is that reasons can serve to keep conversations going.

Furthermore, it turns out that thus used, reasons cannot bring conversations to a close, once and for all. If you accept my reason, then you do not need to offer me a reason in return, but an expression of your acceptance, an expression of your will. If you try to offer me a further reason for cleaning the house, even one that is based on your willingness to do so, then that suggests that the conversation is not over, for you are leaving me room to reject your reasons. Consider the difference between the following responses to my suggestion of cleaning up the house: "I guess you're right. I'll go get the vacuum cleaner out of the basement" and "It would also give us an excuse to miss your nephew's piano recital." In the first case, you do not offer a reason to clean up the house. Rather, you endorse the proposal and begin to carry it out. There is, in the normal course of events, nothing for me to say about the question of what to do this afternoon any more. We have moved on to divvying up the work. Of course, I can reopen the question now or later, but it is no longer what is expected of me, and it requires opening something that is closed, rather than continuing something that is ongoing.

In the second case, however, the conversation about the afternoon has been prolonged. I cannot really go get the vacuum cleaner just yet, because I need to respond in some way or other to the reason you have offered, even if only by now expressing what I am confident can be our joint decision: "Great, then why don't you get the vacuum cleaner while I pick up all the dirty clothes lying around?"

Note that the conversation about what to do this afternoon looks, on pretty much any theory of reasoning, like it involves reasoning: we are deliberating about what to do. And, clearly, in such a case, our deliberation needs to bear some relationship to the decision we ultimately reach if that decision is also to be thought of as reason-guided, and the action it yields rational or reasonable.[34] But there is nevertheless a feature of reasoning that we lose sight of if we think of reasoning as aiming to reach a conclusion, and it is this feature I wish to keep front and center as we proceed: offering someone a reason can be a way of opening the possibility of further conversation, but not, on its own, a means of ending a conversation.

Understanding reasoning as a species of conversation pictures reasoning as an activity that is not episodic but rather forms part of the background of our shared lives. Reasoning, so described, is how we occupy a social space of reasons, just as swimming is how fish occupy water. That is to say that the space of reasons is something we inhabit, not merely invoke and deploy, more like our home than our office, and that reasoning is just the ongoing activity of inhabiting that space. Inhabiting a space of reasons goes beyond merely moving around in it, and navigating through its shoals. As with inhabiting a home, inhabiting a space of reasons involves interacting with it, occasionally changing or remodeling it, and in turn being changed by it.[35]

Thinking of reasoning as the background activity of our lives rather than as episodic also suggests a different focus of attention in order to see clearly this activity of reasoning, and where we engage in it. First of all, if reasoning

---

[34] I return to this example below (towards the end of 1.5) and focus on the question of how to understand the relationship between reasoning and deciding on the social picture.

[35] The image of reason as a home, though most evocative of Hegel's project of reconciliation, finds expression as well in Immanuel Kant, *Critique of Pure Reason*, trans. Norman Kemp Smith (New York: St. Martin's Press, 1933), A707/B735.

is not episodic, then exhibiting neatly packaged episodes of reasoning as cases to study provides a distorted sample. Rather, reasoning also takes place in the more general interactions that shape and constitute our lives, and so an adequate picture of non-episodic reasoning has to include them and describe which of their features make them reasoning. It requires paying attention not to the solving of isolated problems, but all the interactions that Stanley Cavell describes as the "whirl of organism:"

> our sharing routes of interest and feeling, modes of response, senses of humor and of significance and of fulfillment, of what is outrageous, of what is similar to what else, what a rebuke, what forgiveness, of when an utterance is an assertion, when an appeal, when an explanation—all the whirl of organism Wittgenstein calls "forms of life."[36]

This kind of ongoing reasoning takes place in what can be called scenes of instruction, or attunement or the lack of it.[37] These are moments when someone is brought to see the world as another sees it, or is confirmed in her own view by finding that another sees things similarly or is threatened or struck by the recognition that they do not, after all, inhabit the same space of reasons. They are often moments that pass in idle conversation, even if the conversation is emotionally charged. That is, they are scenes of instruction not in the sense that a pupil goes to the teacher and asks for an explanation or help in solving a problem, or where someone sets out to convert another to her point of view, but where, in the course of a conversation that may be aimless and may be aimed elsewhere, something of significance that merits the name of instruction or attunement takes place. They are moments that may only be recognized as such after the fact, and thus are most easily found in literature and other forms of storytelling.

They can, in fact, come in the form of learning to see that a genuine proposal, since it is no more than an invitation, is open to rejection by a rational creature. For Elizabeth Bennet turns down another presumptuously offered proposal in the course of *Pride and Prejudice*, this one from her

---

[36] "The Availability of Wittgenstein's Later Philosophy," in *Must We Mean What We Say?* (New York: Charles Scribner's Sons, 1969). Cavell is unpacking what he takes to be Wittgenstein's understanding of what supports our confidence that others will go on as we do, will understand what we mean by our words.

[37] A focus on scenes of instruction marks Wittgenstein's later philosophy, esp. *Philosophical Investigations*, and it is a point that Cavell continually stresses in his own engagements with Wittgenstein. See, for instance, *Conditions Handsome and Unhandsome*, lec. 2.

eventual husband, Mr. Darcy. And what, apart from money, standing, higher principles, and more intelligence, really distinguishes him from Mr. Collins is how he hears her rejection and what it leads him to. As he tells her upon her much later accepting his second proposal: "You taught me a lesson, hard indeed at first, but most advantageous. By you, I was properly humbled. I came to you without a doubt of my reception. You shewed me how insufficient were all my pretensions to please a woman worthy of being pleased."[38]

If reasoning is an ongoing activity, then understanding it requires investigating the whole range of casual conversation and idle chatter, interactions that have no particular end or aim, but which serve to situate and resituate us vis-à-vis each other in social spaces, and thus not only to invoke shared spaces of reasons but to construct them. Although such interactions do not look like reasoning in the standard sense of the term, they turn out to have what might be called rational significance insofar as they help to shape the spaces of reasons in which we live. Such conversations are the focus of Chapters 3 and 4.

1.5 Reasons as Invitations

If reasoning is episodic and directed at the forming of conclusions or decisions, then it is natural to think of the act of offering reasons as a kind of directing or legislating. Legislating, even in a democracy, is an activity that presumes a kind of hierarchical relationship between the legislator and the subject of the law. In the normal course of events, it is done in a forthright and uncompromising manner: this is what is meant, after all, by saying that someone is "laying down the law." It is this underlying idea of reasons and the thought that reasons function as legislation that both motivates the following passage from Christine Korsgaard's *The Sources of Normativity*, and makes it somewhat jarring:

If I call out your name, I make you stop in your tracks. (If you love me, I make you come running.) Now you cannot proceed as you did before. For now if you walk on, you will be ignoring me and slighting me. It will probably be difficult for you,

---

[38] *Pride and Prejudice*, vol. III, ch. XVI, 282.

and you will have to muster a certain active resistance, a sense of rebellion. But why should you have to rebel against me? It is because I am a law to you. By calling out your name, I have obligated you. I have given you a reason to stop.[39]

Notice here how Korsgaard moves from ignoring and slighting to resisting and rebelling, and then uses the idea of rebellion to introduce the idea of reasons as laws and thus as being able to command.

If I think that by reasoning, I can be a law to myself and others, then I am likely to see reasoning as a process that erects a kind of support and bulwark for my position, and gives me the right to direct things. The result is that, armed with reasons, I am likely to go forth in the world in an arrogant manner, unable to imagine that I might be mistaken, that I might not have a claim on others. If, however, reasoning involves, first and foremost, being responsive to and open to criticisms from others, then it is not a means to put my legislation on firm footing, but is rather what I do when I interact reciprocally with others instead of legislating to them. Thus, on the social picture of reasoning under development here, reasoning rests on an assumption that though my position vis-à-vis others gives me a right to make a demand on them, it is only a right to be heard and to call for a response. As a result, the demands I make in reasoning must be made in a more open spirit, and cannot presume to be the final word. If I call out your name with this picture as background, I am, we might say, not commanding you to stop in your tracks, but asking you to turn your head. And, if you choose not to, although you can do so as an act of rebellion, you need not: you can merely ignore me or slight me and thereby deny my authority. Who am I, after all?[40]

Note that my position in asking you to turn your head rather than commanding you to stop in your tracks is nevertheless not the same as that when I make a plea or supplication. The supplicant forswears all authority, and appeals to our tastes or preferences or whims. And while these preferences may have been reflectively or rationally arrived at, that fact plays no role in their capacity in this matter to render a decision. That is, in appealing to us without invoking any form of authority, the supplicant forswears any criteria on the basis of which she might question our decision.

---

[39] *Sources,* 140.

[40] Though in many cases we can tell which of these kinds of activities someone is engaged in by her body language, affect, and tone, we cannot always. It may depend on how they react to our response to what they say, and even then it may not be determinable at certain moments, by either party. But the possibility of practical muddiness need not undermine the conceptual distinction or obviate its value.

But that is just to say that the supplicant is not reasoning with us but blindly obeying or deferring to us. Supplication, no less than legislation, rests on a hierarchical relationship. If reasoning is being distinguished from commanding, then I also cannot reason with you if I make you issue commands by placing myself under your commanding authority.

This intermediate position from which we reason in the sense being pictured in this book is captured by describing reasoning as a form of inviting or proposing. Thinking of reasoning as inviting has two features it is worth highlighting from the beginning. First, as suggested by the discussion above, it provides a way of understanding the authority involved in reasoning in a manner that is fundamentally different than the kind of authority involved in legislating. Note, in this regard, that inviting is importantly different than licensing or permitting, both of which can be analyzed in terms of hierarchical authority relations.[41] Chapter 2 discusses the mode of authority at work in inviting and how it differs from the mode of authority at work in legislating and licensing.

Second, invitations allow for the creation of relationships that do not already exist, and so capture an essential feature of the activity of reasoning pictured here: that it not only takes place within shared spaces of reasons, but that it can serve to construct and modify those spaces as well. When I invite you to take my words as speaking for you, I open up a space of reasons for us to share, and if you accept my invitation, you thus participate in our joint construction of this space of reasons as one we share. But I can do this without yet knowing whether we do share this space. Moreover, some forms of reasoning with others may not even aim to forge a shared space of reasons, but merely work out what spaces of reasons we each inhabit. In such cases I offer reasons to those with whom I disagree and may not even be trying to convert to my way of thinking. Nevertheless, it is still the case that I cannot offer all invitations to just anyone at any time. In the normal course of events, there is a background that already must be in place for me to offer you a particular invitation, and there is a similar background that is presumed when we reason. I cannot really offer reasons to someone at whom rather than with whom I can speak. Our disagreement cannot be so total that we are mutually unintelligible, or that the person to

---

[41] That reasons function like licenses is central to Brandom's account of what he calls the game of giving and asking for reasons. See *Making It Explicit*.

whom I offer reasons only hears them as noise or a private, inscrutable use of words.[42]

Finally, note that invitations can be offered in all sorts of guises, and these track a number of different kinds of activity that we consider reasoning. Sometimes, we offer invitations that we would be shocked to have turned down. They are invitations, not commands, because it remains open for the person we invite to say no, but we issue the invitation in full confidence that it will be accepted. Similarly, we often have very good grounds for thinking that we share a certain space of reasons with someone and share an understanding of our respective places in that space. Most examples of reasoning in the philosophical literature take this form, and this may explain why they often miss the invitational nature of reasoning.

In other cases, invitations are issued out of a genuine interest to forge a connection that is not already there. In such cases, the possibility of rejection is real and while rejection may be disappointing, it is not a shock. Similarly, I can offer reasons to someone without yet knowing whether I share a space of reasons with them. My offer here is a genuine invitation for them to either enter my space of reasons or affirm that they are already there. Such inviting is at work in cases where people are reasoning about a matter that is not so clear-cut, and so people make suggestions about how to think about the matter, or why certain facts are the salient ones and so forth.

How I respond to an acceptance or rejection of my invitation may depend on what kind of invitation is being offered and to whom. While I might genuinely regret it if you cannot accept my invitation to my wedding, I am unlikely to change the date or my partner as a result. And while it is technically accurate to describe a marriage proposal as an invitation to my wedding, I am likely to have a very different reaction to your rejection of it or your prior commitment to be elsewhere on the wedding day. Sometimes reasoning with someone with whom we don't agree is like inviting them to a wedding, and at other times it is like proposing to them. The differences between these forms of reasoning are the focus of Chapters 5 and 6.

---

[42] I don't mean to rule out here innovative or personal uses of language that, while not inscrutable, require imagination on the part of the hearer to fully grasp, such as those in poetry, literature, or, for that matter, certain forms of humor. It is important that the space of mutual intelligibility is malleable, and changes through our use of language. But we can contrast, at least conceptually, such literary use of language with private use of language characteristic of certain forms of mental illness.

REASONS AS INVITATIONS 35

Third, some invitations are offered out of politeness and we expect them to be refused. Thus, when I offer you reasons merely to explain or justify my beliefs or actions rather than to enlist your affirmation of them, I still offer to speak for you, but my offer is one which I expect you to refuse. Nevertheless, the offer is a way of saying that my world is a world a reasonable person might inhabit, one into which I can in good faith invite you, and so one in which you should feel free to leave me in peace. Certain types of justification, especially of idiosyncratic or unfamiliar practices, make invitations of this sort.

When these practices do not involve issuing invitations, they look less like reasoning. If we are working out what to do and are on sufficiently familiar ground that I can be sure that we agree about the reasons before us, then if I draw a conclusion backed up by my understanding of the reasons we share but take my word on the matter to be final, then I am commanding you to follow, not reasoning with you about what to do. If we are less sure about the reasons we face or whether we share them, and I also draw a conclusion and explain my reasoning, but do not invite you to see it my way, then I am perhaps not commanding you to follow me but I am not reasoning with you, merely explaining my position. And, in the final case, if I lay out the grounds for my behavior without inviting you to share them, then I am not so much justifying what I do as defending it by building up a kind of protective barrier around it.

Trying to picture reasons as invitations nevertheless runs into some obvious objections. Consider, for instance, the following exchanges:

"Why did you cross the street?"
"Because the restaurant is on the other side."

"I don't want to tell him the truth. It will be awkward and uncomfortable for me."
"But it is the right thing to do. Lying would be wrong."

Thinking of reasons as invitations appears not to capture the appropriate finality of what look for all the world like reasons in these two exchanges. It just seems contrived to say of blindingly obvious instrumental reasons or uncontroversial moral ones that they are best thought of as invitations, even invitations that we would be aghast if someone rejected. And this seems in large part because such instrumental and moral reasons are decisive, and properly so. If you explain your crossing the street by pointing to the restaurant where we are headed or explain not having done something by citing moral considerations against it, you are not trying to continue a conversation, but end one. Moreover, such an objection might continue, reasoning together can only help us live together if it somehow connects to action, and not merely to never-ending conversations.[43] If there is not some fundamental link between the reasons that serve as invitations and continue our conversations and our actions, then our actions are arbitrary, mere movements, controlled by something or someone else or merely random, no longer willed but merely willful. So we need to show that our reason-constructing and exchanging conversations also link up to action, that the reasons we offer one another bear some relation to our decisions, conclusions and actions. And then we need to show how these reasons allow us to stop talking and get something done.

Distinguish two activities in which the space of reasons we inhabit play a role. The first activity, which is what the social picture calls reasoning, involves taking part in responsive and reciprocal conversations where we exchange reasons. This activity serves to lay out how the world seems to each of us, and possibly, to us together. Reasons work here in the manner of invitations, asking us to accept or decline particular claims, to rebut or amend them. Offering a consideration as a reason within such conversations can prolong but not end them, and, so, on their own, cannot move us to further action. At the same time, the exchange of reasons within conversations can serve to construct our shared world, our space of reasons, and orient us within it, to set out what is normatively the case for us.

Making and expressing judgments (whether about beliefs or actions) is a different kind of activity we undertake with reasons, and here we need to be able to issue commands, though possibly only self-directed or conditional ones. (This is basically the activity of reasoning as the standard picture describes it.) But what could possibly ground our right to issue such commands? It is precisely the background conversations that have oriented us in our shared world. Go back to my earlier example. We are talking about how to spend the afternoon, and I suggest cleaning up the house

---

[43] Christine Korsgaard, *Self-Constitution: Action, Identity and Integrity* (Oxford: Oxford University Press, 2009), argues that reasoning is essential because it provides a solution to the problem of action, which she describes as our plight.

because it's a mess. If I offer the messiness of the house as a reason for staying in and cleaning, then I invite you to keep talking. Sure, you say, it is a bit of sty, but it's so beautiful out and there aren't going to be many more days like this for a while. Here is a counter-reason, an invitation for me to reconsider our local space of reasons, to see it differently, and so an invitation to keep talking. At any time, however, either of us can try to bring the conversation to a close (otherwise, we will spend the whole afternoon talking). But, if I am to do this, I need to engage in a different kind of activity: I need to stop conversing and (try to) start commanding: "Yeah, never mind the mess, let's go for a walk in the park." Notice that there is not a reason in this statement, only something with the form of a conditional command. I could have said, were I trying to make a philosophical point as well as reach a decision, "Enough talking. Given the space of reasons and our orientation in it that this conversation has helped to bring about and confirm, I have set my will on going for a walk in the park with you, conditional on what I am confident will be your agreement." Note that this command is self-directed and conditional but not provisional. It is up to you to satisfy the condition by commanding your own will, but it is not an open-ended suggestion. To see this, note that, should you agree to satisfy the condition, the matter is closed, and we have, as it were, our marching (or walking) orders.

This suggests that the issuing of commands (whether to ourselves or to others) necessary for action is a different activity, though it takes place against a background of reasoning and makes use of that reasoning to be non-arbitrary. In other words, what grounds my confidence that my conditional self-command will meet with acceptance is that our conversation has revealed to both of us that we see the relative parts of our normative world in similar ways and are similarly oriented within it. We have established (provisionally, imperfectly, but nevertheless solidly) that as far as deciding to go for a walk in the park is concerned, each of us has the right to speak for both of us. This was not exactly the result of a contract, although it was the result of an exchange (or more likely, many exchanges, very few of which may have been concerned with how to spend this afternoon). It was also not the result of a deduction: deciding, on this picture, is not something that follows reasoning like the conclusion follows the premises of a syllogism. It is, rather, a different type of action, and so is guided by different norms. Here I am issuing a command or a report (perhaps only a conditional one) and so what I need is the authority to speak, perhaps only for myself, perhaps for both of us. Such authority, however, comes not from any principles of reason or rationality, for these generate no commanding authority. They will come, instead, from the details of our interactions and our relationships, from the various facts that ground my confidence that you will accept my command, endorse my decision, see things as I do. Since these include our conversations and deliberations, the legitimacy of our decisions, whether shared or individual, can rest in a fundamental way on our reasoning, not because reasons are the name we give to items of reflective success, but because reasoning is what allows us to share a world and thus, to a greater or lesser extent, to know each other and ourselves.[44] Moreover, as we move from talking to acting, it is the background space of reasons and their connection to our joint decision to act that make the parts of that action intelligible or not. If we have decided to clean up to miss your nephew's recital, then my rushing to finish in order to leave in time to catch the recital will seem strange, inexplicable. You will be within your rights to rebuke me by saying, "What are you doing?" And if I reply, "I'm cleaning up the house," then you can retort, "I thought we were trying to miss the piano recital." That is, I have not given a fully adequate description of what I am doing, and so have not rendered my actions reasonable to you. We can sum up these thoughts with the following contrast: on the standard picture, reasoning is an activity that aims at and ends with the drawing of a conclusion, which is thus part of the reasoning process. On the social picture, though reasoning can prepare the ground for conclusions and decisions, the actual drawing of such conclusions is not part of the activity of reasoning, but goes beyond it.

1.6 Speaking for Others

Finally, in inviting someone to share a space of reasons with us, or to affirm that they already do share that space, we are inviting them to take what we say (in describing that space) as speaking for them as well. That our invitation has this basic form and content helps to make sense of the idea that its

---

[44] The idea that reasons are the names we give to reflective success comes from Korsgaard, *Sources*, 93–4.

authority is subject to our interlocutor's veto.[45] If you reject what I say as speaking for you as well, then I have not managed to say something that speaks for you. Now, talk of speaking for others is likely to be misunderstood. It can smack of precisely the arrogance that the social picture of reasoning developed here is in part meant to avoid. So I need to make clear the sense I am giving this phrase.

There are at least three distinct ways of speaking for others. First, there is commanding. In commanding you, I speak for you in the sense of instead of you, overriding whatever you might have said, and thereby replacing your words, in fact, your will, with mine. For me to command you, we need to stand in a hierarchical relationship and my speaking for you must be unilateral. My commanding you rules out your commanding me, at least here and now.[46] To command you, I need to be able to speak to you, but not so clearly to be able to speak with you, though I may need your recognition of my authority over you.

Second, there is the form of speaking for others that tends to be characteristic of intellectuals on the barricades, who claim to speak for the masses. Here one speaks for others in the sense that one claims to represent them, to articulate their interests or desires or ends. Such a claim is also a claim to authority, perhaps the authority of expertise or wisdom. As such, it often rests on a view of the speaker's connection to reasons: it is because of the intellectual's supposed better grasp of the true situation and the reasons it affords that she claims to have the right to speak for others and represent their interests better than they could on their own. Such speech is also unilateral: intellectuals do not expect or allow the masses to speak for them, nor do they think that what they say can be effectively or legitimately challenged by the masses.

---

[45] It also makes clear that treating reasoning as a form of inviting thus treats our reasoning partner from the second rather than the third person point of view. On the importance of the second person in understanding reasoning together, see Darwall, *Second-Person Standpoint*. Habermas criticizes Brandom's "score-keeping" approach to the evaluation of reasons for failing to hold on to this feature of reasoning. Jürgen Habermas, "From Kant to Hegel: On Robert Brandom's Pragmatic Philosophy of Language," in *Truth and Justification*, ed. and trans. Barbara Fultner (Cambridge, MA: MIT Press, 2003), 162–3.

[46] As I discuss in the next chapter, there are some cases where a group of people stands to one another in a series of relationships such that it appears that each can command the other. Think, for instance, of any group that makes decisions by taking majority-rule votes. Each member of the group has, by casting a deciding vote, the possibility of commanding the others, but each is thus also under the command of her fellow members insofar as they, too, can vote. For such cases, the claims above need to be formulated more precisely, but these details do not matter for the contrast drawn here.

The indignity of speaking for others[47] in this sense stems from the fact that it implicitly involves, no less than the issuing of commands does, treating those for whom one speaks as somehow inferior, lacking humanity or at least the capacities necessary to represent themselves. Unlike commands, however, it is a form of speech directed not so clearly to those for whom one speaks but on their behalf to others with whom one may be deliberating or negotiating. To the extent that the intellectual on the barricade's speech calls for a response, the response she seeks is from those in power, not the masses. Note that the indignity here is not built into the activity of representing others by speaking for them in this way, but only to the form this takes when one's representation is not suitably responsive to those one represents.

These forms of speaking for others stand in contrast with the form of speaking for others involved in the social activity of reasoning. This third form of speaking for others can be found in Stanley Cavell's discussion of the authority with which ordinary language philosophers make their claims:

When Wittgenstein, or at this stage any philosopher appealing to ordinary language, "says what we say," what he produces is not a generalization...but a (supposed) *instance* of what we say. We may think of it as a sample. The introduction of the sample by the words "we say..." is an invitation for you to see whether you have such a sample, or can accept mine as a sound one. One sample does not refute or disconfirm another; if two are in disagreement they vie with one another for the same confirmation. The only source of confirmation here is ourselves. And each of us is fully authoritative in this struggle.[48]

He goes on to describe what happens when such offering of instances fails to find confirmation, saying that "At such a crossroads we have to conclude that on this point we are simply different; that is, we cannot here speak for one another. But no claim has been made which has been disconfirmed; my authority has been restricted." It turns out, that is, not that I have "said something false about 'us'," but there is "no us (yet, maybe never) to say anything about." This leads him to conclude that "the philosophical appeal

[47] The phrase is Foucault's, from a conversation with Deleuze. Gilles Deleuze and Michel Foucault, "Intellectuals and Power," in *Language, Counter-Memory, Practice*, ed. Donald Bouchard, trans. Donald Bouchard and Sherry Simon (Ithaca, NY: Cornell University Press, 1977), 209. For some discussion of the problems of speaking for others, see Linda Alcoff, "The Problem of Speaking for Others," *Cultural Critique* (winter 1991–2): 5–32.
[48] *The Claim of Reason* (Oxford: Oxford University Press, 1979), 19.

to what we say...are claims to community...The wish and search for community are the wish and search for reason."[49]

Here I speak for you by speaking for an us of which we are both members, by saying what I take it we would say. Such speech has three distinctive features. In order for us to be connected so that I can speak for you in this sense, you must have the right to speak for me. This already marks a big difference from the first two forms of speaking for others, which are, in the forms that raise concerns, unilateral. But reciprocity requires more than mere symmetry. It also commits me, second, to being answerable to you, to being open to the possibility that you deny my attempts and perhaps, in so doing, distance yourself from me.[50] I only succeed in speaking for you if you accept that my words do speak for you, and thus acknowledge the "us" on whose behalf I have presumed to speak. If I am attempting to speak for you in this way rather than issuing a command, attempting to manipulate you, or doing any number of other things I can do with words, then I must leave open the possibility of your rejecting my offer. Leaving open this possibility not only means that you can say no, but that your doing so has an effect on what has happened, makes it the case that my offer fails, that I have not, in fact, spoken for you. It thus requires that you, too, have authority. Your rejection may, for instance, make it the case that I have failed to speak for myself, either. We are looking at houses. I say, "We'll take it," and you respond, "No, we won't." This does not leave me having offered to buy the house alone. Alternatively, it may leave me reasserting my claim, but now offering more explicitly or clearly my understanding of the connection that I take to support it, a reassertion you can, in turn, accept or challenge. Finally, speaking for others while holding what I say open to criticism also requires that I be vulnerable in the sense that I allow that my position within what I take to be a space of reasons can change as a result of our interaction. Reciprocal, fully answerable attempts at mutual persuasion or conversation, where each nevertheless insists on holding her ground thus do not count as reasoning according to the social picture.

---

[49] Ibid. 20.
[50] Ibid. e.g. 19–27. See also my discussion of "we", –reasons in "Outline of a Theory." On answerability, see Forst, *Right to Justification*. Answerability understood as openness to criticism plays a central role in Kant's conception of reason. See O'Neill "Reason and Politics" and "Four Models."

1.7 Thinking Differently

The full development of the social picture of reasoning occupies the rest of the book. Since, however, the painting of conceptual pictures is not what many philosophers think of as the primary activity of philosophy nor an activity that is familiar outside of philosophy, it is important to try to say something about the kind of activity this is, if only to forestall certain kinds of misunderstandings and frustrations. To begin with, what is meant by talk of pictures? It is a term that Wittgenstein uses in his famous remark about a picture holding us captive, and I mean to invoke his meaning in using it myself. But what is that meaning?

If we take the five features of the activity of reasoning I am trying to describe here one at a time, and note that in each case, there is an alternative way of describing the activity of reasoning, we can naturally ask why a particular set of features must go together. Why, for instance, should we not try to develop a theory that describes the activity of reasoning as social but episodic, or as social and ongoing, but primarily a matter of making assertions, not issuing invitations? Each such possible combination would then yield a kind of theory about reasoning, and we might use such a taxonomy to make sense of the variety of positions philosophers and others take in their discussions of reason and reasoning.

The idea of a picture goes beyond the idea of a bundle of features that categorize a kind of theory in two important ways. First, the image of a picture is of something whose disparate elements fit or hang together in a certain way, so that the adoption of one part of the picture pushes us to adopt its other features. The elements of a philosophical picture, just like the elements of an ordinary picture, fit together because of features that may not be purely logical or conceptual. So describing certain bundles as constituting pictures is not to rule out other bundles as inconsistent or incoherent or even false. The point, rather, is that because the picture as a whole hangs together, we can be led to adopt some of its elements without really noticing that we are doing so. One danger of this, one way that a picture can hold us captive, is that even when we consciously and explicitly reject one feature of a picture, we may be pulled back towards that feature by other aspects of the picture we do not even recognize that we have endorsed. So, for instance, you might not be fully convinced that we ought to conceive of reasoning as episodic, but nevertheless keep finding yourself imagining the activity of reasoning episodically because you are assuming that reasoning cannot merely involve issuing invitations because reasons aspire to be decisive.

Faced with a picture that holds us captive, it can be liberating to entertain a wholly different picture, and thus to expand our imaginative possibilities, even if, at the end of the day, we do not think the new, radically different picture captures the whole truth either. So another advantage of the picture metaphor is that it makes room for a variety of responses, including ones that offer new, possibly hybrid, alternatives to the two I have begun to sketch here or, as my own thinking on the matter currently stands, accepting that each picture captures something different and that in the absence of two distinct pictures, we are bound to misinterpret aspects of our lives and their possibilities.

Because pictures often frame or provide the background to our particular theories, a contrast between two pictures moves of necessity at a high level of generality, often blurring the important distinctions between different theories that rely on a similar picture. And this can lead to misunderstanding. In particular, there are many different ways of developing full-blown theories of reasoning within the two pictures distinguished in this book, and its argument does not, in general, pay attention to these more particular differences. Nevertheless, from time to time, a point is explained by reference to a particular theory that relies on a given picture. In those cases, a proponent of a different theory relying on the same picture is likely to reply that a more sophisticated version of that approach does not run into that particular danger. I ask such a reader for a grain or two of salt at those moments, to see the smaller argument as an illustration of the larger point, not the full argument for it, and to ask whether the more general point being made nevertheless applies to her favored position.

A further way of understanding the idea of drawing pictures is that drawing a picture invites you to adopt an ideal. The offering of ideals does not fit neatly on the standard division of theories into the normative and the descriptive. Ideals, in the sense used here, are akin to what John Rawls calls "realistic utopias."[51] They are descriptions of a world or a social order or, in this case, an activity that we might construct or engage in,

---

[51] *Justice as Fairness: A Restatement*, ed. Erin Kelly (Cambridge, MA: Harvard University Press, 2001), 4.

although we do not always do so now. Offering an ideal sketches a possibility to which we might aspire rather than argues that something is necessary or obligatory.[52] In the sense that it sketches something we might do, it adopts a descriptive tone, and insofar as what it describes is meant to be realistic even if not yet realized, the sketching of ideals borrows from descriptions of what we already do. But the point of sketching ideals is not merely to describe our current activity, but to offer attractive possibilities, and so they play something like a normative role as well. The difference, however, is that their normativity comes from their attractiveness, not their being required. It is important that the ideal being sketched here is realistic in the sense that it can be realized, acted upon, right now by anyone. That is, it is not an ideal in the sense of a distant goal that leaves open the question of its feasibility and the means for reaching it. The ideal of reasonable interaction being sketched here serves as a kind of constraint on our present actions. It tells us not which ends to seek, but the means that would make our actions and interactions more reasonable here and now.

To those used to normative arguments that attempt to ground norms on undeniable or unavoidable foundations, the invitation to consider an ideal and find it attractive will seem hopelessly weak and underwhelming, not a form of argument at all. To dispel such frustrations about the arguments to follow, note two things: (1) we can think of both arguments that invite us to adopt ideals and arguments that aim to force us into certain positions as relying on a similar strategy: making plain the costs of not accepting their conclusions.[53] In painting a social picture of reasoning as the central element in an ideal of living together, this book highlights what we lose in terms of the possibilities of living together to the extent that we do not realize this idealized activity, and suggests some of the attractions for us in living and acting this way. If you accept the account of the costs and the attractions, then you should accept the ideal as your own as well. If you don't, then you shouldn't. (2) Following from this, whether or not you accept the social

---

[52] This marks perhaps the sharpest break between my project here and various Kantian attempts to discuss reasoning as social, all of which search for something like necessary preconditions for reasoning or action so as to show that we are forced to follow the norms that they uncover. See, for instance, Forst, *Right to Justification*, Habermas, "What Is Universal Pragmatics?" and "Discourse Ethics," and Korsgaard, *Self-Constitution*.

[53] I take this way of capturing a broader sense of what might count as philosophical argument from Cora Diamond, "Anything But Argument," *Philosophical Investigations* 5, no. 1 (January 1982): 23–41.

picture as attractive depends not only on where you initially stand in encountering it, but also what can be said in its articulation and development. In other words, I offer a series of arguments on the way to constructing the social picture of reasoning, and, being arguments, they are each open to criticism and challenge. As with any argument, the responses open to you upon reading it go beyond accepting or rejecting it.

What, then, does the fully articulated social picture of reasoning look like? If offering reasons is a matter of offering claims that aspire to be decisive commands, then a theory of reasons should provide prior procedures for determining the reasons we have, whether by laying out a theory of rational choice or something like a categorical imperative procedure.[54] As with procedures for free and fair elections, these need to be worked out ahead of time and then used as the standard to measure what we actually say to see if it rises to the level of a reason.

If, however, reasons are invitations that can only keep conversations going but not end them, then their status as reasons can only be established, as O'Neill points out, retrospectively and recursively.[55] First, they must be treated as reasons by others to vindicate the authority on which they rest. Second, they must survive the test of free and open discussion, and this is not a process that comes to an end. On such a view, a theory of reasons can only be, as it were, negative and defensive. It can tell us what not to do, which utterances cannot ever have the authority of reason, but not positively what reasons we have.

Sometimes conversations are brought to a close, not because the parties stop talking, but because their interaction has collapsed into a series of commands or the babble of mere noise. A theory of reasoning might help us see when this happens and how to avoid it. But it cannot thus provide algorithms for decision-making and acting. Rather, it provides guidelines for what kinds of interaction count as genuine conversation. In short, a theory of reasoning helps us to recognize reasonableness.

---

[54] This is John Rawls's phrase for a kind of schema of practical reasoning to be drawn from Kant's examples in the *Groundwork*. I do not think Kant ought to be read, at least not in the *Groundwork*, as offering us as kind of algorithm for generating a theory of moral, rational choice, nor do I think Rawls read him as doing so. For Rawls's discussion of what he calls the CI-procedure, see John Rawls, *Lectures on the History of Moral Philosophy*, ed. Barbara Herman (Cambridge, MA: Harvard University Press, 2000), 167–70.

[55] O'Neill, "Reason and Politics," 21.

It might also serve to reassure us, to provide a defense of our reasonable faith in the meaningfulness of our words and our mutual intelligibility.[56] Such a defense could aim to show that such intelligibility is not conceptually incoherent, or it might provide some positive support for our confidence in particular cases, positive grounds that are not esoteric or metaphysical, but are bound up in our ordinary practices, even when these fail. Both Wittgenstein and Cavell, for instance, offer reminders of the vastness and depth of the forms of life we share, and how they provide the background against which agreement and disagreement is possible. Such support falls short of a proof or a metaphysical guarantee, but it can be more than sufficient to support our faith and confidence.

Finally, this attention to our ordinary practices of finding common ground and mutual attunement suggests that we think differently about the skills that make for good reasoning. Traditionally, the model of good reasoning has been good decision-making and effective advocacy, the ability to skillfully invoke the rules of reason in service of one's aims. So understood, reasoning is an assertive skill, one which some use effectively to direct and project their wills in the world, a kind of normative bulldozer that clears paths for action and belief. But if the activity of reasoning is the activity of sharing the world, of attuning ourselves to others within reciprocal relationships, then the good reasoner is going to look much more like the good listener: someone who is able to hear others' words as invitations, and be affected or moved by them, and someone who is able to hear and appropriately react to the responses her own invitations prompt. The truly reasonable person, then, is willing sometimes to move to find common ground and forge and maintain reciprocal relationships, and also to understand when not doing so is part of being reasonable. And a social picture of reasoning might serve to provide guidelines for such a reasonable person in how to engage in the very activities her reasonableness directs her towards. Rather than giving us a theory with which to judge interactions as rational or not, a social picture of reasoning might be thought to show its value in animating what might be thought of as the foreign policy of a reasonable person.[57]

---

[56] Kant describes his own philosophy as offering a defense of our reasonable faith. For discussion of this aspect of Kant's thought, see Rawls, *Lectures*.

[57] I mean here to rely on a contrast that is sometimes made in discussions of international relations and global justice, between theories that lay out principles of justice for the global order, and theories that

1.8 The Work Ahead

According to the standard picture of reason, different categories of reason can be seen as occupying sets of concentric circles. At the core are principles of reason that govern the very structure of our actions and beliefs: the requirement that she who wills the ends must also will the necessary means, and the laws of logic. Around this core might be principles telling us that we have reason to promote our interests or overall well-being, or to follow the laws of mathematics, or governing the formation of beliefs on the basis of forms of evidence. At the outer limit would be, for some theories of reason, moral principles and the laws of the special sciences. Thus, the standard picture works outwards from the structure of action and belief to the structure of the self or of reality, and then finally to our relationships with other people and the particular features of our world. Insofar as the social picture starts from the thought that reasoning is always a social activity, it does not work outwards to our relationship with others, but begins there. And instead of working outwards through categories of reasons, it works inwards through different types of reasoning activities.

Part II of this book discusses three such activities: casual conversation, responsive conversation or reasoning, and engaged reasoning. Each category is a subset of the one before it, and the move from the wider activity to the narrower one goes by tightening the requirements on responsiveness that the activity requires. To converse with you, I need to be sufficiently responsive to you to be speaking with and not merely to you. Not all talking in the presence of others counts as conversing. But to reason with you I have to invite you to take my words as speaking for you as well and do so in a way that leaves what I say open to criticism from any quarter. This means that I have to be more responsive to you than when I converse with you, paying greater attention to how you take up my invitations and your grounds for criticizing what I say. If we further tighten the requirements of responsiveness we get a special category of reasoning I call engagements.

work out the principles that ought to guide just democratic states in acting on the international scene; that is, between giving us principles of international justice and principles of foreign policy for a just society. See, for instance, Erin Kelly, "Human Rights as Foreign Policy Imperatives," in *Ethics of Assistance: Morality and the Distant Needy*, ed. D. Chatterjee (Cambridge: Cambridge University Press, 2004). This marks one of the fundamental differences between my project here and that of Habermas, *Theory of Communicative Action*.

When we engage with one another, we are concerned not only to make open invitations, but to make successful ones, and so we are required to be more responsive to those we are engaged with than when we merely reason with them. The discussion of these three activities in Part II elucidates their central characteristic norms, and shows how these shape the activity in question. These norms, insofar as they define the activity of reasoning, are thus the norms that guide the kind of living together the ideal painted here depicts.

All three activities of reasoning are essentially interactive, and they are defined by the levels of responsiveness they require. But defining these levels of responsiveness does not yet help us figure out how to respond to what our conversation, reasoning, and engaged partners say to us and the invitations they offer us. Part III then focuses on how to respond to proposals and invitations. Chapter 7 argues that one constraint on our responding reasonably to the proposals others make to us is that these responses both treat the proposals as proposals and thus not as commands or mere noise, and that they do not undermine our capacity to continue reasoning. In order to meet this requirement, we must constitute ourselves in such a manner that no part of us has dictatorial authority over the rest. Chapter 8 explores the implications of this requirement for the range of reasonable responses that are open to us. Chapter 9 turns to a broader requirement, one that applies to our conversational responses as well. In order to continue conversing with others, we must remain intelligible to them, and this constrains how we can justify and explain our actions and beliefs as well as the ways we structure them. One consequence of the requirement that we respond intelligibly is that we can respond to proposals by pointing to what we do as means to our ends.

Chapters 4–9 thus fill in the details of the social picture of reasoning. The rest of Part I takes up two topics where the social picture enters particularly unfamiliar territory. The social picture of reasoning casts reasoning as a species of casual conversation. Since casual conversation is not an activity that receives much attention from those who think about reason, Chapter 3 brings the phenomenon of casual conversation into view and demonstrates its rational significance. Chapter 2 takes up a general issue about reasoning: the authority that reasoning generates. One way that the standard picture of reason holds us captive is by anchoring our picture of reason in a particular understanding of one of its features: its authority. The standard picture draws a close connection between reason and the authority possessed by laws and rules, an authority that can be described as the right to rule or command or pass judgment. This connection supports a central feature of the standard picture: that reasoning is an activity aimed at reaching conclusions, and thus that aspires to be decisive. In order to open up conceptual space in which to develop a picture of reasoning as an ongoing social activity, we need to loosen this connection between reasoning and the authority of command. Chapter 2 does so not by denying that reasoning has a deep connection to authority, but by loosening up our conception of authority to make room for alternative forms of authority that might be connected to a picture of reasoning as a social and ongoing activity.

2

Authority

2.1 Reasoning and the Authority of Command

Many of the most fruitful recent attempts to picture reasoning as an essentially social activity nevertheless picture reasoning as an activity aimed at reaching conclusions, rather than as ongoing. They do this, in part, because they argue for the social aspect of reasoning by insisting on reasoning as a normative activity, and then accept a connection between normativity and a set of concepts such as obligation, necessitation, rule, and law. In making both of these moves, and especially the second, they see themselves as working downstream from Kant. Robert Brandom, who develops one such picture, describes what he regards as "perhaps Kant's deepest and most original idea" as follows:

What distinguishes judging and intentional doing from the activities of non-sapient [i.e. non-reasoning] creatures is not that they involve some special sort of mental processes, but that they are things knowers and agents are in a distinctive way *responsible* for. Judging and acting involve *commitments*. They are *endorsements*, exercises of *authority*. Responsibility, commitment, *endorsement*, authority—these are all *normative* notions.

But he goes on to say that "Kant talks about norms in the form of *rules*," and so "it follows that the most urgent philosophical task is to understand the nature of this normativity, the bindingness or validity (Verbindlichkeit, Gültigkeit) of conceptual norms...the conditions of the intelligibility of our being bound by conceptual norms."[1]

---

[1] Robert Brandom, *Reason in Philosophy: Animating Ideas* (Cambridge, MA: Harvard University Press, 2009), 32, emphasis in original. Brandom goes on to sketch (and endorse) various Hegelian developments of this insight that wind up with a picture of reasoning as a more fully social and also ongoing activity. Some of these developments will concern me below. But none of the developments he discusses

One can find similar connections between the normativity of reasons and their having the authority of laws or commands in others as well. In analyzing what showing that morality can be justified to us would entail, Christine Korsgaard says that we need to understand the "right of [normative] concepts to give laws to us."[2] Similarly, Jean Hampton, in a book entitled *The Authority of Reason,* glosses her claim that reasons have authority for us by saying "they prescribe a course of action for us," "they *direct* us," "they 'govern' us," and that in speaking of their authority, we speak of their status as "order" or "command."[3] Think here also of the ease with which we talk of good reasons and arguments as being compelling, of rationality as involving submitting to the "unforced force" of the better argument.[4] Now, although commands, rules, and laws differ from one another in ways that are important for their possible connection to reasoning, what they share is something like decisiveness or finality: they tell us what to do or think rather than, say, propose or counsel or suggest what to do or think. They bring our reflections and deliberations and conversations to an end, rather than keep them going.

The right to give laws or make rules or pass judgment are forms of authority, and so it is natural for those who make the connection between reasoning and normativity to speak of the authority of reason and have in mind some form of decisiveness. And it is here, I suggest, that the standard picture can hold captive even those who want to reject a purely individualist or monological conception of reasoning. Thus, to free us from this captivity, it will help to loosen the bonds of this connection between normativity and laws and commands while nevertheless preserving the connection between reasoning and normativity. I will do so in several steps. First, I want to look at a hurdle that any account of reasoning that ties it to the

---

involve a rejection of either the inherent normativity of reasoning or, more significant for my purposes, the connection of authority with something like necessitation.

[2] Christine Korsgaard, *The Sources of Normativity* (Cambridge: Cambridge University Press, 1996), 9.

[3] (Cambridge: Cambridge University Press, 1996), quotes are from 87, 88, 90, 88, 88. Jonathan Dancy takes issue with these characterizations of Hampton's, suggesting that, for one thing, they leave out what he calls "enticing" reasons, reasons that point out that certain desirable consequences will follow from a given action but don't thereby command us to pursue that consequence. Dancy, *Ethics without Principles* (Oxford: Oxford University Press, 2004).

[4] For a delightful meditation on the use and oddness of this kind of language to talk about arguments and reasons, see the opening of Robert Nozick, *Philosophical Explanations* (Cambridge, MA: Harvard University Press, 1981), 4–8. The locution "unforced force of the better argument" comes from Jürgen Habermas.

authority of laws and rules will have to overcome and examine how over-coming these hurdles pushes the sorts of Kantian accounts mentioned above into a set of characteristic positions and moves. Second, I will try to broaden our view of the conceptual space in which authority resides, suggesting that it may be best thought of as what Wittgenstein called a family-resemblance concept, or alternatively, that it belongs to a family of closely related con-cepts.[5] Third, I draw our attention to a set of examples that help contrast a variety of positions within this broader conceptual space. Finally, I distinguish two members of the family that occupy this space: the more familiar conception of authority that I call the authority of command, and a less familiar one that plays an important role going forward that I call the authority of connection. By understanding the normativity of reasoning in terms of the authority of connection, we can break free of the standard picture of reason and develop one that, in the words of Austen's Elizabeth Bennet, would fit us to make proposals to rational creatures.

If the authority of reason consists in its right to command or rule us, then reasoning with someone is, in the end, similar to commanding him. But one who has the right to command is thereby freed of the need to offer reasons, and offering reasons to someone is doing something other than merely commanding them. This difference is why, despite the commonly drawn connection between reason and normativity, the very idea of the authority of reasons can still have an oxymoronic ring to it. Here, for instance, is Hannah Arendt, placing authority *between* force on the one hand and reason on the other:

The authoritarian relation between the one who commands and the one who obeys rests neither on common reason nor on the power of the one who com-mands; what they have in common is the hierarchy itself, whose rightness and legitimacy both recognize and where both have their predetermined stable place.[6]

---

[5] Ludwig Wittgenstein, *Philosophical Investigations*, trans. G. E. M. Anscombe (Oxford: Wiley-Black-well, 1991), §67.

[6] "What Is Authority?," in *Between Past and Present*, 91–142 (New York: Penguin, 1961), 93. Though Arendt ties authority to hierarchy and command, she also develops an account of power and rule that has much in common with what I call the authority of connection below. See, for instance, Hannah Arendt, *The Human Condition* (Chicago: University of Chicago Press, 1958), "On Violence," in *Crises of the Republic* (New York: Harcourt Brace, 1972), 103–98. For an analysis of Arendt's conception of rule that analyzes it as a call for a response, and thus aligns it with what I call here the authority of connection, see Patchen Markell, "The Rule of the People: Arendt, Archê, and Democracy," *American Political Science Review* 100, no. 1 (February 2006): 1–14.

Faced with this tension between the authority of reason and the authority of the commander, philosophers have tried to model the authority of reasons on the authority of democratic law. Democratic laws are command-like in directing what we do, but they do not command in the unilateral way that appears to present the initial problem. This was, arguably, Kant's strategy. As we saw in the last chapter, Kant holds that "reason has no dictatorial authority. Its verdict is always that of free citizens." And we might understand that remark as seeing the need to distinguish the authority of reason from dictatorial authority precisely because of all the other features that they share. For Kant, and those who work in his wake, part of what robs reason of dictatorial authority is that its authority, like that of a democratic government, comes from below, from those who acknowledge its authority by acknowledging their responsibility to it.[7]

Understanding the authority of reason on the model of democratic lawmaking also provides a way of understanding three further features of reason's authority: it is itself norm-governed, reciprocal, and revisable. Reason's authority is norm-governed because not everything we say carries the authority of reason. We must obey certain norms to be reasoning at all.[8] It is reciprocal because the conditions of being subject to reason's authority (being rational and reasonable) are also the conditions necessary to wield it. And it is revisable because, as we saw in the last chapter, reason must always remain open to criticism.

These three features also hold of laws passed by a legitimate democratic government. In order to legitimately legislate, a democratic body must follow a set of procedures and stay within proscribed limits. Not every utterance of the US Congress has the status of federal law. It must be duly passed by the chamber in accordance with its rules, passed by the Senate, signed by the president, and not violate any of the strictures of the US Constitution as interpreted by the federal courts. Second, among the norms

---

[7] Brandom, *Reason in Philosophy*, ch. 2 is helpful here in tying together the role Kant gives to our autonomy in authorizing the normativity of rationality with both a shift towards social contract models of political legitimacy and a rejection of a certain kind of foundationalism in metaphysics.

[8] Brandom, *Reason in Philosophy* and Robert Brandom, *Making It Explicit* (Cambridge, MA: Harvard University Press, 1998) stresses inferential relations as constraining reasoning. Christine Korsgaard, *Self-Constitution* (Oxford: Oxford University Press, 2009) discusses Kant's principles of practical reason as constitutive norms of rational agency. For a helpful discussion of the parallels between procedures of democatic lawmaking and Kant's account of moral reasoning, see Andrews Reath, "Legislating the Moral Law," *Noûs* 28, no. 4 (December 1994): 435–64.

that govern democratic legislating are norms of reciprocity and revisability. There are two senses in which we might describe a legislative body as democratic: it might be democratically elected or chosen and it might operate according to democratic principles. In either case, however, one of the features that makes it democratic is that it embodies a form of reciprocity. In order to combine reciprocity with the capacity to obligate another, thinkers who follow this line of thought analyze democratic governance as involving what we might call mutual hierarchy. A relationship between two people is reciprocal in this sense if each has equivalent command authority over the other one, so that each is both sovereign and subject. Modern democratic legislatures are democratic in both the senses above, and thus are characterized by two sets of mutual hierarchical relationships. Though elected lawmakers command citizens by making the laws that govern them, citizens command their legislators by periodically electing them. And within a legislative body, each member has a conditional authority to decide for the body, and thus command what it does. The condition of wielding such authority is being in a position to cast the deciding vote on a given matter. In casting the deciding vote, I determine what the legislature does, but I only have that conditional authority if all members of the legislature do, and so it also amounts to a kind of symmetrical command structure. This model then shapes how many philosophers think about the reciprocity that is characteristic of reasoning, so that it also turns out to be a form of mutual command.[9]

Finally, though both a commander and a legislature can revise their directives, there is an important sense in which democratically passed laws are in principle open to revision. The difference lies in the source of the impetus to revise. When a dictator issues an order, it is, in general, not open to those being ordered to challenge the order or the dictator's authority to issue the order. In contrast, part of the procedure of democratic lawmaking includes an openness to challenge by the subjects of the law. This doesn't mean that those subject to a law are free to decide whether or not it has authority over them, but that the authority the law wields must be open to challenge from below. If we are reading Kant's remarks about reason's

---

[9] Christine Korsgaard, "Autonomy and the Second Person Within," *Ethics* (University of Chicago Press) 118 (October 2007): 8–23, and *The Sources of Normativity* (Cambridge: Cambridge University Press, 1996). Stephen Darwall, *The Second-Person Standpoint: Morality, Respect, and Accountability* (Cambridge, MA: Harvard University Press, 2006).

authority as these philosophers do, then we will understand the importance of reason remaining open to challenge as requiring that the verdict of reason be always revisable.

Notice, however, that allowing that the authoritative laws that reason gives us are revisable puts pressure on the requirement that reasons aspire to be decisive. Insofar as I am still entertaining possible objections to a decision I am considering, I have not yet made that decision. Decisions bring conversations to an end, it would seem, precisely by closing off the opportunity to raise objections or reasons for revision. In order to square this circle, we can distinguish between two means of remaining open to criticism. On the first, a matter can be closed in a way that allows for reopening. On the second, a matter is never fully closed to begin with. If we want to hold on to the idea that reasons aspire to decisiveness and yet wield an authority that is always subject to challenge, then we can adopt the first of these means. Thus, reasons, like the deliberations of a democratic legislature, lead to a final decision and a closure of the matter. But, in doing so, they leave open the possibility of revisiting the question should objections or further evidence be brought forward. As we will see below, abandoning the demand that reason wields legislative authority allows us to explore the other path.[10]

2.2 In Authority's Family

In distinguishing the authority of democratic legislatures from the authority of dictators, we have already broadened our conception of authority to admit of certain variations. But we can loosen things up even further. Sometimes authorities don't command or legislate or otherwise direct what we do and think, but rather stand in judgment over it. Thus, authority in this case is the right to pass judgment or deliver a normative assessment. Though courts and other ruling bodies do this, it is also how we might think of the role of principles of reason or inference or external facts in our

---

[10] Among the landmarks on this other path will be Rousseau's claim that the general will must constantly be remade, along with Hegel's account of the validation of norms via a process of historical reconstruction of their rationalizing development, a process that must always be open to revision in light of new evidence or ways of thinking. On the latter reading of Hegel, see Brandom, *Reason in Philosophy*, 102–4.

practices of deliberation. That is, what makes a stretch of thinking reasoning is that it is accountable or responsible to these authorities. So I can reason without following the baby steps of formal deductive logic (and even without knowing how to state these laws) but to claim that I am reasoning is to accept the authority of those laws to assess what I am doing. I am accountable or answerable or responsible to those principles.[11] In some sense, the idea of authority as the right to pass judgment is implicit in the idea of the *authority* of law or command. The commander issues a command. The command does not actually cause the commanded person to act a certain way. Nor do laws actually make people behave in accord with them. In both cases, what the command or law does is change what might be called the normative environment by altering the significance of certain actions. If you command me to stop and I nevertheless keep going, then this now counts as disobeying you, and depending on the nature of your right to command me, may also be insubordination or treason. If the legislature passes a 55mph speed limit, then my driving at 65mph becomes speeding. But note that changing the meaning and thus the normative valence of certain actions just amounts to saying that there is a ground for judging an action in a certain way. Depending on the case, we may then want to limit whose judgment counts as determinative or definitive. So we can analyze the right to rule or legislate as the right to appoint and guide a judge on whom is conferred the right to pass judgment.

Thinking of authority as the right to pass judgment also clarifies a further kind of authority, that of the expert. The expert's claim to authority can also be understood as a right to pass judgment over her field of expertise. Being an expert does not give someone the right to rule or legislate the behavior or thoughts of others, and while we may want to consult experts and follow their guidance, their authority ultimately consists in their capacity to determine whether what we do is correct by passing judgment on it.

Moreover, we can also broaden our sense of what authority can do by recognizing that the authority to command or obligate brings with it the authority to issue permissions, insofar as permission involves not being obligated not to do whatever one has permission to do. Thus, authoritative bodies can not only direct and command, but license and entitle. And these capacities can flow from the right to pass judgment as well. The expert can

---

[11] Brandom talks of authority this way in *Reason in Philosophy*.

rule authoritatively on whether a judgment made within her domain is correct, but she can also accept it as not incorrect and thus as permitted.

There are, I think, a number of other familiar uses of authority that would further widen its conceptual boundaries (think about the moral authority of a certain kind of moral exemplar or leader), but rather than survey these, I want to take the material so far gathered and come at it from a somewhat different angle. Thinking about authority in the context of describing various activities can lead us in two different, though related, directions. First, we can attend to what might be the credentials of the person or principle or agency claiming authority. This is a somewhat different question than asking about the source of authority, insofar as the credential is the condition for being invested with the authority, not the source or authoritative body that hands out the credential. So, for instance, the source of Congress's authority is the Constitution and behind that "we the people," but the credential of the current Congress is its having been duly elected in accord with the procedures laid out in the Constitution. I have the authority to give grades to students registered in my courses and to determine whether some dissertations submitted to my department merit the award of a doctorate. The source of both authorities is the university I work for, but my claim or credential to wield this authority is my being a professor there. In asking for the credentials that yield a certain form of authority, then, we are asking "Who must one be to do that? On the basis of what authority can we so act?" And of course, the answer will depend on what "that" is.

Second, we can attend to the activities our authority authorizes: grading and passing dissertations in the case of a professor, passing laws in the case of a legislature. As I suggested above, having authority involves the capacity to change the normative environment. We can thus call this aspect of authority, "normative capacity." So, my authority to issue grades goes beyond being able and allowed to report a letter between A and F to a student at the end of a class. It is, rather, that by so reporting, I change that student's normative environment, in part by changing her status within the university setting. Similarly, the police officer's authority to arrest those suspected of crimes is not merely a permission or ability to interrupt their activities, put them in handcuffs, or transport them to a court or a jail. It involves changing their status by putting them under arrest. To understand the police officer's authority in this sense, then, we have to know what this normative capacity amounts to, which may require knowing what the relation of arrest to punishment is, what counts as resisting arrest, and what sort of record is made of arrests and how that affects one's civil and social status.

Part of the structure of authority, then, is a pairing of credential and normative capacity, along perhaps with some connection between the two, some explanation of why this credential should entitle its bearer to wield this normative capacity. Passing judgment, ruling, commanding, licensing, entitling, and legislating are then all kinds of normative capacity, and depending on their extent and scope, can be acquired through a variety of credentials. And while such language derives from a consideration of people or groups of people wielding authority, it can also be used to think about the authority of reasons or principles. Rational principles thus have the capacity to pass judgment on stretches of reasoning or decisions or actions on the basis of their credentials as, perhaps, grounded in metaphysical truths or insofar as they are constitutive of thinking or acting at all, or because we recognize this authority and take ourselves to be responsible to it. And we have the normative capacity to mean something by our words, refer to the world, and render judgments in virtue of a set of credentials, whether the structure and size of our minds or brains, or by accepting responsibility for our thoughts and actions.[12]

But now note that the list of normative capacities listed above is incomplete, and that there are a number of activities we engage in that involve a normative capacity which we have in virtue of some credential that are not well captured by the canonical examples of authority canvassed above. Consider, for instance, the following list of activities that a least some people engage in legitimately: arresting someone, performing a legal marriage ceremony, voting in a municipal election, voting in a vote in Congress, conferring a degree, giving a grade on a term paper, giving you a reason to get off of my foot, assuring you that a mathematical proof is correct, showing you that a mathematical proof is correct, offering an idea in a brainstorming session, offering an idea in a joint deliberation, inviting you to join an organization of which I am a member, inviting you to dinner, inviting you to my wedding, proposing marriage, licensing you to attribute a belief to me, saying something to you by way of continuing or initiating a conversation. What I think unifies this disparate list is that in each case, one

---

[12] Again, one can find arguments of this form and with something like this content in the work of Korsgaard and Brandom, among others.

requires some form of credential to legitimately perform the action, and as a result of the action, some normative environment is changed. To see that some credential is required, note that in all cases, there are people who would be so ill-positioned to perform each action that we would say that they were doing so illegitimately. Thus, while anyone can, technically speaking, invite me to dinner, there are a fairly limited number of people who could appropriately do so, including centrally, people I know well, people representing organizations I belong to, people having a reason to want to know me better or to thank me for some prior action or to entice me to some future action. So, even if the credential here is vague and its boundaries less well defined than those necessary to pass a law or arrest someone, there are some credentials nevertheless. Similarly, while it is clear how passing a law changes the normative environment by changing the set of obligations those subject to the law are under and giving certain people the right to pass judgment along with guidelines for how to do so, there is also an important way that a normative environment changes as a result of the cases that involve inviting or offering. In these cases, once a legitimate offer or invitation has been made, though one may be free to turn it down, one has nevertheless been called on to respond, and, under normal circumstances, one's failure to respond will now count as a snub or a denial of the invitation's legitimacy.

Even if these and similar cases are similar in these ways, it would be an important mistake to unify them further, and to try to assimilate the cases of inviting and offering and proposing to those of ruling and directing and licensing. And because these are fundamentally different kinds of normative capacity, we should not be surprised if the credentials they require are also fundamentally different. What this suggests, then, is that there is a family of such activities. It is, I think, a purely terminological matter whether we want to call all members of this family forms of authority and thus broaden our concept of authority, or keep the concept of authority narrow and admit that it has an interesting set of cousins.

Broadening our vision of the conceptual terrain inhabited by "authority" has important effects when we return to the question of the authority of reason. For the most part, philosophers who have thought about the authority of reason have focused on the question of reason's credentials, assuming that the question of reason's normative capacities was settled. This has meant that they have not focused on the kind of authority that reasoning involves, but rather the grounds on which reasons might claim authority. And so questions about the authority of reasons become questions about the nature of reason or, perhaps, for those less metaphysically inclined, about our nature as reasoning beings: what grounds the right of reasons to command us, or our right, in invoking reasons, to command one another? So conceived, the problem looks ontological or at least theoretical: showing that a certain kind of entity or being has a certain property.

But if we want to take seriously the idea that reasoning is, fundamentally, an activity, then framing the problem this way leads us to grasp the wrong end of the stick, and ask the wrong question. Rather, reasoning is the name we give to our interactions when we claim they have a certain kind of structure, and in doing so, we also claim that the reasons that emerge from that interaction have a certain kind of authority insofar as they shape our normative environment. So the question we need to ask is not, "how could our reasons have the authority of commands or the right to pass judgment on us?" but "how could our utterances have the authority that would lead us to call them, and acknowledge them as, reasons?" Furthermore, if the nature of authority is an open question, then merely calling our authoritative utterances reasons is not yet doing much work, since it doesn't specify the nature of the normative capacity that we want our utterances to have. In that case, we are left with the following questions: what sort of capacities do we need our utterances to have, and how might they have those capacities?

This question is not ontological but practical, and so the answer will depend not on the nature of reason (or anything else, for that matter) but on what it is we want and need to do, what problems we face that might be solved through speaking to and with one another, by reasoning. Rather than focusing on our credentials as reasoners, understanding the authority involved in reasoning requires a focus on the capacities we need to reason as this activity is conceived according to the social picture.

2.3   Some Examples

To aid in this process of analysis and reimagination, it helps to have some examples of people altering normative environments, and to ask what their capacity to do so consists in and what it allows them to do. My aim in

bringing these examples forward is not to survey the whole field of normative capacities but to give us material to think through two positions within
that field. Consider, first, the following three cases: (1) A sergeant leading
her platoon on some military exercise orders one of the soldiers under her
command to go on ahead and scout for the enemy. (2) It is the beginning of
the semester and the professor tells his students that they will have a paper
due on a particular date. (3) The official at the Department of Motor
Vehicles verifies that I have the requisite skills to drive a car and issues me
a driver's license.[13] In the first two cases, someone tells someone else what to
do and their relationship to one another (commander–subordinate, teacher–
student) means that the mere fact that the person said it in this context turns
it into a kind of command, something that they must either obey or rebel
against. In the final case, though the issuing of a license is not a command,
something similar goes on. First, the licensing is done on the basis of a
credential that is connected to the relationship between the parties. And,
more importantly, the license can be seen as comprising a set of commands,
both to me and to others. Licensing me to drive removes the otherwise
standing command not to drive, just as all permissions can be understood as
the lack of obligations to refrain. And, moreover, in licensing me to drive,
the state, in the person of the DMV official, commands all others to
recognize me as a licensed driver, and thus not, in normal circumstances,
to prevent me from driving, deny me permission to drive, and so forth.
Thus, in all three cases, what is said or done alters the normative environment of those addressed, as well as of others: it changes the meanings of at
least one of their addressees' subsequent actions. Moreover, in all of these
cases, that change takes a particular form. The object of a direct command is
limited to obeying or rebelling: in the face of the legitimate order, failure to
obey just is rebellion, perhaps mild and worth overlooking, perhaps warranted, but rebellion nevertheless. And while it may appear that the latitude
in actions that follow the granting of a license (I can drive or not as and
when I please) makes the case of licensing different in kind, once we
recognize that a license is just a set of commands, we can see that it also
sets up a set of actions as counting as obedience or rebellion. If someone

---

[13] I include licensing here in part because it plays a large role in Brandom's account of reasoning. One
of the ways the account under development here differs from his lies in the difference in the nature of the
authority involved in licensing vs. inviting.

subsequently denies my right to drive, they are rebelling against the authority of the state to issue the license. This also brings out that even in the case of direct commands, there is always latitude in how the command is carried out. The soldier can head off to scout ahead by leading with his left foot or his right, with a song running through his head or while wondering when he will eat again, and so on. So what is crucial to the capacity invoked by commands and acts of licensing is that it involves establishing certain actions as obedience and others as rebellious, and, moreover, does this in a way that counts as definitive. (In these cases, if the one ordering is asked "why?" the response, "Because I said so" is not wholly inadequate).[14]

Now consider a second kind of case. A couple live together and are deciding how to spend the afternoon, and one suggests cleaning up the house because it is a mess. At a hiring meeting in an academic department, one faculty member says "We should hire candidate A because she will one day make a great chair." In the course of a debate in parliament, an MP objects to a new anti-terrorism law because it will curtail certain civil liberties. In these cases, someone says something that he thinks someone else ought to hear, pay attention to, not dismiss. That is, he regards himself as being entitled not only to say what he says but to demand to be heard and paid attention to in saying it. Those who are addressed in these examples are responsible to the speaker in the very literal sense that they are called on to respond to what was said. Moreover, the capacity to call for a response is a result of having certain credentials, certain standing, and not the content of what was said. Whether the MP offers a good reason for his vote or not doesn't change the call for a response that it creates, though it may change the particular responses his action calls forth. But if a foreign journalist makes the same criticism of the anti-terrorism law, she cannot thereby call for a response from the other MPs, and this is precisely because she lacks the credential to participate in parliamentary deliberation and debate. The journalist cannot change the normative environment of the other MPs in

[14] Of course, just how adequate it is will depend on the relationship in question and the stringency of the authority it establishes, and what other ends it may have. Though the teacher may be within her rights to respond so, she may thereby miss an opportunity for educating her students. Furthermore, in all three of these cases, it is possible that the parties stand in a variety of relationships to one another, and so although questioning an order from the point of view of the commander–subordinate relationship is a form of rebellion, it may be demanded and licensed by the soldier's relation as friend or fellow citizen or human being.

the same way that their fellow MP can. Whereas the failure to heed the journalist may be a sign of inattentiveness or moral callousness, it will not count as the same kind of rebuke or rejection, as it will when their fellow MPs' words are ignored.

Though both kinds of cases involve a credential–normative capacity pairing, the capacities that they involve are importantly different. The issuing of a command or a license leaves those governed by the action with the choice of obedience or rebellion. But when someone suggests a course of action, there is nothing to obey and nothing to rebel against. Those to whom these suggestions have been addressed can show that they have heard and taken seriously what was said to them by agreeing with it *or* by arguing against it. Though *a* response has been called for, there are a variety of responses that will answer the call. Moreover, there are two forms of response that will fail in some sense to count as recognizing the change in normative environment, and thus the capacity and credential of the speaker to affect it. One can flatly ignore what someone has said, treating their words as mere noise, or dismiss what they say out of hand. But, interestingly, one can also fail to recognize the normative capacity being invoked in these cases by unreflectively accepting what was said as if it were a command. I can't reason with you if you don't take seriously what I say, but I also can't reason with you if you take my every suggestion as a command or a definitive conclusion.[15]

We have here, then, two different constellations of normative capacity, each of which will require a different kind of credential to invoke legitimately. In the rest of the chapter, I explore these constellations more systematically, and begin to explore what a picture of reasoning that relied on the kinds of authority at issue in the second set of examples might look like. Since the cases in the first group all involve the capacity to issue legitimate commands, I call such authority the authority of command. I argue that in the second set of cases, the normative capacity of the parties arises from their connection to one another, and so I call this the authority of connection. By so naming it, I mean to highlight the fact that when the

---

[15] In a passage I quoted in Chapter 1, Stanley Cavell discusses the difference between claims that must be obeyed or rebelled against and those that can be acknowledged or dismissed in the context of describing the authority of ordinary language philosophers claiming that "we say..." (*The Claim of Reason* (Oxford: Oxford University Press, 1979), 19–20; see also his discussion of speaking for oneself (at 27–8). I mean my discussion here to be moving in basically the same direction as his.

speaker is ignored in these cases, it is not his status as commander that is being rebelled against, but his status as part of a "we" with those with whom he is speaking that is being denied.[16]

2.4 Authority of Command vs. Authority of Connection: Five Differences

2.4.1 Normative Capacity: Unilateral vs. Mutual

Building off these examples and my initial remarks about them, I explore five key differences between these forms of authority. My primary aim here is to flesh out the idea of the authority of connection and its central differences from the more familiar authority of command. The first and clearest difference involves, as I suggested above, the particular normative capacity that each involves. The authority of command gives me the right to issue commands (including in the form of granting permissions and licenses). This right is a capacity to determine unilaterally some piece of the normative environment of those I command. This has two related dimensions: my commands, in general, alter the normative environments of my subordinates independently of what they do or think or say. It may be, of course, that my right to command depends on their prior agreement to place themselves under my command, but once my authority is established, I don't need further contributions from those I command to effectively shape their normative environment. Second, the unilateral character of the capacity requires a credential that rests on a similarly asymmetrical relationship: the commander's capacity to effectively shape his subordinate's normative environment does not entail and may even preclude that his subordinate have a similar capacity vis-à-vis the commander. As we will see below, there are cases where each of us is the other's commander, but in this case, there are two separate asymmetrical relationships in place, not one reciprocal one.

---

[16] It is important to note as well that these are not cases where I try to wield an altogether different kind of authority: that of the authority figure who presumes to speak for us because he knows better. You can also challenge and call into question my advice when I assume this kind of authority without rebelling against me, but my claim to be able to advise you comes, in such a case, not from my connection to you but from my connection to or knowledge of, some set of facts or truths or traditions.

When we converse with each other on the basis of our connections, on the other hand, our capacity is a capacity to try to shape a normative environment we share, that we inhabit together. There are two features of this description that bear further discussion. First, the capacity here is essentially mutual: we are both entitled to try to shape each other's normative environment in part because we are each shaping a normative environment we share. Moreover, what gives me the capacity to shape our normative environment (membership in a "we" of which we are both a part) in these cases also gives you that capacity, and so in trying to shape that environment, I also accept that you can as well. Thus, the authority of connection is essentially reciprocal.

Second, the capacity in question here is a capacity to try something, and this brings out another way that the capacity is mutual. I have the capacity to call forth some response from you, but no particular response. So, that while my speaking changes your normative environment in one sense, it only changes our normative environment if you respond to what I say by accepting it. That means that the capacity I have in virtue of the authority of connection is, in part, answerable to you. Your response to what I say plays a role in determining what I have managed to do. In many accounts of authority, the fact that I am answerable or accountable or responsible to you amounts to saying that you have authority over me. And so the fact that my normative capacity here is both a capacity of mine and answerable to you will mean that the authority of connection is not something that can be wielded or established unilaterally or asymmetrically. In claiming the normative capacity at issue here, it turns out that I acknowledge yours as well.

All of the examples of the authority of connection I gave in the previous section relied on the speaker having an established credential in virtue of an already established standing as a member of a group with an established right to speak and demand a response. That means that what each of these people say is answerable to those with whom they are speaking, but that their right to speak is not itself dependent on the current acknowledgement of their interlocutors. The MP who blithely ignores the comments of her fellow MP has failed to give proper recognition to his standing, not called that standing into question. But we can also imagine relationships that are neither formalized nor fixed, where this standing is not assured ahead of time. If we are in the process of becoming friends, for instance, then not only may it be uncertain whether you will agree to my suggestions and

invitations, but it may also not be a determined matter whether in even
trying to make them I am presuming a level of relationship that does not yet
exist. In such a case, my presumption as well as my suggestion will be
answerable to you and you can legitimately deny both what I say and my
right to say it.

2.4.2 Relationship: Hierarchical vs. Reciprocal

The second difference involves the nature of the relationship on which our
authority rests. To command another, I need to stand in a hierarchical
relation to him, to be in a superior position that gives me the right to
command. This is true even if we accept that the only thing that can
legitimately grant the right to command is the acknowledgement of the
one commanded. For in such a case, even though there is no prior hierarchy, the acknowledgement establishes one. But to speak for another from
the authority of connection does not require hierarchy; only our standing
in a relationship that creates an "us" that can be spoken for, about this, in
this way.

   The reciprocity required to construct the authority of connection is not
the mutual hierarchy characteristic of democratic legislatures. As I suggested
above, two people stand in a relationship of mutual hierarchy if each stands
to the other in a hierarchical relationship where she commands the other.
The possibility that I can command you while at the same time you can
command me is made possible by considering each member of such a
relationship under at least two aspects: as both sovereign and subject, to
use Rousseau's terms.[17] Contrast this with a relation of reciprocal connection. We stand in such a relationship not in virtue of our ability each to
command the other, but rather in virtue of our ability to express, to use
Kant's language, our veto, to answer each other's attempts to alter our
normative environment. To put the point in the terms developed above,
our reciprocal connection consists in our capacity to respond to one another
and to call for such responses. In a reciprocal relationship, what we suggest
to or urge on each other is fully answerable to that other person's uptake or
rejection of it. In virtue of such a relationship, either party can demand to be
given a hearing, but cannot issue a command. Calling for a response goes

---

[17] "The Social Contract," in *The Social Contract and Other Later Political Writings*, ed. and trans. Victor
Gourevitch (Cambridge: Cambridge University Press, 1997), 49–51 (bk. 1, chs. 6–7).

beyond calling for a reaction, requiring that one heeds that response, which in turn requires that the other's response itself calls for a response. Thus in calling for a response from someone, I must simultaneously acknowledge their capacity to call for a response from me. Moreover, in acknowledging that, I do not acknowledge an additional relationship in which we stand, but merely the features of this one.[18]

Apart from personal relationships such as friendships and egalitarian marriages, the most familiar example of relations of reciprocal connections in the philosophical literature is also among democratic citizens, although considered in a different light. As democratic citizens we partake of our reciprocal relationship when we deliberate politically and reasonably, rather than when we vote. Reasonable deliberation requires that each participant be properly responsive to the rejection of his reasons by his fellow deliberators.[19] Such deliberation does not work by each party issuing conditional commands and waiting to see if the commands of others serve to satisfy the conditions. Deliberation on its own does not yield laws or decisions. So when I offer reasons in the course of deliberation, I am not commanding anyone or (even conditionally) determining the law. That would be to regard deliberation on the model of voting. Rather, I invite my fellow citizens to accept what I say and must be responsive to their rejection of my proposals. Authority in such a relationship is only eventually constructed when all come to agreement, rather than when a set of conditions on conditional commands are met.

The point of distinguishing relationships of mutual hierarchy from those characterized by reciprocal connection is to make clear that the authority of connection requires more than mere symmetry in our relationships, and that relationships can be symmetrical while still being hierarchical. Although symmetrical relationships of command are not hierarchical in a straightforward way, they must, nevertheless, rely on an existing hierarchical structure, a structure that is not necessary to generate the authority of connection.

---

[18] Relations of reciprocal connection thus share fundamental features with the relations of reciprocal recognition that are central to Hegel's account of normativity, and the work of contemporary Hegelians. For discussions of recognition, see Brandom, *Reasons in Philosophy*, ch. 2, Axel Honneth, *The Struggle for Recognition*, trans. Joel Anderson (Cambridge, MA: MIT Press, 1996), Robert Pippin, *Hegel's Practical Philosophy: Rational Agency as Ethical Life* (Cambridge: Cambridge University Press, 2008). The shift from relations of mutual hierarchy to relations of reciprocal recognition as central to the activity of reasoning is one of the central ways that the picture on offer here is Hegelian.

[19] Chapter 6.3–6 discusses reasonable deliberation in general, and this requirement in particular.

2.4.3 Credentials: Backward-Looking vs. Forward-Looking [20]

From these first two differences follow two further ones. The third difference involves the nature of the credentials needed for each kind of authority.
In the case of the authority of command, credentials must be "backward-
looking" in the sense that whatever it is that establishes them must be prior
to the exercise of the capacity they authorize: do we already stand in a
relationship that gives me the authority, the superior position, to command
you? One reason the source of my authority to command must be backward-looking is that only then can the question of my authority remain
properly normative, by being independent of its being effective. If I try to
establish my authority to command by commanding you and take my
authority to have commanded you to depend on my success, then my
command has no normative effect. Your failure to follow my command in
this case would not count as disobedience, but rather would show that
I lacked the capacity to command you in the first place.

In the case of the authority of connection, however, things are different
and more complicated. When I attempt to alter our normative environment
in this way, I rely on my understanding of the relationship between us. But
whether or not our relationship is such as to support my capacity to alter it,
or alter it in this particular way, may depend not merely on my understanding of our relationship or on firmly established, verifiable facts, but also on
your understanding of our relationship. Furthermore, the final status of my
authority may depend not only on whether I have the right to try to alter
your normative environment, but whether my attempt actually succeeds.
Since even if there are definite facts that establish our positions vis-à-vis one
another in a way that grounds my right to call for a response, these facts may
very well not fully determine whether I should succeed in eliciting the
response I hope for. Thus, the question of whether I have changed our
normative environment as I intended may not be settled until after I have
spoken because it may depend on whether you acknowledge what I say as
what you would say as well.[21] And so my normative capacity can at times

---

[20] I have drawn the contrast between backward-looking and forward-looking conceptions with
regard to democratic legitimacy in my "Democratic Legitimacy and the 2000 Election," *Law and
Philosophy* 21 (2002): 197–220.

[21] And given that intentions are not always fully formed prior to what we say and do but often only
become fully formed as we act, it may be the case that what I intended to do will depend on what
happens after I speak. On this general point about intentions, see Robert Pippin, *Hegel's Practical*

remain indeterminate until you either acknowledge or refuse what I said. But that means that in an important sense, my authority to speak this way, at least here and now, need not be something that is established ahead of time, but can be constituted, as it were, after the fact.[22] Thus, it must at least be possible for the credentials that ground the authority of connection to be forward-looking.

The distinction between the capacity to call for a response and the capacity to elicit the response I wish and thus the capacity to change our normative environment in this way can help make sense of understanding relationships, like that between citizens, that are a mix of legal, political, and social status. Thus, it is in virtue of our legal relation as citizens, a relation that is established ahead of time, that we have the credentials and thus the right to speak to one another on political matters, whether through deliberating or voting. But this legal status may not on its own establish a social and political relationship wherein one can fully reciprocally speak for and be spoken for by one's fellow citizens. Groups that are legally granted citizenship but are stigmatized or marginalized in various ways will often have the legal right to speak and be heard, but not the social authority to be heeded as representative of the whole. Whatever such citizens say will be taken as articulating their particular group interests or viewpoint, and not as possibly speaking for other citizens outside their group. They will be heard, for instance, as raising "women's issues" or "black issues" or "gay issues" rather than as raising questions of equality, fairness, or justice, or of social and economic organization more generally. In those cases, though they may invoke the commanding authority of the law to be able to give voice to their positions, their fellow citizens prevent them from also having the authority of connection.

Philosophy: Rational Agency as Ethical Life (Cambridge: Cambridge University Press, 2008), Talbot Brewer, *The Retrieval of Ethics* (Oxford: Oxford University Press, 2009). Thanks to David Owen for pointing out its relevance here.

[22] More needs to be said about this point to make it fully precise and convincing. By making the establishment of the authority of connection forward-looking I do not mean to rule out the possibility that some failures to acknowledge connection are wrong, inappropriate, or unreasonable. But, even in such cases, it will be the case that in dismissing the connection, one breaks or alters it. Also, in some cases, invocations of connection will also rest on fixed norms or status, such as legal status that is established ahead of time. Nevertheless, there is plenty of room between allowing another to speak and taking seriously what they say. I can invoke the authority of command of the law to make you let me speak, but I cannot so force you to take what I say seriously. There I am dependent on your attitude towards me and what I say.

2.4.4 *Loci of Authority: Internal vs. Distributed*

The fourth difference between the authority of command and the authority of connection concerns where authority resides. I label it by saying that whereas the authority of command is lodged in the hands of the commander, the authority of connection rests in part in the hands of the listener rather than the speaker. This point is somewhat tricky but vitally important if we are to understand why the authority of connection is fundamentally different from the authority of command, including the authority to license, and how it might thus alter our picture of reasoning.

Imagine that when the sergeant orders one of his soldiers to scout on ahead, the soldier, or someone watching the scene, questions the sergeant's authority. What kinds of facts might establish that the sergeant had the authority to issue this order? We would first need to look to facts about the sergeant: that he is in fact the commanding officer, that he has a right to order his soldiers in this way in these circumstances. This might, admittedly, require looking to the general context that places the sergeant in the position of authority: the military code, the authority of whoever placed him in command, and so forth. And it might also require answering questions about the soldier's standing: that he is under the sergeant's command, that there aren't extenuating circumstances that block such command, and so forth. Nevertheless, what we are trying to establish in establishing the sergeant's authority to command is that here and now, giving this order, the final decision of what order to give and whether or not, in speaking, to give an order, are his to make. It is in this sense that the authority lies, as it were, in his hands. Again, this feature of the authority of command is a result of the unilateral nature of normative capacity it involves. Once I am entitled to issue commands (or grant licenses), then whether or not my words count as commands depends entirely on me.

Now take the case where I make a suggestion to you about how to spend the afternoon, and rather than acknowledging my suggestion by either endorsing it or responding to it, you question my authority to make it. There are at least two ways you might issue such a challenge. You might be questioning whether we stand in the kind of relationship that would entitle me to make suggestions to you on this matter. If a stranger joined our discussion about where to have dinner we would question his authority thus. In this case, a response would have the same structure as the one above: I would need to point to our relationship (or lack thereof) and thus to where each of us stands vis-à-vis the other. Even here, however, there is another possibility. Not all of the relationships that ground the authority of connection are firmly and publicly established ahead of time. So there is the possibility that in making my suggestion I am also at the same time inviting you to understand our relationship in a new or not yet fully established manner. Whether I have the authority is not yet settled, but open to you to accept or reject.

Furthermore, you can also challenge the authority of what I say by challenging not my right to make suggestions about this to you but rather what I have suggested. Here you challenge, as it were, not the existence of our "we" but its intimacy, its scope. In political contexts, this might happen when you reject my proposal on the grounds that it is not based in what John Rawls calls "public reason," but instead on the basis of religious beliefs that we do not share.[23] In doing so, you accept that our status as fellow citizens entitles us to try to speak politically for one another. But you object to my proposal because it presumes that we form a kind of community of believers that we do not form. By denying that we form a "we" in the way I imply, you reject my capacity to shape this part of our normative environment. It is not just that you disagree with the content of what I say but rather that you reject the extent of the authority I am presuming in saying it here. To see this, note that you might also so object to a fellow citizen who makes a non-pubic reason argument you think is sound for a position you agree with because it rests on a presumption about the scope of the "we" we form as citizens. The objection, then, is not to the proposal itself, or even to the argument for it, but to my authority to make this argument in this context.

Faced with these sorts of challenges to my authority, what sort of facts would determine whether our relationship supported the authority I have implicitly claimed? Unlike in the case of commanding, they are not primarily about me. If my attempt to alter the normative environment rests on the authority of connection, then it rests on there being a "we" whose environment can be changed in this way. What does there being such a "we" depend on? Among other things, it depends on us, on our acknowledge-

[23] See *Political Liberalism* (New York: Columbia University Press, 1996), esp. 212–54, and "The Idea of Public Reason Revisited" in his *Collected Papers*, ed. Sam Freeman (Cambridge, MA: Harvard University Press, 1999), 573–615.

ment of such a unit. In relying on what I take to be our connection, I have acknowledged it, and so what is left to determine is whether you, too, will acknowledge it. Thus, in order to establish my authority in this case, we need to determine something about you, not me. It is in this sense, then, that the authority of connection rests not entirely in the hands of the one speaking, but also in the hands of the one being spoken for: at the moment when I make my suggestion of how we should spend the afternoon, the final decision of whether or not I have the capacity, here and now, to alter our normative environment with this suggestion is no longer mine to make but yours to acknowledge or refuse or even ignore. This means that particular instances of the authority of connection are not wielded like a sword, but jointly constructed like a bridge.

Now, suggesting that there is a form of authority whose status can be determined after its invocation by those over whom it is invoked will and should raise eyebrows. How, it will be asked, could such a form of authority be normative at all and thus how could it be a genuine form of authority? If every failure to acknowledge an attempt to speak for another, or to respond to a call for response dissolves the basis of that authority, then it will be impossible to rebel against such authority, which is to say that it won't be normative at all.

There are several things to be said in reply to this worry. The first requires that we appreciate the kind of concept "authority" is. It is not a purely normative concept, but rather a descriptive term that refers to the normative order. To say that a given situation is one where someone has authority, or that a relationship grounds a particular form of authority is to describe something, to make a claim which can be true or false, albeit to make a claim that is about something normative. And so to say that your refusal to acknowledge my authority makes it the case that I don't have authority here is to make no kind of normative judgment as to whether your refusal was proper or not, justified or not. We can, for instance, say of the socially marginalized citizens mentioned above, that they lack the authority to participate as full equals in political deliberation, but it is unjust that they do so. Nor must it deny the further claim that I had the initial entitlement to make the suggestion in the first place. That of course can also be denied, but it is important in understanding the authority of connection to see the possibility of denying part of the authority without denying all of it.

Second, as I have already said, the authority of connection differs from the authority of command in terms of the options it leaves open to the recipient of the authoritative statement. Refusing my suggestions does not involve rebellion but a failure of acknowledgement, a kind of dismissal. Furthermore, I can reject what you say either by denying there is any kind of an "us" whose normative environment you have the capacity to alter or by merely denying that what you have said does alter that environment. In the latter case, I reject your suggestion but accept our connection. I do not undermine your authority but (re)constitute it, by acknowledging that you have the capacity to change our normative environment, even though you have failed this time to exercise it effectively. Put differently, in responding to you, I answer your call and thus acknowledge its authority, while at the same time denying you the capacity to elicit the particular response you were hoping for.

Finally, to say that the authority of connection has forward-looking credentials and a distributed location does not imply that its invocation is not norm-governed. That is, even if you can undermine my authority through your response or lack of it, not everything you do to ignore me will have that effect. Just as not every utterance in the imperative mood is an authoritative command, not every failure to respond is an authoritative denial of authority. It will be the work of future chapters to work out some of the central norms of the activity of reasoning that make it a site for the construction of the authority of connection.

2.4.5 *What Authority Does: Ending vs. Continuing Conversations*

The fifth difference between the authority of command and the authority of connection has to do not with what they are but with what they do. Whereas the authority of command serves to end our conversations, the authority of connection leaves room for them to keep going. That commanding another serves to end a conversation should be clear enough. After all, the only appropriate response to a legitimate command is to carry it out, perhaps adding in a "yes, sir" by way of acknowledgement that the command has been heard and will be obeyed. Commanding is not a way of initiating or continuing a conversation but of bringing about action. What is perhaps less obvious but no less important is that the issuing of commands cannot serve to prolong a conversation. Questioning a command itself, and not merely how to implement it, is questioning its authority and thus a form of rebellion. Of course, rebellion need not be violent, and it can be carried out with words, so that in rebelling against an authoritative command I can engage the commander in a conversation. But even when I do this, I am engaging the commander in a *different* conversation than the one that issued the command, a conversation about the extent of his authority, not about the considerations that went into the decision to issue the order in the first place.[24] The command has not prolonged the initial conversation but rather set the stage for a new one.

When I make a proposal or offer an invitation with the authority of connection, however, things are rather different. First of all, the capacity I exercise is a call for a response, and as we have seen, calling for a response as opposed to a mere reaction is to call for something that will require a response in turn. Moreover, since among the things your response may do is confirm or challenge or reconfigure my authority, there is ample opportunity for my invocation of authority to open space for our conversation to continue in any number of new ways. Calling for a response in this sense is not merely initiating a final sequence of words in the way that issuing an order that calls for a "yes, sir" is.[25]

Moreover, it turns out that I cannot bring conversations to a close by invoking the authority of connection. This is obvious in the cases where I aim to alter our normative environment by making suggestions or offering criticisms as in the examples with which I began. In response to a suggestion whose authority you recognize, you need to make some sort of response, even if only to accept it. As I argued in Chapter 1, if I say, "I think we should clean up the house this afternoon because it's a mess," you can't just go and get the vacuum cleaner without somehow signaling your agreement. Since against a wide background of shared understandings, one way to accept a proposal is to begin wordlessly to act on it, you may be able to signal your agreement by getting the vacuum cleaner. But there is

---

[24] That isn't to deny that among the things I might raise in the conversation that follows my refusal to obey are criticisms of the commander's decision and questions about what considerations went into that decision. But the point of raising these at this point in the story is not to figure out what the commander should have commanded, but to show that his incompetence unfits him for his authority, at least in this instance. In that sense, they form, as I say above, part of a new conversation about the extent of the commander's authority.

[25] The connection of authority and beginning as it figures in Hannah Arendt's work is the focus of Markell, "Rule of the People."

nevertheless an important difference between assenting to a proposal and obeying an order, and I mistreat your suggestion if I treat it as calling for obedience and not assent. We can make this clear by making explicit what will, in the normal course of things, often go unsaid: in response to a suggestion made and heard as a suggestion, you need to at least express agreement and issue a judgment: "Yeah, you're right. Why don't I go get the vacuum cleaner while you start picking up the dirty clothes." As we saw in the last chapter, this conversation-sustaining capacity is characteristic of the activity of reasoning pictured as social and ongoing.

But, even in the case where I try to decide for us on the basis of our connection, rather than just try to speak for us, there is an important sense in which this does not end our conversation so much as put it on hold. Because my authority in trying to decide for us in this case is established in part by being answerable to your acknowledgement of it, you must be free to withdraw that acknowledgment in the future. So my authority, even if accepted for the moment, is not thereby established once and for all. There is still room for it to be challenged or denied, and so the conversation in which I attempted to speak authoritatively is not closed, even if we have stopped talking for now. If I am authorized to make suggestions, but not to command you, I overstep that authority if I try to speak for you in a way that leaves no room for you to criticize what I say. I also overstep my authority if I try to close off room for later criticism for good.

Speaking in a manner that ends our conversation would require declaring that the time for objections and criticisms is over, and thus fail to give others a chance to express their reservations or veto. But that would be to undermine the reciprocal nature of our relationship that establishes and maintains the connection on which the initial capacity to affect our normative environment is based. A definitive ending of the conversation, then, whether in the form of a command that no more be said, or in an unwillingness to hear any objections as more than "merely words," does not protect and establish once and for all my authority. Rather, it undermines that authority.

There are at least two ways that a conversation may stop and begin again. In the first, the conversation is in a kind of lull. Neither party has anything to say, but the conversation has not come to a stop, even if it is not continued here and now. If, during the current lull, one of the participants was called away or engaged on another topic (even by the same people), we would say that the first conversation had been interrupted, and were one of us to try to pick up the original thread later on, we might say that we were hoping to continue our earlier conversation. All this suggests that the conversation has not come to an end but was still open.

Contrast this with a case where a conversation comes to an end, but nothing in the way it ends prevents one of the participants from reopening it later. In such a case, we stop talking not because we have nothing more to say here and now, but because we have reached a kind of accord or agreement. If another person or topic were to be introduced at this point, it would not count as an interruption. In fact, if a person intruded and asked if it was alright to join us or take one of us away, we might reply that it was fine, as "we were finished talking." Such a conversation may be something we can revisit or reopen later. I may change my mind about its topic or come to have new information. This may prompt me to suggest that we return to the topic, rather than continue discussing it. This suggests that the conversation had indeed come to an end, and that we would now be reopening it.

As with the discussion of symmetrical relationships above, the point I want to make here can be usefully made in terms of two types of democratic activity. When citizens have voted, then, barring irregularities, the decision has been made and the activity of deciding by voting is finished. This need not preclude any of us returning to the question later on and reopening our consideration of it, but barring that, the thing is at an end. In the case of deliberation, however, though we may run out of things to say on a given topic, we can't thereby declare the matter closed, only leave off discussing it (perhaps to now call a vote). What this means for our pictures of reasoning is this: earlier I suggested that those who picture reasoning as like democratic legislating accept that reasoning is open to revision, but that in doing so, what they imagine is not that reasoning never comes to an end, but that it can always be revisited. If, however, we picture reasoning as invoking the authority of connection, then we get a different way of picturing it being revisable. Reasoning, so conceived, is ongoing not because we can return to it, but because declaring that we have come to an end of reasoning is not a move that is authorized within the activity itself.

2.5 Back to Reasons

At the beginning of this chapter, I suggested that the authority invoked in reasoning would have to be norm-governed, reciprocal, and revisable, and I laid out how these features could be captured on an analogy with democratic legislation. If we picture reason as having the authority of command, then this analogy will hold a certain promise for us, one that might capture Kant's insight that reason has no dictatorial authority. But my hope in this chapter has been to open up space for a more radical inheritance of Kant's claim, one that does not merely distribute command authority among the members of a democratic assembly, but which imagines reasoning as the attempt to construct the authority of connection. And that then points to a different way to understand what might be involved in claiming that reasoning is a norm-governed, reciprocal, and revisable activity. As we have just seen, reasoning that constructs the authority of connection is revisable in the sense of always ongoing and social. In order to be reasoning and *not* commanding, one needs to continually hold open what one says to criticism and to regard one's moves in reasoning as calls for the response of others. But calling for a response from others is, as we also saw, an activity that must simultaneously accept their right to call for our response, whether directly when they criticize what we say, or indirectly, when they make claims that they hold open to criticism. To say that reasoning is reciprocal is to acknowledge just this point: that I cannot participate in the activity of reasoning without simultaneously acknowledging your participation and actively inviting your active participation. Finally, because the authority of connection that the activity of reasoning constructs is established in a forward-looking manner, the sense in which reasoning is a norm-governed activity must also shift. The model of democratic legislation imagines a set of authoritative norms that are established ahead of time, perhaps theoretically grounded, and which are not, at least in the normal course of legislation, up for grabs through the activity itself. This means that the activity of working out or establishing the norms is potentially of a different sort than the activity that the norms define. Constitution-writing and legislating are different activities, and their standards of excellence and the skills they require are also different. But if we are to picture reasoning as establishing its authority in a forward-looking manner, then this also involves imagining that it establishes and authorizes the very norms that govern its activity. This means that the process of drawing out these norms and eliciting their authority is not different from the process of reasoning itself, and thus that it cannot be done in a manner that is final, monological, or decisive. Instead, in what follows, I will make a proposal about the norms that govern a set of reasoning activities, by trying to describe what is characteristic of those activities and doing so in ways that obey the very norms I elicit. The success of that effort, like any attempt to construct the authority of connection, depends on the response it brings and the conversations it begins.

3

The Rational Significance
of Conversation

3.1 Introduction

Conversation is an activity in which we speak with others. If one were to look at the descriptions of our speaking with others found in the philosophical literature, one might come to the conclusion that we only speak with others when we have a purpose in view: to reach a joint decision, pass along information, or convince someone of something. But, of course, most of the time we actually spend in conversation is not so purposeful. Much of it is idle.

And yet, much of that idle conversation plays a significant role in our lives, a role that is significant because of, among other things, how it shapes both the activity of reasoning and the reasons we exchange. I don't mean to claim here that all forms of idle conversation involve reasoning, though some do. But it is important to my argument to understand that even those forms of idle conversation that do not involve reasoning are governed by norms that also shape the spaces of reasons we can come to inhabit together. According to the social picture of reasoning, reasoning is a species of conversation. So what is distinctive about this picture becomes clearer if we examine conversation more generally. Since casual conversation is not generally taken as a subject of philosophical attention, it first needs to be brought more clearly into view. We can then see why some of its central features make it a feasible site for thinking about reasoning. In order to begin, consider two scenes from *Pride and Prejudice*:

"My dear Mr. Bennet," said his lady to him one day, "have you heard that Netherfield Park is let at last?"

Mr. Bennet replied that he had not.

"But it is," returned she; "for Mrs. Long has just been here, and she told me all
about it."

Mr. Bennet made no answer.

"Do not you want to know who has taken it?" cried his wife impatiently.

"You want to tell me, and I have no objection to hearing it."

This was invitation enough.[1]

Mrs. Bennet has some information she wants to give, and tries to get her
husband to ask about it: in that sense their conversation engages with the
world and they, through it, with each other. It may also in various ways
have the effect of altering or reinforcing their relationship and giving each
other more confidence about when and how they might offer to speak for
one another. The particular give and take here also relies on the Bennets'
having a long history together, and knowing each other well. But in the
exchange itself, no one is attempting to or offering to speak for the other,
even if we might agree that what Mrs. Bennet will go on to tell Mr. Bennet
will have to be answerable to facts about the world, and thus to whether he
might also assent to them. (What she goes on to tell him, after all, are pieces
of ordinary empirical information: the name of the tenant, his eligibility and
standing in the world). Even though Mrs. Bennet has an agenda here, her
engagement with Mr. Bennet is also about trying to pass the time at
breakfast *with* him, rather than letting him hide behind his newspaper. If
there wasn't this bit of neighborhood news to impart, she would have no
doubt found something else to talk to him about.

Contrast this with a second case, where the conversation is, in one sense,
even more completely idle: there is no decision to be made or information
to impart, and no one even seems to have an agenda, only an evening to pass
engaged in conversation. Nevertheless, both participants take much of what
they say as offering up a view of things that they are offering to the other to
accept and their exchange shows that they are concerned not to be misunderstood:

"Mr. Darcy is not to be laughed at!" cried Elizabeth. "That is an uncommon
advantage, and uncommon I hope it will continue, for it would be a great loss to
me to have many such acquaintance. I dearly love a laugh."

---

[1] Jane Austen, *Pride and Prejudice*, Oxford World Classics, ed. James Kinsley (Oxford: Oxford
University Press, 2008), vol. I, ch. I, 1.

"Miss Bingley," said he, "has given me credit for more than can be. The wisest and the best of men, nay, the wisest and best of their actions, may be rendered ridiculous by a person whose first object in life is a joke."

"Certainly," replied Elizabeth—"there are such people, but I hope I am not one of them. I hope I never ridicule what is wise or good. Follies and nonsense, whims and inconsistencies do divert me, I own, and I laugh at them whenever I can.—But these, I suppose, are precisely what you are without."

"Perhaps that is not possible for any one. But it has been the study of my life to avoid those weaknesses which often expose a strong understanding to ridicule."

"Such as vanity and pride."

"Yes, vanity is a weakness indeed. But pride—where there is a real superiority of mind, pride will be always under good regulation."

Elizabeth turned away to hide a smile.[2]

At the end of this conversation, Elizabeth and Mr. Darcy have a clearer sense of where they stand vis-à-vis each other, at least on this tiny bit of terrain.

Here each offers reasons and not mere information, in the sense that they are inviting the other to accept what they say as speaking for them as well, even though neither is trying to convince the other of the aptness of those reasons.[3] It is, at this point in their relationship, a matter of some indifference whether or not either of them takes up what the other says. Each marks a position and is sufficiently responsive to the other to be concerned that the other has properly grasped what that position comes to. It is this responsiveness that I will claim marks their exchange as reasoning. It is of far less concern to either that the other accepts the invitation to occupy the position as well, or that they find, together, a position that they might inhabit together.[4] The full support for this claim will develop over the next three

---

[2] Ibid. ch. II, 42–3.

[3] Note that we can see here what will become a major difference between the picture offered here and both Habermas's theory of communicative action, and Brandom's account of the game of giving and asking for reasons. Elizabeth and Mr. Darcy are not communicating with the aim of reaching a "rationally motivated agreement" (Habermas) and while each makes assertions that enters them into the game of "giving and asking for reasons" by licensing others to draw conclusions about their beliefs (Brandom), this is also true of the earlier conversation between Mr. and Mrs. Bennet, and so doesn't mark out the particular feature of this exchange I mean to bring into view.

[4] The smile that marks the end of their conversation is a sign that Elizabeth feels she has fully understood Darcy's position and wants nothing more to do with it. It is a sign of Darcy's beginning to have feelings for her that he is left ultimately unsatisfied with this conclusion, not because he is concerned that she should think him right. Rather, he worries, or at least comes over the course of the novel to see that he should worry, that she might find his position uninviting.

chapters. To begin, we need to consider why casual conversations might have any rational significance at all by getting clear on what they are and how they work. I discuss three central features of casual conversation in the next section: casual conversation is endless, can be playful, and the point of what we say in the course of it has to do with our attunement to one another.

3.2 Causal Conversation Is Endless

Casual conversation is endless in two related senses. First, it neither aims to do anything or get anywhere in particular: it does not have an end in the sense of a goal.[5] It also does not have a built in termination point: when we enter a casual conversation, we cannot say when or where it will count as finished. It is the type of activity that Amy Dickinson describes in her memoir:

My mother and her three sisters, Lena, Millie, and Jean, have been engaged in a conversation about nothing in particular that started in 1929. To successfully track a typical encounter with the four of them would require a team of linguists with clipboard and sensors, feeding streams of data into a supercomputer.

Conversational categories include: Ancestor Trivia, Politics and You, Jellies and Preserves, Movies, Books and Popular Culture, Humidity, *Law & Order* (the television show), Pets: Dead or Alive, Snow Removal, Cold and Ice, Offspring, Curtains.[6]

Note that it is both these forms of endlessness, rather than any particular description of the content or weightiness of the topics of casual conversation, that mark it as casual. That is to say, what marks the kind of talk I want to focus on is not that it is concerned with trivial matters, although it can be, nor that it is negative or scurrilous or about others,[7] though it may be. In fact, many so-called casual conversations will comprise some of the momentous activities of a person's life. It is often while engaged in such

---

[5] Suzanne Eggins and Diana Slade, for instance, define casual conversation as "talk which is NOT motivated by any clear pragmatic purpose" (*Analysing Casual Conversation* (London: Continuum, 1997), 19).

[6] *The Mighty Queens of Freeville* (New York: Hyperion, 2009), 33.

[7] These are features generally used to define gossip, an important variety of casual conversation.

conversations that we fall in love, or come to understand who we or others are, or cement the bonds of friendship. Further, if I am right about the role casual conversations play in the construction of the reasons we have, then such conversation is, in general, one of the more important activities we engage in qua reasoning beings.[8] What defines a conversation as casual is that it is a form of interaction that is in principle ongoing as a result of the fact that it is going nowhere in particular.

If we are trying to decide where to have dinner or whom to support in the next election or even trying to decide what to do, we will be engaged in a goal-directed activity, and if and when we reach our goal, the activity will come to a close. Once we agree on a restaurant, there is nothing more to say on the topic, and it will be odd for one of us, having agreed to the decision, to start bringing forth further considerations that bear on the choice, just for the sake of keeping the activity of deciding where to eat going. The same is true in the theoretical case: reasoning as a path to forming conclusions and belief is end-directed, and once the goal is reached, there is nothing more to say. Of course, part of reaching a reasonable decision is that it we regard it as open to revisit and revise in the light of new or newly remembered information or a change in attitude. Having chosen a restaurant, I may subsequently remember that it is closed today, or suddenly develop a craving for a different kind of food, and these shifts give me good grounds for reopening the decision. But what I cannot reasonably do is to keep discussing where we should eat merely for the sake of prolonging the activity of making *this* decision.

In the case of casual conversation, however, such attempts to continue talking are the norm, and not an odd exception. If a topic of conversation comes to a close or peters out, we move to other ones. In contrast to goal-directed conversations, when we are engaged in casual conversation, the odd thing would be for one of us to peremptorily say at a pause in the conversation, "Well, we've finished that. Good-bye." As Erving Goffman puts the point:

Once individuals enter a conversation they are obliged to continue it until they have the kind of basis for withdrawing that will neutralize the potentially offensive implications of taking leave of others. While engaged in the interaction it will be

---

[8] Eggins and Slade argue that it is "concerned with the joint construction of social reality" (*Analysing Casual Conversation*, 6).

necessary for them to have subjects at hand to talk about that fit the occasion and yet provide content enough to keep the talk going; in other words, safe supplies are needed. What we call "small talk" serves this purpose. When individuals use up their small talk, they find themselves officially lodged in a state of talk but with nothing to talk about; interaction-consciousness experienced as a "painful silence" is the typical consequence.[9]

The claim that casual conversation is not goal-directed is a claim about the activity itself rather than the motivations of the participants in the activity. To get clearer on this point, it helps to distinguish the activity itself and its possible aims and goals from the ends or motivations of the participants in engaging in the activity on the one hand, and the reasons that they have for saying various things within the conversation on the other. Often, and even perhaps always, we enter into casual conversation with an end in view: to pass the time or to get to know someone better. In other cases, we might enter a conversation in response to social norms: because to fail to do so would be rude. Even if I enter the conversation with an end in view, the conversation itself isn't directed at such a goal. While an engaging conversation may serve me well as a means to pass the time, what makes it a success as a conversation is not that it satisfies the ends that led me to it, but something internal to the kind of interaction it is.

Moreover, casual conversation, being a norm-governed activity, provides a kind of guidance to what people say at each moment in the conversation. But these norms and the guidance they provide are not connected to nor do they derive their authority from some overall end that the conversation has in the way that they would be for a more goal-directed interaction like making a joint decision. The claim being made here, then, is about the activity as a whole, and neither the motivations of the participants for entering it, nor what guides them as they make particular moves within the conversation.

It is this open-endedness of casual conversation that makes it a useful context in which to think of the activity of reasoning. If reasoning is a species of conversation, then we can picture the activity of reasoning without having to describe it as goal-directed. We can imagine the activity of reasoning as open-ended and ongoing. When we engage with one

⁹ "Alienation from Interaction," in *Interaction Ritual: Essays on Face-to-Face Behavior*, 113–36 (New York: Pantheon, 1982), 120.

another with a common goal in mind, to solve a problem or come to a decision, this goal serves to structure our interaction, and in various ways determine its bounds and provide markers for its progress and success.[10] If we regard such activity as our model of reasoning, then we are quickly drawn towards the standard picture of reasons as aspiring to be conclusive or decisive and reasoning as episodic.

Keeping in mind the activity of casual conversation and entertaining the thought that such conversation is the genus of which reasoning is a species, avoids prematurely accepting that it must be an essential feature of reasons that they aspire to decisiveness or of reasoning that it comes to an end. Rather, the category of possibly conclusive or decisive considerations would be narrower than the category of reasons, and only be relevant to a range of activities narrower than the full scope of activities that involve reasoning, namely that subset whose context makes them goal-directed. Paying more attention to the nature and norms of casual conversation thus makes it easier to appreciate the role reasons play in maintaining and shaping our relationships and constructing the social space in which we live our lives together, an activity that is neither goal-directed nor has a natural stopping point. This is not yet to say conclusively that engaging in casual conversation does have anything to do with reasoning, but only that if we want to break the hold that the standard picture has on our conception of reasoning as episodic, posing this question will be a fruitful way to do so.

3.3 Casual Conversation Can Be Playful

Second, casual conversation leaves room for playfulness. Even though conversation is a norm- and rule-governed activity, its rules and norms do not firmly insist that one stands completely behind everything one says in the course of casual conversation. We may try things out, say something because it is amusing or what is called for or merely to keep the conversation going, without articulating a position we are ready to defend or whose consequences we are willing to accept. We can, in the course of such

---

[10] These are the sorts of markers that Candace Vogler takes as markers of it being reasoning at all. See my discussion in Chapter 1.4, and Candace Vogler, *Reasonably Vicious* (Cambridge, MA: Harvard University Press, 2002), 157–70.

conversations, let our words run somewhat freely. Contrast this freedom with the rules that govern a negotiation, for instance. If we are negotiating, and I make an offer, I can't later withdraw it by saying I didn't really mean it. Such behavior would call into question the extent to which I am negotiating in good faith, and thus, in a sense, negotiating at all. Responsibility is, in this sense, a constitutive requirement of negotiation, and in fact, most if not all forms of goal-directed reasoning. In fact, failure to stand behind what one says in the course of goal-directed forms of reasoning is generally taken to be a prime example of irrationality: a case of not taking appropriate means to one's declared ends.[11] It also explains the recurring tendency to try to analyze failures to keep promises as involving some kind of failure of reason or reasoning capacity.[12] In a casual conversation, however, I might say something and later withdraw it or fail to stand by it without calling into question my good faith participation in the conversation. It was just a joke, perhaps, or meant to provoke a response, or a mere idle speculation.

The possibility of playfulness in casual conversation has two consequences that make such conversations a good place to begin an investigation of the activity of reasoning. The first is that it provides for a kind of freedom in our interactions that allows us to use those interactions to change our relationships from within. The possibility of somewhat playful talk gives us the ability to rearrange and alter the spaces of reasons we inhabit without abandoning them or seeking some Archimedean point outside them from which to judge them. I can try to change our relationship by offering to speak for you in a new way, by offering you a new kind of reason. Doing so leaves me vulnerable to your rejecting my offer, however, and if my offer is one I am bound to stand behind, then I am not only vulnerable to having my reason rejected, but to thereby losing our relationship. So the possibility

---

[11] Vogler, for instance, offers such cases as instances of irrationality: searching for her keys, she unpacks her purse and does not find them, but then continually returns to her purse to hunt for her keys; from Anscombe, continuing to pump in order to fill a bucket despite being made aware that there is a leak in the pipe; offering to do a card trick when one has no idea of how to go about it, and then moving the cards around for a while as if the trick will happen on its own (ibid. 172–5).

[12] There are several variants of this attempt: Friedrich Nietzsche, On the Genealogy of Morals, ed. and trans. Walter Kaufmann (New York: Random House, 1967), 57, argues in the second essay that having the right to make promises requires having a certain sort of capacity that he describes as a memory of the will, but involves something like the ability to stand behind what you say, to take it as a reason for later action. See also John Rawls's discussion of promising in "Two Concepts of Rules," Philosophical Review 64, no. 1 (January 1955): 3–32, and David Gauthier's discussion of the rationality of constrained maximization in Morals by Agreement (Oxford: Oxford University Press, 1986).

of playful talk within casual conversation gives me a lower-cost means of testing the waters, so to speak. It gives me a way of risking the rejection of my proposal without thereby risking the dissolution of our relationship.[13]

Of course, the value and appropriateness of such play depends on its falling within certain limits. The attraction, but also arguably the virtue, of charming conversationalists comes in large part from their willingness to be playful, to be more faithful to the animation of the conversation than to their own positions and those of their conversational partners. But such virtue easily slips into the vice of roguishness, which we might characterize as an inability or unwillingness to forgo such play, to ever stand behind what one says. At some point, play slips into irresponsibility. As Mr. Darcy says of the charming rogue Mr. Wickham, "Mr. Wickham is blessed with such happy manners as may ensure his *making* friends—whether he may be equally capable of *retaining* them, is less certain."[14]

The possibility of playfulness in idle talk comes with the ever-present possibility of irresponsibility. This possibility represents another aspect of conversation that gives them rational significance. When we engage in casual conversation, if we are to be responsible for what we say, for which reasons we offer and stand behind, this will have to be because we take responsibility for our stands ourselves. If nothing binds us to our words, then we must make our word our bond, must endeavor to stand behind what we say. If we are used to searching for the foundations of reasons' authority in something beyond the activity of talking to one another, in fundamental facts about human nature or the way the world is or in the logic of communicative action, then this feature of casual conversation will look like a recipe for anarchy, and lead us to think that casual conversation will be a singularly unhelpful place to look as we try to understand reasons and reasoning.

---

[13] As John Morreal puts the point, "we are allowed to think and say almost anything in bantering conversation, just as the traditional court jester could say almost anything to the monarch" ("Gossip and Humor," in *Good Gossip*, ed. Robert Goodman and Aaron Ben-Ze'ev, 56–64 (Lawrence, KS: University of Kansas Press, 1994), 63). In a different register, the freedom available in casual conversation is similar to the kind of freedom Michel Foucault tends to celebrate that comes from recognizing the contingency and constructedness of our social norms, from no longer seeing them as inevitable or natural or God-given. See Michel Foucault, "What Is Enlightenment?," in *The Foucault Reader*, ed. Paul Rabinow, 32–50 (New York: Pantheon, 1984), and for a discussion of this theme in Foucault, James Tully, "To Think and Act Differently: Comparing Critical Ethos and Critical Theory," in *Public Philosophy in a New Key*, vol. 1, 71–132 (Cambridge: Cambridge University Press, 2009).

[14] *Pride and Prejudice*, vol. I, ch. XVIII, 70.

But if we want to learn to think about reasoning and its authority differently, then the need to take responsibility for what we say in casual conversation turns out to point us in a helpful direction. To see why, consider a point Stanley Cavell makes about our attitudes towards other norms, whether of language or morality. Cavell argues that the wish to ground our authority, and thus the responsibility we bear in exercising that authority, in something beyond or below or outside what we do and say is ultimately a way of *not* taking responsibility for our stands and positions, of seeing those positions as more or less forced on us and others.[15] Cavell's thought, or at least what I want to take from that thought, is that in looking for firm and unimpeachable grounding for our norms or for an authority that would stand behind our words, we are inevitably sloughing off our own responsibility for them. If, for instance, what assures either of us that I will stand behind my words is that there is some external force requiring me to, then though I may be held responsible for what I say, I have not *taken* responsibility for it. Kant helpfully describes the reliance on transcendental or anyways external grounds of our norms and their authority as "tutelage."[16] It is this kind of tutelage that Kant thought Enlightenment had the aim of escaping. From this perspective, the fact that we must on our own take responsibility for what we say is not so unattractive. And if the possibility of irresponsible talk is what makes this taking responsibility possible, even necessary, then we can also come to see the possibility of irresponsibility in casual conversation as one of the reasons to pay closer attention to it and its rational significance. Casual conversation, according to this view, turns out to be, much more than its more rule-bound cousins, a site in which we *take* responsibility for what we say.

---

[15] *The Claim of Reason* (Oxford: Oxford University Press, 1979), 215–16: "we sometimes feel about our more obviously moral commitments that they are more or less arbitrary, and that if they are to have *real* or full power they must be rooted in, or 'based upon', a reality deeper than the fact of morality itself. It is as though we try to get the world to provide answers in a way which is independent of our responsibility for *claiming* something to be so (to get God to tell us what we must do in a way which is independent of our responsibility for choice)."

[16] Immanuel Kant, "An Answer to the Question: What Is Enlightenment?," in *Kant's Political Writings*, ed. Hans Reiss, 54–60 (Cambridge: Cambridge University Press, 1991).

3.4 Conversation as Attunement

The third feature of casual conversation is that though the activity is aimless, what is said within it is not pointless, and its point has to do with what I call attunement. This is a slightly more difficult point to make, and will require a bit of a detour into ordinary language philosophy in order to make clearly.

Let me start with Cavell's interpretation of Wittgenstein and J. L. Austin. Cavell takes them to be arguing that in order to for me to understand what you have said when you say something, I need to know not only what the words you utter mean, but what you take the point of uttering them here and now to me to be. That is, there is a difference between knowing what your words mean, and knowing what you mean in uttering them, and I can only determine the latter if I know what you take the point of saying them to be. I can know what your words mean by looking them up in a dictionary. But this will not tell me what you mean by uttering them.[17]

The importance of this argument for Wittgenstein and Austin is that it provides them with a diagnosis of what goes wrong when someone who is skeptical about the possibility of our really knowing anything pushes his position by repeatedly asking someone who makes an ordinary claim to knowledge, "But how do you know?" The skeptic's mistake, here, is to assume that what is meant by words is fixed by the meaning of the words alone, so that a sentence being meaningful is a context-independent feature.[18] Thus, to take Austin's famous example, the words "But how do you know it's a goldfinch?" have a more or less clear meaning in a variety of contexts where we might ask this question (when, for instance, we are questioning the speaker's knowledge of ornithology or her line of sight or

---

[17] This analysis of what we mean when we say something in conversation is importantly different from the analyses favored by Habermas and Brandom. For Brandom, what I mean is determined by the inferences I license in asserting it, and this, as Habermas notes, seems to come apart from my point in saying it to you. Habermas goes on to describe his own view of what we mean by uttering something "in communication" in terms of the "goal of communication" being "rationally motivated agreement": "we understand a speech act when we know the conditions and consequences of the rationally motivated agreement that a speaker could attain with this speech act" (Jürgen Habermas, "From Kant to Hegel: On Robert Brandom's Pragmatic Philosophy of Language," in *Truth and Justification*, ed. and trans. Barbara Fultner, 131–74 (Cambridge, MA: MIT Press, 2003), 165). Habermas's approach makes the activity of reasoning end-directed, however, in a way that the phenomena I am trying to picture here is not.

[18] Cavell, *Claim of Reason*, 206–11. For a more extensive discussion of Cavell's argument and its importance to philosophy, see Avner Baz, "On When Words Are Called for: Cavell, McDowell, and the Wording of the World" *Inquiry* 46 (2003): 473–500.

trying to learn how to identify goldfinches ourselves). It is, however, these contexts that make this sentence meaningful, make it something it would be meaningful for a speaker to say. There would be a point to saying these words in those contexts. But the skeptic is imagining giving these words a different meaning without providing them a context in which those words could be uttered to mean that, where asking the question the skeptic wants to ask would have no point. The skeptic wants to suggest that we can utter these words to ask, in effect, "How do you know that it is a real goldfinch, not a figment of our collective imagination?" in a context that is otherwise unremarkable. In such a context, the argument continues, there can be no point in asking this question, and so it turns out that he cannot mean this by uttering those words.

I wish to take two lessons from Cavell's analysis: (1) claiming that the meaning of what we say depends on its point is to treat our utterances as act-like, as doing something, and so to call forth J. L. Austin's speech-act theory and the variety of things we do with words.[19] (2) Because we cannot just read the point of saying something off of the meaning of the words said, and because, moreover, the point of saying certain things in certain kinds of conversations may not be obvious, the point of our utterances is something to which we need to pay attention. Unpacking this second lesson will lead us back to Austin and also to the point of casual conversation.

To get there, it helps to look at more familiar terrain. When we engage in goal-directed conversations, the point of our contributions is set by the goal of the conversation. If we are making vacation plans together, we take it that the point of saying one thing rather than another, here and now, is that it contributes to our reaching a joint decision. If we begin to talk about last night's match, or the latest political scandal, we will be rightly rebuked for wasting everyone's time, for making pointless and irrelevant comments.

When we focus on such goal-directed conversations, the importance of Cavell's insight can be missed precisely because the structure of the activity apparently provides everyone with a clear answer.[20] But when we turn to

---

[19] J. L. Austin, *How to Do Things with Words* (2nd edn, Cambridge, MA: Harvard University Press, 1975).

[20] This appearance turns out to be mistaken in a manner that will be made clear in Chapter 6 as a result of the analysis presented in this one. To rush ahead briefly, there are at least two different activities we can engage in with others that aim to reach joint decisions: deliberation and negotiation or bargaining. As I will define them later, in deliberation we seek common ground, and so the point of our claims is to find

casual conversation, we can lose sight of Cavell's point in a different way: since casual conversations do not have a goal in this sense, the goal cannot determine the point of what we say, and why we say this rather than that. So it may seem that there can be no real point to saying anything in particular in a casual conversation. It is thus tempting to dismiss the whole range of things that are said in casual conversations as meaningless (or at least lacking in significance) because pointless. This conclusion would also go a long way to explaining their irresponsibility. Such conversations lack a goal or end, and thus they seem to lack a point. Therefore, the argument goes, what is said in them also appears to lack a point. And this means that what is said in casual conversations is not the kind of thing anyone could stand behind because, in the end, nothing is actually said when we speak in such contexts. Such a conclusion suggests that the rogue's failure is not *how* he participates in idle conversation, but *that* he does so, that it is a mark of a virtuous character not to have "the talent of conversing easily with those I have never seen before."[21] But it thus speaks with the voice of prejudice and misses the import of Cavell's point.

I describe this as missing Cavell's point because it takes the point (or lack of it) of our speaking to be obvious from its context, and so not something to which we need to pay attention. Taking Cavell's point seriously in our thinking about casual conversation would mean thinking more seriously about the norms guiding such conversation and thus about the point of saying particular things at particular moments within it. And here we need to go beyond what Cavell says in *The Claim of Reason* and the standard fare of philosophers who think about skepticism and our capacity to make meaningful assertions.

The examples encountered in such work almost always involve someone informing another and the question they raise is whether or not there is a point in doing so. For Cavell, this emphasis on informing is tied to his project of unpacking what the skeptic about knowledge might be up to.[22] But the emphasis on informative utterances also reflects a widespread view

---

and map that ground, whereas in negotiation, we aim for a mutually acceptable compromise, and so the point of our claims is to find the compromise that is best for us. In either case, the structure of the activity determines the point of our utterances, but if we fail to distinguish these two activities, we may not properly see what it so determines.

[21] *Pride and Prejudice*, vol. II, ch. VIII, 135. This is again Darcy listing his character traits.

[22] Cavell explicitly discusses utterances whose aim is not to inform in Stanley Cavell, "Passionate and Performative Utterance," in *Contending with Stanley Cavell*, ed. Russell Goodman, 177–98 (Oxford: Oxford University Press, 2005), where he points out that among the things Austin's *How to Do Things*

that what we primarily do in conversation is what socio-linguist Deborah Tannen calls report-talk.[23] Report-talk is a means of transmitting information and can include straightforward reporting, but also the telling of jokes and the recounting of stories.[24]

Tannen argues that not all conversation consists of report-talk. To make clear this thought, she contrasts report-talk with what she calls "rapport-talk," talk whose aim is not to inform but to forge connections with others. Rapport-talk works by establishing common features of our positions and outlooks, for example by exchanging stories which serve to place each of us in a similar world rather than by evaluating the information reported on to see if it is true, useful, justified, and so forth. Unlike report-talk, which is directed towards the transmission of information, the point of rapport-talk is the conversation itself, and thus in part, making sure that it keeps going.[25] Rapport-talk, then, is one of the primary forms that casual conversation takes.

To see the difference between report-talk and rapport-talk, imagine that we are chatting at a reception, and I tell you about the difficulty I had concentrating on the train on my way here because the person sitting behind me was having a particularly loud and inane conversation on his cellphone. If you understand me to be engaging in report talk, then you will take me to be giving you some information about my day or the condition of train travel, and, taking a page from Cavell, you might wonder what my point is in bringing this up here and now, to you. If you decide that my point is to place a problem before you, then you will think that I am requesting a solution. So, you might respond by giving me strategies for getting people to talk less loudly on cellphones or by recommending a certain brand of earplugs.

with Words was meant to challenge was a widespread philosophical view that the importance of our utterances lay in their capacity to inform or describe.

[23] A similar assumption seems widespread in the philosophy of language, where assertions are taken to be the central form of language use that raises questions of meaning and content. The depth of this assumption is apparent even in as social and pragmatist a view as Robert Brandom's inferentialism (see Making It Explicit (Cambridge, MA: Harvard University Press, 1998)). For instance, on p. 647, where he argues that it is our norms of ordinary conversation that determine our norms for interpreting what others are saying, claiming that "The only answer to the question of what makes one interpretation better than another is what makes one conversation better than another," but goes on to make clear that what makes a conversation better is purely a matter of whether the participants properly understand the assertions each makes.

[24] You Just Don't Understand: Women and Men In Conversation (New York: William Morrow and Co., 1990), 77.

[25] Ibid. 102.

If, however, you take me to be engaging in rapport-talk, then the point of my comment will be very different. Rapport-talk is meant to forge connections, and this often begins by making clear where I stand so that you can assure me you stand with me. My story is meant to place me in a world of technology gone wild that amplifies the powers of inconsiderateness and leaves those of us devoted to certain kinds of quiet, contemplative activity less and less space to engage in them. And I tell you this story not to inform you of a fact about the world I think you somehow don't know, or to ask you for a solution to a problem I have, but to solicit your agreement and recognition of my description. I am not expecting you to respond with solutions but solidarity, commiseration. You can affirm our connection, our shared placement, by telling me about all the loud TVs in bars and cafés or about an experience of yours with a loud person on a cellphone. Or you can disavow my attempt at connection by defending my tormentor, and singing the praises of all of this now public conversation.

What, then, is the point of saying one thing rather than another in the course of rapport-talk? As Tannen develops the idea, there are two related reasons for saying certain things in rapport-talk: to keep the conversation going and to place oneself vis-à-vis one's conversation partner. That is, one point of rapport-talk is to forge, develop, and determine the shape and limits of our relationships. But that means that in engaging in such talk, we test to what degree we can talk with and for certain others and to what degree we are prepared to let them talk with and for us. And now we can see why paying attention to casual conversation and rapport-talk will be important to developing a truly social picture of reasoning. In working out where we can speak for each other, we work out what reasons we are likely to share. Having told you my story about my experience on the train, and having been met with your story about a loud TV in a café, I now have grounds for thinking that somewhere being quiet or cut off from such behavior is a reason in its favor for both of us. If we are trying to decide on a place to meet, I can suggest some place and recommend it to you by saying that it's quiet, and not be terribly worried that it's also a place with bad cellphone reception.[26] More broadly and more vaguely, it might give me grounds for

---

[26] I mean this example to be suggestive, nothing more. Clearly the defender of the standard picture can handle this case as one where our conversation reveals basic facts about our preferences, and these are relevant only because of the type of decision we try to reach, one that aims to satisfy those preferences.

confidence in thinking that we will have more to say to one another talking about books than reality TV shows or day trading on the stock market. But if reasons are invitations to take our words as speaking for others as well, then figuring out the reasons we share is tantamount to figuring out the reasons we have. And so casual conversation looks as if it will play a significant role in the determination of the spaces of reasons we each inhabit.

3.5 The Ends of Casual Speech Acts

There is, however, a problem with the argument above. If there is a point to saying something in a casual conversation, it appears that there is something suspiciously like a goal in the terrain of casual conversation after all: we seem to have merely moved the goalposts rather than eliminated them. It appears that even the reasoning that goes on in casual conversation is end-directed and episodic. It is just directed at a different kind of goal: fostering relationships rather than making decisions. In order to find a point for our utterances in casual conversation, we have to treat them like actions. In so doing, we reintroduce the whole goal-driven structure of reasoning that the standard picture assumes. Just as the activity of deciding what to do aims at something and so has success conditions that derive from that goal, so the activity of attuning myself with others has an end (our attunement) and thus must have success conditions that derive from this goal. Thus, what differentiates conversational moves that partake of the activity of reasoning from those that don't, the objection continues, is whether they promote the end of attunement. And that suggests that even casual conversation, insofar as it is meaningful, a site of rational significance, is fundamentally end-directed, and so merely a variation on the kind of reasoning we find in more conventional reason-guided activities such as deciding and concluding.[27]

To respond to this challenge, then, we need to understand what is fundamentally different about the activities of casual conversation that

---

[27] I suspect that this is Jürgen Habermas's position. At the very least, it would parallel the basic distinction he makes between strategic and communicative action, both of which are directed at ends, but fundamentally different kinds of ends (see *The Theory of Communicative Action*, trans. Thomas McCarthy, 2 vols. (Boston: Beacon Press, 1984)).

produce attunement and those directed at more familiar goals such as decisions and conclusions. The relation between what is said in casual conversation and what that brings about is not best thought of in terms of steps and goals or means and ends. There is a difference between what an activity brings about and its end or goal. In the course of playing a game of soccer, the players may burn calories, get some fresh air, have fun, and build camaraderie, but none of these are properly speaking, the end of the activity itself. The end of the activity itself is to win by scoring more goals than your opponents. My claim above is that casual conversation is a site of rational significance because through our participation in it, we work to construct and situate ourselves within spaces of reasons. But though this is a product of casual conversation, it is neither the end of the activity nor even necessarily the goal we have in entering such conversations.

In addition, it turns out that there are important differences between how what we say in casual conversation brings about attunement and how activities directed at a goal bring about that goal. Getting clear on this point, however, requires yet another detour into ordinary language philosophy. We can begin by distinguishing two pathways by which we might act in order to bring about an end. The first is straightforwardly causal: I pull a lever and this engages the mechanism that moves the piece of track that directs the trolley to the left rather than the right. The second relies on certain given normative structures, authoritative conventions: I say "I do" while standing next to the right person, in front of the right person, in the right context, and I thereby marry the person I am standing next to.

In *How to Do Things with Words*, Austin argues that many of our words can bring about ends, can serve as actions, in this second manner, through what he called their "illocutionary" force. Austin distinguishes the illocutionary act, what I do in saying X, from two other kinds of speech acts: the locutionary, what I say in saying X, and the perlocutionary act, what I do by saying X.[28] Saying "The cat is on the mat" performs the locutionary act of asserting that the cat is on the mat. Saying "I do" at the right moment in a marriage ceremony performs the illocutionary act of marrying someone. And shouting "Fire!" in a crowded theater performs the perlocutionary act of starting a panicked rush for the exits. Austin provides detailed analysis of the illocutionary act, its success conditions and its various types. Much

---

[28] *How to Do Things with Words.*

subsequent work that relies on speech-act theory has followed Austin in focusing on the illocutionary act as distinguished from the locutionary act. This, however, leaves the category of the perlocutionary act rather unanalyzed. It is generally assumed that perlocutionary acts work through basically causal mechanisms, albeit psychological ones. If by shouting "boo" at you from my hidden spot in the darkened room you have just entered, I scare you or get your heart racing, I have performed a perlocutionary act with my words, and we can trace the effects of this action to your startle response. I could have made any loud noise and had the same effect: the words don't matter. In other cases, they do: I come home from the doctor and say, "He wants to do more tests." In so saying, I may alarm you or worry you, and again, these will be through the perlocutionary action of my words. But the explanation of this effect will go via certain psychological theories about the effects of certain stimuli on your emotions. This suggests that analyzing perlocutionary acts will not tell us much about *language* or at any rate about the particularly linguistic things we do with words.[29] This apparent consequence is no doubt why the category has gone relatively unexplored.

The need to assimilate the effectiveness of perlocutionary acts to causal mechanisms while at the same time treating them as *speech* acts creates a problem when we try to analyze words that might be categorizable as perlocutionary (the way "I promise" is illocutionary). As Cavell points out, whereas the "illocutionary act is built into the verb that names it" so that "to say them is to do them," this will not (cannot) be true of perlocutionary verbs.[30] He thus concludes that we need a different way of understanding particularly perlocutionary words, since it looks like they cannot work through either causal mechanisms or authoritative structure:

If to say "I alarm you" (or chastise, or seduce, or outrage, or discombobulate you) *were (eo ipso)* to chastise or seduce or outrage or discombobulate you, I would be exercising some hypnotic or other raylike power over you and you would have lost

---

[29] See, for instance, Habermas's discussion of perlocutionary actions in *Theory of Communicative Action*, vol. 1, 286–95. Habermas claims that perlocutionary actions are essentially strategic, unlike illocutionary and locutionary actions.

[30] Stanley Cavell, "Passionate Utterance," in *Contending with Stanley Cavell*, ed. Russell Goodman (Oxford: Oxford University Press, 2005), 187. In what follows, I use Cavell's discussion of the perlocutionary nature of passionate speech to make clear the distinction between the end and point of saying something. Cavell's reading of Austin is not the only one in the literature, and many would object to it as a reading of Austin (it differs from Habermas's, for instance). Those interpretive debates have no bearing on the discussion below.

your freedom in responding to my speech. Contrariwise, if I could not rationally expect, by expressing myself to you, fairly reliably to have the effect of alarming you or reassuring you, of offending or amusing you, boring or interesting you, exasperating or fascinating you…I would lack the capacity to make myself intelligible to you. And what you would lack is not some information I might impart to you.[31]

In other words, perlocutionary verbs must make a difference, but not via the determinate mechanisms of either straightforward (ray-like) causation, or via the authoritative structures of conventions that make illocutionary acts possible.

Cavell argues that we can understand perlocutionary words by understanding how they work in what he calls passionate utterances. Rather than focus on what delineates passionate utterances, I want to look at Cavell's understanding of how perlocutionary effect is brought about by such utterances, for it leads to an understanding of speech acts, and thus of reasons, that are not end-driven despite there being a point to uttering them.

Since perlocutionary acts, unlike illocutionary ones, do not rely on established procedures, but must create their own effects, Cavell claims that in attempting to bring about a perlocutionary effect I "am not invoking a procedure but inviting an exchange" by declaring myself to "have standing with you" in this case, here and now. Note here the close connection between Cavell's account of perlocutionary effects and the picture of reasoning being developed here. What Cavell's analysis adds to that picture comes out in his further conditions, which turn in large part on the connection between an utterance being passionate, and passion being something we are passive in the face of, so something that is not entirely in our control. He suggests that passionate utterances are grounded in "my being *moved* to speak, hence to speak in, or out of, passion, whose capacity for lucidity and opacity leaves the genuineness of motive always vulnerable to criticism."[32] This creates a kind of sincerity condition on success, since it is only in virtue of actually being moved to say what I say that I have any kind of right to "demand from you a response *in kind*, one you are *moved* to

---

[31] Ibid. 187–8.

[32] Ibid. 193. Note here that this makes passionate utterances importantly different from expressive ones, which are generally thought to be more fully under the control of the speaker. Habermas's account has room for expressive but not passionate utterances as forms of communicative action (see *Theory of Communicative Action*, I: 296–305).

offer, and moreover *now*."[33] Since what I demand from you is a response in kind, I demand of you something that is not in your conscious control either. Nevertheless, it is not the result of having produced something in you: since my attempt to so move you comes in the form of an invitation, "You may contest my invitation to exchange, at any or all of the points marked by the conditions for the successful perlocutionary act, for example, deny that I have that standing with you, or question my consciousness of my passion, or dismiss the demand for the kind of response I seek, or ask to postpone it, or worse. I may or may not have further means of response."[34]

To see Cavell's point here, consider the difference between the speech of the lover and that of the seducer. The lover is moved by love to invite his beloved's reciprocation. He thus speaks in the hope that his beloved will reciprocate, but what he says, if it is to be honest, a genuine expression of love, must express how he feels rather than be designed to elicit the response he desires. To speak with the goal of eliciting love is to speak as a seducer, not a lover. The seducer speaks with an end in view, and the point of what she says is that it will, she hopes, bring about that end. Though the lover also hopes to bring about that end, he does so not by causing it (via ray-like powers) but because he has appropriately invited it. The point to take from this contrast is that the perlocutionary effect of passionate speech, not being straightforwardly causal, does not work via an end-driven logic. So here we have an example of meaningful moves in a conversation that have a point and felicity conditions but do not themselves have an end or goal.[35]

The argument to this point suggests that moves in casual conversations partake more fully of the perlocutionary than the locutionary or the illocutionary. This would help to explain how our casual utterances can thereby qualify as acts because they have a point, without thereby having a goal, even the goal of attunement. It would also explain why many philosophers who are nevertheless concerned with the role speech acts play in communication have not fully seen the significance of casual conversations.[36] Though this comes out most clearly when we fix our attention on the category of the passionate, I think the claim can be extended beyond it.

---

[33] Cavell, "Passionate Utterance," 193.   [34] Ibid. 192–3.
[35] To someone like Habermas, who only has the end-directed categories of strategic and communicative action to work with, we might ask where the lover's declaration of love fits?
[36] This strikes me as true, though in different ways and to different degrees, of both Habermas and Brandom.

For what we really have here is a third model of impacting the world (primarily other people) with our words. Cavell says that straightforward performatives work via an "offer of participation in the order of the law." Second, there is the category of what we might call manipulative speech, where my words cause their effects via the workings of psychological rather than mechanical causal pathways. Cavell's category of passionate utterances appear to work, when they do, by offering the authority of connection: an authority, as we have seen, that is brought about by issuing genuine invitations that are accepted. Thus, even the non-passionate parts of casual conversation that also establish the authority of connection will function according to the logic of perlocutionary effect and have something like the success conditions that Cavell claims passionate utterances do.

To finally return to the worry that our utterances having a point makes them actions and thus end-directed after all, note that this conclusion rests on a reduction of all utterances to the locutionary (which aim to inform), the illocutionary (which aim to act within the confines of established conventions), and the manipulative (which aim to cause certain reactions). To the extent that casual conversation will be replete with attempts at perlocutionary action, it will be replete with utterances that have a point while nevertheless not having the kind of end that ordinary actions do, and so, once again, such conversations will be fruitful ground for finding reasons that do not aspire to be decisive.

To see that casual conversation will be replete with such perlocutionary action, return to the case of rapport-talk: I complain to you about being disturbed by someone having a loud cellphone conversation in the train car where I was hoping to get some work done. In saying this to you, I am not pursuing any particular goal, except perhaps that of avoiding a painful lapse in our conversation. I am not trying to cause you to react one way or the other: my remark will be equally successful as a move in our casual conversation if you respond with a story about loud TVs in bars or if you reject my offer to stand where I stand, and distance yourself from me by celebrating public cellphone conversations as a triumph over outmoded notions of privacy.[37] In this, my move is very different from one directed at reaching

---

[37] This may not always be true. I may be engaging in what Tannen and others call "troubles-talk" and not only aiming to keep the conversation going but to solicit your solidarity. In such cases, my effort has gone awry if it meets with distancing. Interestingly, it has also gone awry if you take it up as a piece of report-talk, and offer me a solution to the problem you think I have laid before you. More generally,

a decision or convincing you of a point. In those cases, its success is measured by some noticeable movement towards my goal. Here, there is no applicable sense of "towards" to apply, and in that sense, there is no goal I am aiming at, even though my remark has a point.

We have to be careful about the metaphor of attunement. If our idea of attunement is what happens before a symphony orchestra plays, where the oboe lays down the law, as it were, and it is then up to everyone else to follow, we will miss what happens in casual conversations and why they are important for my picture. In casual conversation, two other results are equally admissible: first, we can reach attunement by any one of us, or even all of us, changing our position to move it closer to that of others, and second, we can decide that on this issue, here and now, we are neither in tune nor wish to be. Because these results also count as a kind of success in a conversation, it will be impossible to describe moves in the conversation as necessarily aiming for one of them, and also impossible to say which of many moves open to me at a given moment in the conversation are the ones that bring it closer to its aim. That is, it may be wholly undecidable whether my moving my position towards yours or standing fast in my initial conviction is bringing us closer to a resolution, or even whether a resolution of our positions vis-à-vis one another will signal the success of the conversation. It might very well leave us with nothing further to say to one another (even if we have come to agreement). Thus, while my saying any number of things in the conversation may have a point, the point of what I say is not that it moves us closer to a particular goal, even the goal of attunement. Moreover, since the particular attunement that a conversation produces cannot be determined ahead of time, participants cannot enter conversations with the goal or end of producing the eventual outcome. The next chapter turns to a discussion of the norms of conversation, and argues that one set of those norms concerns the role of conversations in producing attunement. In order to mark the possibility of a successful conversation that does not lead any of its participants to change their position vis-à-vis various spaces of reasons, the norm requires only that the parties are open to being touched or

---

even if there isn't a particular goal in light of which we can assess perlocutionary success, this does not imply that there are not success and failure conditions for perlocutionary utterances. It is these conditions that distinguish perlocutionary utterances from merely making noise.

affected by what others say rather than that they are open to being "moved" as Cavell has it.

To recap, then: unlike the goal-oriented activities of deciding and persuading, investigating and understanding, casual conversation is an activity that not only has no natural end, but which is structured as ongoing. It engages with the spaces we share not as tools but as the background against which and in which we live out our lives together. Because, however, casual conversation is casual, it leaves room for playfulness, for offering new ways of seeing or occupying or shaping the spaces of reasons we inhabit which can be rejected without offence or a disruption of our relationships. It thus affords us low-cost opportunities to attempt to reshape those spaces and low-cost opportunities for others to either accept or reject our suggested changes. At the same time, it provides us opportunity to take responsibility for our positions, and thus to fully engage in the reciprocal and open-ended offering of invitations that my alternative picture says is definitive of the act of reasoning. Finally, since casual conversations serve, inter alia, to build, develop, and otherwise shape our relationships, the meaning and import of what we say to one another concerns not merely the fittingness of a consideration for a particular end, but the larger question of when and how we can speak with and for one another. All this, then, suggests opening up to the thought that something of fundamental rational significance takes place within casual conversation.

The last two chapters have tried to dislodge two aspects of the standard picture of reasoning that hold us captive—that if reasons have authority, it is the authority of command, and that if reasons have a point, it is in moving episodes of reasoning closer to their ends. The possibility that reasons might carry the authority of connection and find their point in our mutual attunement in the context of ongoing conversations provides conceptual space to stand in as we build up a social picture of reasoning by working out some of the central norms that both govern and characterize it as the particular activity that it is. Over the next three chapters, I fill in that picture by considering in turn casual conversation, reasoning in general, and what I call engaged reasoning.

PART II
Reasoning Together

Every universe, even our own, begins in conversation.

Michael Chabon, *The Amazing Adventures of Cavalier and Klay*

4

Norms of Conversation

Although casual conversations are aimless, they are not formless. Not all instances of human beings gathered together and speaking are forms of conversation. Sometimes we speak past one another and sometimes our words are heard as mere noise. Sometimes we lecture or hold forth or pronounce our sentiments. Sometimes we talk without meaning what we say. Sometimes we cry out. Part of what makes such instances of speaking not forms of conversation is what we try to do with our words, and part is how those words are received. Conversation can be distinguished from these other forms of speaking in each other's proximity by saying that while they may involve speaking at or to someone, conversation involves speaking with them. Doing so allows for the derivation of a set of characteristic norms of casual conversation whose authority does not stem from a specification of the ends of the activity. These characteristic norms then play two roles in shaping the activity of reasoning. First, since reasoning is a species of conversing, the norms of casual conversation also apply to reasoning. Second, as we saw in the last chapter, one result of our conversing with one another is to form, maintain, and shape our relationships to one another, and thus, inter alia, the spaces of reasons we share. Thus, the norms that characterize the activity of conversation also turn out to help shape the spaces of reasons we inhabit.

4.1 Norms and Principles: Some Background Remarks

Before turning our attention to the norms of conversation, it will help to have a vocabulary for discussing types of norms and their relationships to the activities they govern. We can start with a common distinction in philosophy: between constitutive and external norms. As the name suggests, the constitutive norms of an activity are the norms that constitute the activity as the particular activity that it is. They are the norms that must be followed if one is to be engaged in that activity at all. Constitutive norms thus derive both their content and their authority from the nature of the activity itself, rather than from external considerations. So, unlike other kinds of norms, they do not represent external constraints on someone performing the activity, the following of which would distinguish some examples of the activity from others. The difference is easily seen in the case of games and other rule-governed activities. If we are sitting across from one another with a chessboard and chess pieces between us, but only one of us is moving the pieces in a way that is properly guided by the rules of chess, then we aren't actually playing chess. The rules of chess may limit how we move the pieces, but they don't limit our ability to play chess. They make it possible. They are thus constitutive norms of the game of chess. Similarly, I can't walk if I don't put one foot in front of another, and I can't construct a well-formed English sentence if I don't have a subject and a verb.[1]

Though following the constitutive norms of an activity may be necessary in order to engage in the activity, it may not be sufficient. Someone can follow the constitutive norms of an activity and yet fail to engage in the activity in two ways that will be important when we turn to conversation and reasoning. First, if the activity is interactive, my doing my part will go for naught if my partners fail to do theirs.[2] If we are sitting down on opposite sides of a chessboard and I am moving my pieces in accordance with the

---

[1] Both Christine Korsgaard and Jürgen Habermas derive moral norms by working out the constitutive norms of some necessary activity (action or communicative action), and then grounding these norms as the necessary presuppositions of the activity. Jürgen Habermas, "Discourse Ethics: Notes on a Program of Philosophical Justification," in *Moral Consciousness and Communicative Action*, trans. Christian Lenhardt and Shierry Weber Nicholsen (Cambridge, MA: MIT Press, 1990). Christine Korsgaard, *Self-Constitution* (Oxford: Oxford University Press, 2009). In line with my aim to offer an ideal, I take the norms I work out to specify the ideal picture I offer, and not, thereby, to provide necessary grounding for our engaging in this activity, but merely to highlight what makes such engagement worth doing.

[2] I leave aside here the question of whether or not all activities are in some sense interactive. It is enough for my purposes that the activities on which this book focuses are interactive. For an argument in support of the importance of interactivity to the understanding of all sorts of action central to human life and the way that one person's failure to interact can affect the possibility that others perform interactive activities, see Tamar Schapiro, "Compliance, Complicity and the Nature of Nonideal Conditions," *Journal of Philosophy* 100, no. 7 (July 2003): 329–55.

rules of chess, and following a recognizable strategy and so forth, but you are not, then we are not playing chess and so I am not playing chess. Second, since activities unfold over time, there is no guarantee that our having engaged in the activity up to this point implies that we will continue to do so. And this can have retrospective consequences. If, as we proceed, our actions begin to violate the constitutive norms of the activity, then this cannot only call into question what we are doing now, but what we have been doing all along. I thought we were playing chess, but you were just preparing to ridicule me.

In contrast with constitutive norms, there might be external norms governing an activity, and these can be helpfully divided into two types. First, there may be norms that govern the activity because of its placement within a larger network. Such norms are not constitutive of the activity, and their justification must go beyond the nature of the activity itself, though it can also appeal to that activity. Perhaps my chess club has a rule about talking during games or touching the board or wearing loud ties or earphones. These rules may be justified by the club authorities because of their impact on the quality of the game or the quality of the club. These restrict how I play chess at my club, and require some sort of external authority (the club) to impose.

Second, there are what, for games, might be called strategies but more generally are something like norms of excellence. These, like constitutive norms, make internal reference to the activity itself rather than to an external authority. They are not however, constitutive of engaging in the activity, but of engaging in it well. In the case of games, these norms will have to be constrained by the constitutive norms. There are no strategies for playing chess well that do not involve playing by the rules. Moreover, though norms of excellence are thus constrained by constitutive norms, they can go beyond what those norms require. Though I cannot play chess well without playing chess, I can arguably play chess without even aiming to play well, perhaps as a means to idly pass the time with a less skilled player or to spend time with a child who is just learning to play.[3]

---

[3] Some would deny this, at least with regard to some activities which we might call teleological. In particular, Christine Korsgaard, relying on Aristotle, draws the connection between constitutive norms and norms of excellence much more tightly than I have here (*Self-Constitution*, 27–34). I don't think it matters for what I want to say whether or not the loose or tight connection is correct, so I set aside the difference.

For my purposes, what is interesting about these norms of excellence is that while they are not constitutive of the activity, they also make reference to the internal structure of the activity. What makes writing or chess playing or, as we will see, conversation excellent is tied to the nature of writing or chess playing or conversation. So while I can write or play chess or converse poorly and still be engaging in these activities, the norms that shape excellent engagement in these activities do not come from outside of them.

One of the advantages of conceiving of the principles that govern an activity as either constitutive norms or norms of excellence is that their connection to the nature of the activity itself serves to ground their normativity. If I ask why I shouldn't move my king two spaces or why I shouldn't sacrifice my pawn here, the answer can be given in terms of the activity of playing chess. If I move my king two spaces, then I am no longer playing chess. If I sacrifice my pawn here, I give my opponent checkmate in four moves, and so, assuming there is a better move, stop playing chess well. And given that I am engaged in that activity and thus, barring special circumstances, trying to do it well, there appears to be no room for me to challenge these answers with a further "why?" question or a dismissive "so what?"

When we turn our attention to activities that are less clearly defined than games, we need a further category: characteristic norms. Characteristic norms function like constitutive norms but allow some wiggle room around the edges. When an activity is governed by characteristic norms, it is possible for the norms of excellence of the activity to conflict with the characteristic norms. Sometimes, the excellent performance of an activity involves knowing when and how to bend or break the rules. So, for instance, though the norms of English grammar govern writing in English, many examples of excellent writing will include phrases marked off as a sentence without a subject and a verb. Because such writing defies norms of the activity without ceasing to be an instance of the activity, it makes more sense to describe the norms violated as characteristic rather than constitutive. In fact, many "unofficial" plays of games allow for similar wiggle room. If we are playing a friendly game of chess and one of us distractedly takes two turns in a row, and we don't realize it until several turns later, we may decide to keep playing and take it that we are continuing to play a game of chess.

Although constitutive and characteristic norms and norms of excellence are all internal to the activity, it is helpful to distinguish among them, and to keep in mind that for many kinds of activities that are less rule-bound than games, doing them excellently may involve some violations of what we have taken to be at least their characteristic norms.[4] This is especially true when we turn to the activities of reasoning, where it is easy to slip from talking of rationality or reasonableness as a basic requirement to thinking of them as virtues. The norms in the two cases will be related, but not the same, and perhaps not even entirely consistent.[5]

Finally, it is important to note that conversation, unlike playing chess or even negotiation or argument, is a rather vaguely defined activity with fuzzy borders. That vagueness means that the norms that I discuss are better thought of as characteristic norms. That is, given the fuzzy boundaries, it may be possible to violate some of them and still be engaged in the activity of conversing. In that sense, the norms of casual conversation discussed below don't give shape to the activity by marking out its boundaries, but rather by describing the topology of its central regions. While it helps to consider some of the activities that lie over the border by way of contrast, this comparison can be fruitful without knowing exactly where those borders lie.

---

[4] We may also take such cases as a sign that we have characterized the activity in question incorrectly, and so need to revise our account of its norms, or that we need to distinguish between the activity we were trying to get into view and the one the norms we have articulated characterize. Though making an assertion with propositional content requires a subject and a verb, communicating effectively does not. We might thus conclude that there are more things to do with language than make assertions, and so the norms that characterize asserting may not fully capture the more wide terrain of linguistic interaction. Note, in passing, that this is one place where my project and Robert Brandom's in *Making It Explicit* (Cambridge, MA: Harvard University Press, 1998) diverge.

[5] This final claim will strike many readers as far too hasty and loose. Assume, for instance, that the laws of logic are among the constitutive norms of reasoning. How could one reason well while violating them? Wouldn't the violation render what was said nonsense? Yes. But if we take seriously the idea of reasoning as a social activity, then it is a mistake to think of that activity as necessarily involving taking the baby steps of deductive logic. Reasoning excellently often requires imagination and creativity and leaps of intuition and a willingness to follow a path that hasn't (yet) been fully laid down. And though to count as reasoning it must remain open to censure from the principles of logic, or any other principles, it can outstrip those principles as it proceeds. Or so I want to claim. For a similar point, see J. David Velleman, *How We Get Along* (Cambridge: Cambridge University Press, 2009), 20–1, and Brandom, *Making It Explicit*, 97–102, where he discusses and adopts Wilfrid Sellars's category of "material inference" and its answerability to but not derivability from logical inference.

4.2 Conversational Norms I: Agreement and Continuation

Consider four features of conversation, and the types of norms to which they give rise. First, conversation involves speaking with (and so not merely past) others. Participants in a conversation thus must reach or rely on certain forms of agreement about the meaning of words and terms of reference and be able to find routes to agreement where it is lacking. Second, conversation is aimless, but particular conversations come to an end. Casual conversation thus turns out to have rules governing how to bring the activity to an end that also shape how it proceeds. Together, these first two norms shape the kind of unity that conversations tend to produce among their participants. This section focuses on them. Third, conversation involves speaking with rather than merely at or to others, and so is distinct from one-way forms of address, including commanding, lecturing, and holding forth, even when these activities are done by all parties to an interaction. As a result, conversations require certain levels of equality, and tend to flourish more fully and easily when that equality is entrenched and supported. The next section takes up these kinds of norms. Finally, conversation can be distinguished from a kind of empty prattling where those involved speak with one another, but don't mean what they say. Because conversations allow for some playfulness, they also require a certain level of sincerity in order for them to do the work of constructing, maintaining, and forming our relationships. Norms of sincerity take up the following section. As these norms get developed throughout this chapter, a set of distinctive conceptual models emerge from thinking about the structure of conversations. These models of unity, agreement, and responsiveness help shape the full social picture of reasoning developed in later chapters.

In order to speak with someone I cannot talk past them, and that means that in order to converse, we have to make ourselves intelligible to each other. This requires that what we say is intelligible to the other. As we saw in the last chapter, such intelligibility goes beyond my partner knowing the meaning of my words; it requires also that she understand my point in saying those words to her, here and now.[6]

---

[6] David Velleman also makes the aim of intelligibility central to his account of human action and interaction, most recently and thoroughly in *How We Get Along*. Though I find much in that work

Some norms of conversation govern this need for a certain form of mutual intelligibility. At the most basic level, we need to agree about the meanings of our words, and in particular to the kind of shorthand we use in casual conversation.[7] The need for agreement about the reference of casual terms is not merely placed on us by the demands of intelligibility. The flow of conversation is interrupted by the need to spell everything out and also by failures of referential convention, the need to stop and explicitly ask, "What do you mean by . . . ?" So even if conversations permit the overcoming of failures of referential agreement, these reparative moves cannot be invoked too frequently.

Susan Brennan and Herbert Clark argue that the choice of terms to refer to objects in a conversation rest on what they call "conceptual pacts" between speakers. Their research focuses on situations that push participants to work out agreements to conceptualize and refer to a given object in a given way.[8] Such pacts can change over time, and are subject to breakdown, but they ground our choice of words. They determine, for instance, whether we refer to a given shoe as "a shoe" or "a loafer" and whether we use certain forms of slang, for instance using "my dogs" to refer to my feet. The point to take from their research is not that all our agreements in reference are explicitly worked out. To claim that the path to referential agreement is via conceptual pacts suggests that the needs of conversation drive our modes of reference and not the other way around. That is, according to their theory, we don't come to referential agreement as a happy by-product of each of us aiming to refer correctly to an objective reality, to speak the truth, as it were. It isn't that in conversation we aren't concerned to speak the truth, but rather that how we do so is a result of the social need for intelligibility brought on by our participation in the social activity of conversation rather than directly through the pressures placed on us by the realm of objects.

---

attractive, I note here a key difference in our approaches. Whereas he begins from a connection between individual agency and the intelligibility of one's own actions to oneself, I work in the opposite direction: starting with our intelligibility to others in conversation, and only later taking up its connection to self-intelligibility and individual agency.

[7] See the work of Herbert Clark and Susan Brennan on referential agreement, e.g. "Conceptual Pacts and Lexical Choice in Conversation," *Journal of Experimental Psychology* 22, no. 6 (1996): 1482–93.

[8] Ibid. 1491. They contrast this theory with others that, for instance, following Grice's work on conversation, argue that speakers choose in terms of efficiency: picking out the simplest term that they think will sufficiently precisely pick out the object referred to in the circumstances.

Two features of these conceptual pacts affect the shape of casual conversations. First, they are pacts, that is, agreements. The necessity of such pacts for smooth-flowing communication and thus conversation suggests that among the things we do in casual conversation is find our way to agreement about the referents of our words. Second, the pacts are conceptual, not merely conventions about which words name which objects. They involve an at least tacit acceptance to conceptualize the object one way rather than another, and thus to construct our conceptual landscape in a particular way. The importance of such conceptual agreement is most clear when it is absent or resisted. Clark and Brennan discuss a 1975 trial of a Boston doctor who was accused of murder for having performed an abortion. In the trial, the defense lawyer talked about "the fetus" while the district attorney spoke of "the baby" and neither yielded in their use of terms throughout the trial.[9]

What Brennan and Clark describe as conceptual pacts are thus similar to Wittgenstein's notion of a criterion, as this is developed by Stanley Cavell.[10] Because Cavell is particularly concerned with and attuned to the possibility of, as he puts it, disappointment in our criteria, it helps for what follows to develop these connections here. Cavell argues that Wittgenstein's notion of criteria differs in a number of important ways from what he calls our "ordinary" notion of criteria. Three differences concern me here. First, whereas ordinary criteria are developed by some or other group with the vested authority to establish criteria, the criteria that Wittgenstein discusses are invariably "ours," and the authority we have in invoking or relying on these criteria is something like the authority of connection.[11] Second, the use to which we put Wittgensteinian criteria is not establishing certainty in our judgments but in laying out our conceptual terrain. As Cavell puts the point, "Criteria are 'criteria for something's being so' not in the sense that they tell us of a thing's existence, but of something like its identity, not of its

---

[9] Ibid. 1492. I take it this example does not show so much a failure to reach agreement as a rhetorical attempt by each attorney to get the jury to adopt a larger conceptual frame for addressing the case.

[10] The importance of criteria and Wittgenstein's particular use of the term is a central theme of Cavell's reading of Wittgenstein in *The Claim of Reason* (Oxford: Oxford University Press, 1979), and is covered again in Stanley Cavell, *Conditions Handsome and Unhandsome* (Chicago: University of Chicago Press, 1991), lec. 2, e.g. 64.

[11] Cavell, *Claim of Reason*, 18–20.

being so, but of its being *so*. Criteria do not determine the certainty of statements, but the application of the concepts employed in statements."[12] Third, our relation to and acceptance of some set of criteria is a matter of, as Wittgenstein puts it, "agreement in" rather than "agreement to" something. That is, criteria are not established outside of our practices and then presented to us for our consent or acknowledgement or acceptance. Rather, our speaking with one another insofar as that involves our mutual intelligibility requires that we share a piece of conceptual terrain, and that is what we achieve when we share, or agree in, our criteria. As Cavell explains, "The idea of agreement here is not that of coming to or arriving at an agreement on a given occasion, but of being in agreement throughout, being in harmony, like pitches or clocks, or weighing scales, or columns of figures. That a group of human beings *stimmen* in their language *überein* says, so to speak, that they are mutually voiced with respect to it, mutually *attuned* top to bottom."[13]

Our agreement in our criteria and conceptual pacts is wide and deep and thus conversing with one another is, in some sense, the most ordinary activity in the world. However, it is also agreement that can come apart. At some point in our interaction, if we refuse to make such conceptual pacts or if I find that my criteria are not in agreement with yours, we will no longer be conversing, but talking at or past one another. So even if the activity of conversing tends to push us to produce agreements in our use of words and concepts, it is also the case that establishing and acknowledging such agreement is a characteristic norm of participating in conversation. Without such pacts, conversation stops flowing smoothly, and, at the limit, dissolves into talking past one another. In the absence of such agreement, it isn't merely that our conversation is halting and clumsy, but rather that it is not genuine conversation at all.

One of the things that supports referential agreement, both in cases where the reference is common and established, and also in the projection of meaning into new cases, is a broader background of agreement in what Wittgenstein called "forms of life."[14] This need for background agreement

---

[12] Ibid. 45.   [13] Ibid. 32.

[14] See, for instance, *Philosophical Investigations*, trans. G.E.M. Anscombe (Oxford: Wiley-Blackwell, 1991), §241. Cavell also emphasizes the place of sharing a form of life in providing the widespread background of agreement which provides all the foundation our shared language needs and could have (see *Claim of Reason*, e.g. 178–9 on the foundations of language and initiation into a shared form of life, and 180–90 on projecting a word).

in form of life thus pushes conversational partners to find and construct more substantive common ground, of common interest and mutually supported attitudes. Note that this doesn't mean that we have to start from or come to agreement either about particular conclusions or decisions or about more large-scale theoretical or moral commitments. Since casual conversation is not aimed at conclusions or decisions, we need not reach full agreement for the conversation to succeed. Sharing a form of life may require, as Wittgenstein says, agreement in judgments, but it does not require agreement in all judgment, even importantly those that are under discussion.[15]

Norms governing the sharing of criteria not only stand in the background of the possibility of our conversing, but also push the very activity of conversation itself into certain characteristic forms. Conversing requires that we sustain a kind of involvement with one another, and this requires effort of accommodation by each of us. As Erving Goffman puts the point, citing Adam Smith's *Theory of Moral Sentiments*:

the individual must phrase his own concerns and feelings and interests in such a way as to make these maximally usable by the others as a source of appropriate involvement; and this major obligation of the individual *qua* interactant is balanced by his right to expect that others present will make some effort to stir up their sympathies and place them at his command.[16]

So the very activity of speaking with others, of conversing, turns out to push us towards a kind of accommodation with them that is nevertheless somewhat loose. According to Suzanne Eggins and Diana Slade, "While YEAH occurs very frequently in casual talk, NO and its conversational derivatives . . . are relatively infrequent."[17] Interestingly enough, the same authors point out that "casual conversation thrives on confrontation and wilts in the face of support," so the agreements signaled by all those YEAHs and conceptual pacts do not serve to force us into more high-level agreements, but merely to place us in a position to speak with and not merely past one another.[18]

---

[15] Cavell talks of the need to share a sense of what is interesting. Suzanne Eggins and Diana Slade, in their introduction to the linguistic study of casual conversation, discuss, among others, the work of Michael Halliday, who argues that conversation serves to construct our shared social reality, *Analysing Casual Conversation* (London: Cassell, 1996), 50–51.

[16] "Alienation from Interaction," in *Interaction Ritual: Essays on Face-to-Face Behavior*, 113–36 (New York: Pantheon, 1982), 116.

[17] *Analysing Casual Conversation*, 97.   [18] Ibid. 224.

That casual conversation is also ongoing and aimless creates similar kinds of pressures. Some social scientific work on casual conversation analyzes it as a kind of self-propelling social mechanism with a set of rules that are designed to make sure that conversations continue without lapses.[19] We give one another cues, for instance, that say whose turn is next or when a turn has come to an end, and we generally have ready a set of material to talk about should one subject run its course and not lead naturally to another.[20] In addition to the rules of conversation working to keep conversation going, it is also the case that since conversations have no internally deter- mined end point, bringing casual conversations to a close can be a tricky and delicate business. One can't just walk away from a conversational partner mid-discussion even if the conversation arrives at a lull unless certain conditions have been met. One way to understand those conditions is that they establish the bases that would allow another conversation among these people to start up again later.[21] This suggests that successful conversa- tion requires ongoing accommodation by participants so that the conversa- tion doesn't reach a point where its termination is, in some sense, final. Should we be having a casual conversation and come to a topic on which we irreconcilably disagree, then there is a certain pressure on us to find a new topic of conversation before we can stop talking. The point is not that deep disagreements are impossible in casual conversation. Such disagree- ments animate conversations. The point is rather about what is necessary for us to draw our conversation to an appropriately satisfactory close: either we must find some common ground on our current topic even if only by agreeing to disagree, or we must find a new topic where such ground is more evident.

While these mechanisms of conversation place us each under this obli- gation to attune ourselves to our conversational partners, they do not require us to find complete agreement. As we saw above, conversation actually wilts in the face of complete agreement. One needs to have something to talk about, and at least one way to generate such talk is to

---

[19] This is the starting point for the approach known as "conversational analysis" developed by Harvey Sacks. This work is discussed in ibid. 25–32.

[20] Goffman, "Alienation from Interaction," 120.

[21] Both of these points are made by Goffman in, among others, "On Face-Work" and "Alienation from Interaction" in *Interaction Ritual*, see esp. 38, 120.

dispute each other's claims, or at least their interpretation or implications.[22] Eggins and Slade argue that:

The frequency of rejoinders in causal talk and their relative absence from more formal spoken interactions, relates to their potential to sustain the interaction. While pragmatic interactions aim at closure and completion, casual conversations need to be sustained if their goals are to be met. The building and reaffirming of relationships and identity is never fully achieved, hence the need to use the linguistic resources to keep the channels open for as long as possible.[23]

Being attuned to one another does not require always playing in unison and the interest of talking together comes, as it does in music, from the harmonies and discords, from the interplay of different voices. The fact that casual conversation is characterized by the ongoing activity of speaking with others thus generates a norm of attunement: in conversing, we work to position ourselves vis-à-vis our partners so that we are attuned with one another, not so that we agree about everything, but enough that we can continue speaking with and not merely to or at one another.[24]

Note, to return to a conclusion from the last chapter, that our capacity for achieving this kind of attunement requires that we are open to being touched or moved by what our conversational partners say. If I am exchanging words with you and am not willing to be touched or affected by what you say to the extent necessary to be able to keep talking with you, then we are not conversing. Perhaps I am lecturing or holding forth as Oscar Wilde's Lady Bracknell or Jane Austen's Lady Catherine de Bourgh are wont to do. Perhaps we are fighting: hurling words at each other like weapons. Though we sometimes have good reasons for lecturing or fighting, neither are forms of conversation in the sense I am using

---

[22] Eggins and Slade, *Analysing Casual Conversation*, 223–4.

[23] Ibid. 212.

[24] The possibility of a kind of solidarity that falls short of complete agreement or consistency is often overlooked in discussions of agreement and disagreement in casual conversation, and so this norm is rarely if ever described or tested in that literature. Conceiving of conversation as requiring effort at attunement in this sense might help resolve seemingly inconsistent conclusions about the threat of disagreement to conversation found in the literature. See, for a sample of the disagreement I have in mind, ibid. 223–4 (disagreements are one of the engines of conversation), Deborah Tannen, *You Just Don't Understand: Women and Men In Conversation* (New York: William Morrow and Co., 1990), 72–3 (disagreements are troubling), and Robin Dunbar, *Gossip, Grooming and the Origin of Language* (Cambridge, MA: Harvard University Press, 1997), 105 (disagreements are made possible by language, and these make possible recognition of objective, shared reality).

the term. So my claim here is not that being open to being touched by others is always a virtue. It is merely that it is necessary for the activity of conversing.

One interesting feature of the analysis above is that it gives us an interesting model of unity. To the extent that the standard picture of reasoning includes reasoning together in its purview, it tends to conceive of the unity that reasoning brings about in terms of complete agreement or consistency. But this obscures important aspects of our social lives. In particular, it leads us to imagine the role of reason in our social lives as producing a form of living together marked by pressures towards uniformity: successful living together as more or less a matter of marching in lockstep, all singing the same tune. This, in turn, can lead those who champion plurality and individuality to be critical of reasoning as a social activity of living together.[25]

But if casual conversation lies at the base of the spaces of reasons we inhabit together, then we can picture sharing these spaces differently. And rather than looking for moments of complete agreement and uniformity as a mark of community or common ground, we can look to the looser model of being able to continue speaking with one another. That might provide a new way of thinking of all sorts of entities whose unity has been a topic of philosophical concern, from states and societies to individual persons. In particular, it gives us a new model for thinking about the kind of unity reason imposes on us and our activities. The importance of such a model will be explored in later chapters.

4.3 Norms of Conversation II: Equality

Although I cannot speak with you if we are not intelligible to each other, I can speak intelligibly to you and yet not be genuinely conversing with

---

[25] This point echoes a line of criticism often leveled at theorists of deliberative democracy by those sympathetic with the radical potential of a more agonistic picture of democracy. See, for instance, James Tully, *Strange Multiplicity* (Cambridge: Cambridge University Press, 1995), Iris Marion Young, "Communication and the Other: Beyond Deliberative Democracy," in *Democracy and Difference*, ed. Seyla Benhabib, 120–36 (Princeton, NJ: Princeton University Press, 1996), Bonnie Honig, *Political Theory and the Displacement of Politics* (Ithaca, NY: Cornell University Press, 1993), though Tully, in general, is less critical of the place of reasoning in our practices of justly living together.

you. Conversation involves speaking with others, and so is also fundamentally different from a variety of activities that involve merely speaking to others. These activities, such as issuing orders, lecturing or otherwise informing, reporting, and generally holding forth can be thought of as forms of one-way communication. The differences between these and conversation reveals another set of characteristic norms of conversation. Two differences are relevant here. First, the kind of attunement described above as the result of casual conversation involves a certain balance in the participants' openness to touch and be touched (and, sometimes, to move and be moved) by the positions of others, so that the attunement can be a process of mutual adjustment. Second, conversation involves an ongoing process of adjustment: there is no point at which conversational partners could declare themselves attuned and then move on to something else.

Before expanding on these differences and drawing out their implications, note that the lines between these kinds of communication can, in practice, be blurry. Even the most ideal forms of communication will involve periods of one-way communication: telling stories and jokes, reporting information, laying out one's views in detail. Nevertheless, should a conversation include nothing but such activities, it will be at best a degenerate form of conversation and at worst no conversation at all. Moreover, when these activities take place within the confines of genuine conversation, then they are open to challenge and rebuke in ways that make them importantly different than in the purer forms in which I will discuss them here.

The first difference between conversation and one-way communication concerns not so much whether a speaker is responsive to her audience, but how. To see this difference, consider the age-old dispute between philosophers and rhetoricians. Students of rhetoric since Aristotle have insisted that skillful performance of any of the one-sided activities listed above requires knowing one's audience and adjusting one's presentation to their capacities, prior interests, and positions. Such adjustment is basically a matter of how what is said is presented, not in the basic content of what is communicated. That rhetoricians not only alter the form of what they say but its content in response to their audience has been the central charge leveled against them by philosophers since Socrates. The fact that one might change one's position to appeal to one's audience is a failure, however, only if one is engaged in a form of one-way communication that is not answerable to what one's audience says.

If I adopt the position of an expert informing an audience of some facts within the purview of my expertise, then what I say is answerable to those facts, and misrepresenting those facts to appeal to my audience is failing to inform them. But a similar shift in the content of what I say in the course of a casual conversation may not be a failure in the same way, or at all. When I converse with someone, I must be interested in how they take up what I say. Moreover my interest in their reaction to what I say is not merely as a check on the clarity of my presentation, but whether my words move my interlocutor to say something in response. Proper interest in that response involves being open to being moved in turn by it—not merely to alter my articulation of my position, but to alter the position itself. That is, the very susceptibility to change my position in light of my audience that is the characteristic vice of the rhetorician in the mind of the philosopher is, in the context of genuine conversation, a characteristic virtue.

Conversation also thrives on a certain degree of surprise. In contrast, surprises in one-way communication are a sign of failure. My students regularly school me in possibilities for misunderstanding what I have said in a lecture or on an assignment. This makes teaching an ongoing challenge because it points to a need to improve the clarity of what I say because my students' surprising (to me) ways of taking up what I say in lecture suggests that my lectures are insufficiently clear. In contrast, a conversation partner who finds hidden meaning or unintended implications in what we say can be delightful and make for excellent conversation. When Mr. Darcy says to Elizabeth Bennet that her defect "is willfully to misunderstand" people, he says it with a smile because he is not, in fact, criticizing her failings, but expressing his admiration for her conversational abilities.[26]

The different attitudes to surprise here point to the kind of attunement that each activity requires. In one-way communication, success involves the audience adjusting to the speaker, even if this requires the speaker adjusting her speech to the audience. Genuine conversation, on the other hand, requires all parties to be open to adjusting where they stand as a result of what others say. Being thus open to such adjustment does not imply that

---

[26] Jane Austen, *Pride and Prejudice*, Oxford World Classics, ed. James Kinsley (Oxford: Oxford University Press, 2008), 43.

one cannot converse if one has strong principles, but only that the activity of conversation requires that we regard those principles in a certain way: as strong and central commitments, rather than as unimpeachable certainties. To see the difference, consider two ways we might understand a phrase that has come to play a central role in much moral philosophy: "claims that cannot be reasonably rejected."[27] On the first reading, a claim that cannot be reasonably rejected is one that is foundationally grounded in such a way that the very fact that one rejected it would be taken as showing one's unreasonableness. If I regard my principles as ones that cannot be reasonably rejected in this sense, then I am not genuinely conversing with you in any area where these principles play a role. On the second reading, however, to say that what stands behind my claim that they cannot be reasonably rejected is to say that my commitment to them is dependent on their not being reasonably rejected, and is thus consistent with an openness to considering challenges to them as giving me reason to abandon these commitments. If my commitment to my principles takes this form, it is entirely consistent with my engaging in genuine conversation. Being open to the possibility of the reasonable rejection of what we say does not, however, require laxness in our own commitments, but merely an openness to the possibility that someone who does not agree with us about them could nevertheless be fully reasonable. So, for instance, devout religious believers and secular atheists can converse with one another without being open to conversion if they can accept that agreement on religious matters is not determinative of one's rationality.

Third, all of these one-way forms of communication come naturally to a close: if I am lecturing you or otherwise trying to inform you of something, then, barring any clarificatory questions you may have when I am done, once I have said my piece, the activity is finished. If you have asked me for directions, and I have given them to you to your satisfaction, then we have nothing more to say on the matter. But rather than this leading to the painful silence that running out of material leads to in casual conversation, it will prompt you to say, "thanks" and go on your way. The ongoing nature

---

[27] The phrase is T. M. Scanlon's. See, for instance *What We Owe to Each Other* (Cambridge, MA: Harvard University Press, 1998). But it finds its way into much Kantian writing on moral philosophy that stresses the role of offering justifications as constitutive of the moral nature of our relationships to one another. See, for instance, Rainer Forst, *The Right to Justification*, trans. Jeffrey Flynn (New York: Columbia University Press, 2011).

of conversation, as we saw in the last chapter, means that we cannot describe conversation as aiming at any particular attunement or even at agreement itself. Moreover, it means that in a genuine conversation, no one has the authority to declare any position reached in the conversation to be final, and this further distinguishes the authority structure of one-way communication from that of genuine conversation.

If these forms of one-way communication differ fundamentally from casual conversation, then the differences between them point to a further set of constitutive norms of conversation. In particular, a form of equality among the participants turns out to be a necessary feature of a conversation being a genuine conversation. The kind of equality required here is weaker than the reciprocity that is necessary in order to reason with someone. In order to offer you reasons, I have to offer to speak for you with the authority of connection, and that means that my offer has to be fully answerable to your response to it, and simultaneously open up the possibility that you can speak for me.[28] Neither of these conditions is necessary for genuine conversation to take place. I can, after all, say something in conversation in order to stake out my position without thereby making an assumption that it is yours or making an attempt to bring you towards it. I can also say something merely to keep us talking: "How about them Red Sox?", "Nice weather we're having", "Did'ya hear the latest?" All of these are invitations to keep (or start) talking with me, but none need be even the beginnings of invitations to take what I say (or will say) as speaking for you.

On the other hand, one of the things that marks a conversation as different from reporting or lecturing or commanding is that all its participants have a claim to control its direction and what is said. There must be some mutuality of influence in the process of attunement as we keep talking. Such mutuality may be merely potential: in some conversations, one person's position will be unassailable or backed by more convincing evidence, more complete knowledge, or better considered, and the conversation will achieve attunement by everyone else coming around to that position. But what differentiates such a conversation from a lecture by the same person is that the very structure of the conversation holds out the possibility that the movement could have been different. If his evidence had been less solid than he initially thought, then he would have changed his

---

[28] I take up these requirements of reasoning in the next chapter.

position. If what he said wasn't of interest to the others, they would have found a new topic. In other words, there is, built in to the structure of a genuine conversation a mutuality of influence that amounts to a kind of equality. The requisite level of equality obtains when each participant in a conversation is open to being affected by her conversation partners. In the absence of such mutual openness to being affected, the exchange of words, mutually intelligible though they be, will amount to someone speaking to, rather than with, the others. Being open in this way is something on the order of a disposition rather than a conscious attitude or commitment. We can be unclear or deceived about the degree of our openness and, as with all dispositions, it can sometimes be hard in actual cases to tell whether it is present. None of that, however, need obscure my point here: that in the absence of such a disposition, conversation shifts into a different activity. Note that the difference between one-way communication and moves in a conversation lies in the mutuality of this openness to being affected. When I give you a lecture, I expect or hope that what I say will affect you, but do not also think that what you say, perhaps in the course of asking questions or raising objections, will affect me. When we converse, this further possibility comes into play.[29] Moreover, there are many ways to be affected by what our conversation partner says. I can learn to see the space of reasons and the positions it affords differently without also changing my position in it. The religious believer who is affected by her conversation with the atheist may, for instance, be moved to a new or better appreciation of his reasonableness without thereby being moved to give up her own religious beliefs.

To further clarify the importance of this norm and its model of equality, consider two basic obstacles to such mutual affectability: one lodged in the dispositions of the participants, and one in their relative social position. If I am stubborn or haughty or both, and so do not accept you as the kind of person whose words could move me, then I cannot genuinely converse with you, but merely hold forth. The same problem arises if I am sure that my position is unassailable, that it is backed up by incontrovertible foundations, whether in the nature of reason or language or the universe.

---

[29] Those familiar with the academic ritual of a talk followed by a period in which the audience can ask questions might here note the difference between cases where this period is one of question and answer and times when it is a discussion. Which happens will depend on both speaker and audience and what they take themselves to be doing and perhaps the relative level of status and expertise and respect in play. The mere fact that many people talk does not make the interaction a discussion.

Conversation involves engagement that requires a kind of vulnerability, and so if I am not open to being touched by you, then I cannot converse with you. Contrast, for instance, the reactions that Elizabeth Bennet's two suitors have to her rejection of their proposals. Although Mr. Collins alters his plans, he is not much affected or changed by her refusal. Darcy, on the other hand, is utterly transformed by her rejection, and in that transformation shows himself to be someone with whom she might engage in the "meet and happy conversation" that is marriage, someone who has been touched by her words and so presumably is open to being so in the future.[30]

A similar problem arises if I am overly deferential or lacking in self-respect, and so do not regard myself as someone whose words could or should move you. The middle ground in which we can genuinely converse with each other rests on two further attitudes: respect and trust. My treating what you say as something that could move me is one way that I manifest respect for you as someone whose words are worth taking seriously, even if they initially strike me as unfamiliar or hard to understand. But it also requires that I trust you, that, for instance, I am not worried that you will use my capacity to be moved by what you say to manipulate me with your words. Participation in genuine conversation, because it requires an openness to being affected by others, requires dropping our guard, as it were, and thus making ourselves vulnerable. Again, these facts about conversation cut both ways: sometimes there will be good reasons not to enter into conversation, here, now, with you, precisely because I do not want to be affected by what you say, or because you are not trustworthy or have not sufficiently manifested your trustworthiness to me. If I don't want to buy a car, it's advisable to rebuff the salesman's attempt to start chatting.

Perhaps more interesting is the role played not by our dispositions but by our relative social positions. One way that social inequality manifests itself is in undermining the mutual openness to be affected or the conditions that warrant such openness. This is especially true in cases where the inequality in question can be understood as an inequality in power. One of the characteristics of a social scheme where some have power over others is that those with power get to decide, unilaterally, where they stand. That

---

[30] The idea of marriage as a meet and happy conversation comes from Milton's treatise on divorce, and is much discussed by Cavell. See, for instance, Stanley Cavell, *Conditions Handsome and Unhandsome* (Chicago: University of Chicago Press, 1991), 104–5.

means that those with power do not, as a matter of course, make themselves vulnerable to those without power, and those without power have no choice but to be vulnerable to those who have power, though their vulnerability is a result of neither respect nor trust.[31] To the extent that interaction between groups with different levels of power leads to attunement and movement, it will often not be the result of any mutual influence. Note that this can be true even when the powerful decide to change in a way that benefits or answers to the demands of the less powerful. If such movement remains in the gift of the powerful so that they can choose to move or not, acknowledge the importance of what the powerless say or not, but are not, except as they choose to be, necessarily open to being affected by them, then any movement is not the result of the mutual openness to being affected that is characteristic of conversation.

This obstacle to genuine conversation takes a particularly subtle form when the inequality of power involves the capillary forms of power that, since Foucault, are called "disciplinary" or "constructive."[32] Constructive power works in part by shaping our conceptual landscape and, in particular, in determining what counts as standard or normal, and thus, in turn, what routes of criticism and argument are within the bounds of reason, and which are confused or special pleading or just "silly." It is often distributed asymmetrically: some have this power over others who do not have it over themselves or the others. In such cases, it is not only that those with power get to decide where they stand and root themselves to the spot, but that their standing there serves to establish that spot as standard and thus the standard for having standing at all.

Note two consequences of this point. First, what renders an exchange of words under conditions of inequality not a genuine conversation is not always something that can be read off of the transcript of that conversation.

---

[31] I don't mean to close off the possibility that there are ways to forge genuine respect and trust or establish trustworthiness in the contexts of inequalities of power. I will discuss these possibilities below. But it is worth saying here and often that doing so is truly difficult, and that even powerful people of good will fail at it much more often than they succeed. On these points, see María Lugones and Elizabeth Spelman, "Have We Got a Theory for You!," in *Hypatia Reborn*, ed. Azizah al-Hibri and Margaret Simons (Bloomington: Indiana University Press, 1990).

[32] Michel Foucault, *Discipline and Punish* (New York: Random House, 1975), Sandra Bartky, "Foucault, Femininity and the Modernization of Patriarchal Power," in *Femininity and Domination*, 63–82 (New York: Routledge, 1990), Catharine MacKinnon, *Towards a Feminist Theory of the State* (Cambridge, MA: Harvard University Press, 1989).

There may be what appears to be genuine back and forth, roughly equal amounts of time in which each participant speaks, and nothing said that sounds like a lecture or a command. And yet, if, at the end of the day, it is the case that only some participants are open to being moved by what is said, perhaps because the underlying conceptual landscape in which the exchange is taking place obscures or flatly rules out other possibilities, then what is going on is not people speaking with one another, but some speaking to others. Thus, the norms of conversation go beyond shaping the moves we make in our exchanges with others to features of a conversation that lie in its background.

Second, since it may be the case that nothing in the words themselves will tell us whether or not we are conversing or doing something more one-sided, we are very likely to give the outcome of such exchanges a similar place in our further discussions. That is, whether we all tune ourselves to the oboe or all find some pitch to which we can mutually adjust, we will still, at the end of the day, be in tune. And, similarly, whether we are genuinely conversing or merely appearing to converse as a result of a combination of politeness and inequality, our exchange of words brings us into relationships with one another where we can be confident about which spaces of reasons we all occupy. This confidence, in turn, allows us to offer seemingly genuine invitations to speak for others. And so it can be tempting to say that such attunement, no matter how it comes about, leaves us sharing spaces of reasons, occupying them together, and thus sets the stage, as it were, on which we can fruitfully decide or act together.

The arguments above suggest that this conclusion is too hasty. For when our attunement is the result of my speaking to you and you being moved by my words, then we have not established that we live together in a shared space of reasons, but merely that there is a space of reasons that I inhabit and that you inhabit alongside me. Such a position, however, does not (yet) leave us ready to reason together, for since our reasoning takes place in a space that is basically mine, there is a sense in which my capacity to speak for you within that space is not fully answerable to your criticism. Such failure of answerability can happen in two rather different ways: first, I may not be able or willing or required to respond or react to your criticisms. Such an attitude can be fostered by social attitudes about members of a powerless group: that they are, for instance, overly emotional or self-interested. It can also be fostered by social attitudes about the proper bounds of criticism, by what is so thoroughly entrenched in our ways of thinking as to set out the limits of reasonable objection in a way that excludes the very grounds on which one's position is vulnerable.

Second, your lack of social power may serve to deprive you of the means of easy access to terms of criticism. The space of reasons I inhabit and construct may be your home as well, even if you have no hand in its construction, and so you may not be able to think well outside of it. As Catherine MacKinnon says of women under patriarchy who are silenced in various ways by sexual inequality:

when you are powerless, you don't just speak differently. A lot, you don't speak. Your speech is not just differently articulated, it is silenced. Eliminated, gone. You aren't just deprived of a language to articulate your distinctiveness, although you are; you are deprived of a life out of which articulation might come. Not being heard is not just a function of lack of recognition, not just that no one knows how to listen to you, although it is that; it is also silence of the deep kind, the silence of being prevented from having anything to say.[33]

Though you may not need to occupy this space, and may be able to abandon it, what you cannot do is participate in its (re)construction, and so it is not a shared space of reasons. The requirement of basic forms of background equality does not arise from the features of reasoning that requires the offering of a reason to be a reciprocal and answerable attempt to speak for another. These features of offering reasons will also place egalitarian pressure on the activity of reasoning, but in doing so, they merely extend and solidify a feature that is inherent in the wider activity of conversing.

Faced with this diagnosis of how the sorts of inequalities of power that are a deep feature of all human societies can distort and disable our attempts at genuine conversation, it is tempting to conclude that in the absence of full equality, we cannot converse, and thus cannot reason. Such a conclusion would be devastating for the project of this book, however. First, it would make the ideal of reasoning offered here ideal in all the wrong ways: a kind

---

[33] "Difference and Dominance: On Sex Discrimination," in *Feminism Unmodified*, 32–4 (Cambridge, MA: Harvard University Press, 1987), 39. A related point is made by Sandra Bartky, talking about the psychologically oppressive nature of cultural domination that leaves those dominated without a standpoint from which to mount resistance because, as she says, "the limits of my culture are the limits of my world" ("On Psychological Oppression," in *Femininity and Domination*, 22–32 (New York: Routledge, 1990), 25).

of pie-in-the-sky abstraction that has no clear bearing on the problems we face in living together here and now because it abstracts away from the very features of our current predicament that make living justly together so difficult. Second, it would imply that the only way to make the world a fit place for the realization of this ideal would be to go through a period in which we violate it. That is, if we can only reason once we have established symmetric distributions of power, then we cannot reason with one another in order to establish them. The end of being able to reason together would have to be achieved through unreasonable means.

Luckily, however, there is another way to understand this diagnosis without diluting its severely critical bite. Return to the idea of criteria. Cavell insists on the ever-present possibility that we are disappointed with our criteria. Disappointment in our criteria involves coming to see our norms as failing, but in a very particular way. One familiar way that our norms can fail us is when they are corrupted through systematic violation. In the case of rule-governed, interactive activities such as games, the systematic violation of norms can undermine our capacity to play the game. So, to return to an earlier example, if I think we are playing chess, and we are, for a time, both moving our pieces in accord with the rules, I can find myself disappointed when you start to move the pieces in a random fashion or otherwise alter your activity in a way that shows that all along we have not been engaged in the same activity. Here, the norm fails to guide your actions and in so doing, corrupts our activity. Nevertheless, it doesn't call forth any skepticism about the possibility of playing chess.

But the disappointment that we can feel in our criteria does not come about in that way. Rather, in the cases that interest Wittgenstein and Cavell, it turns out that our criteria do not guide us as we thought they would, so that there turn out to be ways of obeying the criteria that nevertheless leave us feeling as if we no longer share a sense of what is meant by what, or what the point of a given statement is, or, in the extreme cases, that we are mutually intelligible, that we share a form of life. Our criteria disappoint us, that is, when our words or the words of others somehow fail to mean what we or they intended them to mean. And, Cavell insists, it is just as much a part of our condition as users of language that we can be intelligible to one another on the basis of nothing firmer than our shared criteria as that nothing in this basis absolutely guarantees that we will not fall out of attunement, that our criteria will not disappoint us: "criteria and skepticism are one another's possibility."[34]

One lesson to be learned from this connection between criteria and the possibility of our disappointment in them, is that the mere possibility of disappointment in our criteria should not be taken as grounds for either abandoning them or searching for firmer foundations for them. It should not, as Cavell puts this point, push us to turn away from the ordinary, but rather to return to it. Similarly, I want to say that the obstacles to genuine conversation that inequalities of power present work by undermining our criteria, and thus that the response to such a diagnosis should not be to turn away from conversation, but to return to it.

Put in somewhat less elusive language, when someone criticizes the very terms in which a conversation proceeds as themselves set and structured by inequalities of power, and thus unable on their own to make those inequalities visible and thus to challenge them, that is itself a move in a conversation, and one that any norms of genuine conversation must find a way to regard as open. In practice, this openness takes work, as one common way the criticism above begins to find voice is in the exasperated cry of the powerless that they cannot talk about these matters with those who are powerful or speak in their idiom, that on this point, in these circumstances, conversation is impossible.[35] These claims do not signal that we should stop talking until we bring about justice, however, but that we have reason to be disappointed in our criteria, in the concepts that shaped our conversation to this point. What looked for all the world like a conversation is in danger of not being one, and we may have to find new terms on the basis of which to continue if what we will say to one another from here on in is not to fall into this familiar pattern. Looking for new terms, however, is just to join the conversation anew, not to abandon it as a hopelessly corrupted endeavor, for there is no other route to a set of shared terms than through conversation. Voicing and hearing such criticisms is not at all easy, nor is managing to do so once or many times a guarantee against further disappointment. It is, rather, that the possibility of such moves as moves within the activity of conversation shows that the obstacles that inequalities of power place in the

---

[34] Conditions Handsome and Unhandsome, 64.

[35] This, of course, is the position that Nora finds herself in at the end of Ibsen's A Doll's House. I discuss the relevance of Nora's predicament in Chapter 8.3. Cavell discusses it in, among other places, Conditions Handsome and Unhandsome, 108–15.

way of genuine conversation are ones that we are, in principle, able to overcome through participation in the very activity itself.[36]

Beyond this conceptual point, there are at least four practical lessons to be learned from thinking of the problems that power poses to the activity of genuine conversation in terms of leaving us disappointed in our criteria. First, it points to an intriguing set of conversational virtues that turn out to be central to conversing and reasoning, but which are all too often neglected in philo-sophical discussions of the intellectual virtues. We have already seen that a willingness to make oneself vulnerable, to let down one's defenses, is a necessary attitude for entering into genuine conversations. We can now add to that a certain receptivity to unfamiliar lines of criticism, especially those that may initially seem as if they are themselves incoherent or conceptually confused because they challenge the basis of one's conceptual map. If there is a conversational path back to genuine conversation that has been distorted by the effect of inequality in power, then it will require such openness. This openness involves certain skills of listening and heeding what others say, and it is particularly important that those who are privileged by inequalities of power possess and deploy it. By and large, societies that are characterized by patterns of unequal constructive power tend to train those who are privileged by such distributions to be sure and confident in their views and oblivious to their dependence on privilege.[37] If, however, the intellectual virtues such a society requires include the ability to listen and be open to these forms of criticism, then such societies need to be teaching their children different skills.[38]

---

[36] The claim that the shortcomings in our conversations might be fixed through conversation, rather than a shift to a different kind of activity marks a difference with at least one reading of Habermas's account of the norms of communicative action, and in particular, his discourse ethics ("Discourse Ethics," 93–4). For Habermas, it appears that when an ordinary claim is challenged, this can lead us to move up to the level of discourse to work out if certain necessary norms have been violated. Though discourse, like the base-level conversation, proceeds in a natural language, and so the shift is not one of moving to a meta-language, the justification of the norms at each level work differently. In particular, whereas the norms of ordinary communication are dependent on our acceptance of them, the norms of discourse are to be reconstructed by philosophers who can tease out the necessary presuppositions of argument as such. On the view being developed here, there is only one level, and so no space for a specifically philosophical form of expertise. I discuss the question of philosophical expertise and its relation to political deliberation in Habermas's work, with reference to his debate with John Rawls in my "The Justice of Justification," in *Habermas and Rawls: Disputing the Political* (New York: Routledge, 2010).

[37] For a vivid account of this form of reasoning and its class basis in the United States, see Annette Lureau, *Unequal Childhoods: Class, Race and Family Life* (Berkeley: University of California Press, 2003).

[38] I have explored what this might look like in my "Learning to Be Equal: Just Schools and Schools of Justice," in *Education, Justice and Democracy* (Chicago: University of Chicago Press, 2012).

Second, the ease with which we can come to see the above skills and attitudes as virtues of reasoning will depend on our picture of reasoning itself. If the activity of reasoning is pictured as aspiring to reach decisions and conclusions, then reasoning is primarily a tool for reaching conclusions and defending the positions reached against criticism. This makes the prime virtues of reasoning the capacity to defend against challenges, and the ideal reasoner someone who is thus invulnerable to criticism, "above reproach."[39] From within this picture, it will be hard to see the kind of openness and vulnerability I am here championing as natural virtues of reason. One advantage, then, of picturing reasoning as a form of conversation is that being reasonable will naturally involve the kinds of virtues discussed above, and that will make it easier to counsel reasoning and conversation as an appropriate response to inequality in power while at the same time taking seriously just how deep such inequality can cut.

Third, we have here a model of equality that makes equality not a matter of a static set of positions or distributions of certain goods, but rather a kind of practice. That is, the equality that conversation requires is not that we all have the same or similar piles of resources, whether within the conversation or beyond it, or that we stand in certain fixed relations to one another, but rather that we treat each other in accord with certain norms, norms of respect and trust and openness.

Finally, since the boundaries of conversation are fuzzy, these norms of equality cannot be hard and fast. As a result, the important consequence of seeing that such norms exist is not that they can give us precise methods for evaluating the genuineness of conversation. Rather, I think their value lies in directing our attention to a certain set of questions and issues and remedies, and helping us to fill out a picture of what excellent conversation is and does.

Contrast the view outlined above with a different account of the effects of inequality on our ability to reason together, one that begins from the standard picture. If the point of exchanging reasons is to forge some kind of agreement, and excellence at this activity is measured by the goodness or

---

[39] This characterization comes from a much criticized claim in John Rawls, *A Theory of Justice* (Cambridge, MA: Harvard University Press, 1971) that if one had a rational plan of life and carried it out, then one would be above reproach (422). For criticisms of this claim, see Bernard Williams, "Moral Luck," in *Moral Luck* (Cambridge: Cambridge University Press, 1982), and Cavell, *Conditions Handsome and Unhandsome*, lec. 3.

wisdom of the outcome, then the problem with unequal levels of power is in the content of the agreement reached. Unequal amounts of power can distort our deliberations because those with more power wind up having a greater influence on the final decision, whether because others yield to them out of prudence or because one way that social power manifests itself is in having the resources of persuasiveness at one's disposal.[40] These count as distorting effects on the standard picture to the extent that they affect the outcome of those deliberations. So, in order to argue that inequality is in part bad because of its deleterious effects on our reasoning together, we have to provide an argument as to why decisions reached under conditions of equality would be better. Some argue, for instance, that the powerful are likely to be blind to features of the world that ought to impact what they say, and so by exerting undue influence on the final shape of the space of reasons, they distort that space or ill-fit it for navigating the world around us. But this need not always be the case. Sometimes, the powerful are also wise and knowledgeable. If the only problem with decisions and conclusions reached under conditions of inequality were epistemic, then we could solve them, as Plato wanted to, by educating the powerful just as easily as we could follow Rousseau's recommendation of undoing the inequality. Even if there are further purely epistemic arguments to be made in support of Rousseau and against Plato, the point here is that thinking about the dangers of inequality in this way gets us into this debate, and it is the wrong debate to be having.

By thinking about the deleterious effects of inequality within the context of the conversation itself, where the problem is a lack of mutuality, we get a rather different picture. As we have seen, when our idle conversation takes place against the background of inequality, it easily ceases to be a genuine conversation. And while a world without genuine conversation would be a duller and flatter world, it would also be a world where we don't engage in the very activity that constructs shared spaces of reasons. In such a world, we can't live together but merely side-by-side. The joint construction and maintenance of shared spaces must be mutual and reciprocal, and thus must involve not only persuasive articulation, but attentive listening, and

---

[40] One can find such diagnoses in republican thought and in a somewhat different key, in feminist thought. See, for instance, Philip Pettit, *Republicanism: A Theory of Freedom and Government* (Oxford: Oxford University Press, 1999), and Iris Marion Young, *Justice and the Politics of Difference* (Princeton, NJ: Princeton University Press, 1990).

with it, the capacity be touched and an openness to being moved by one's conversational partners. One of the effects of inequality in such interaction is that those with more power or status talk more and listen less and the result is that they bring their conversation partners to them, and not the reverse. Another effect is that powerful people protect themselves against vulnerability, and so even if they aren't doing most of the talking, they are rarely doing the kind of listening that makes conversation an activity of mutual attunement.

As a result, even when the outcome of unequal conversation is agreement, and even when that agreement is wise and thoughtful and concerned for all, it does not create a shared space of reasons. Those who occupy it are not thereby living together but merely side-by-side. If we are conversing, but I am doing all the talking and you all the accommodating, or the presuppositions of our conversation include a conceptual space that marks me as the standard, then what we will build is not a space of reasons we share but one in which I reside and you know how to live alongside me. This is because, while it may look as if we are talking with one another, and are working out when and how to talk for one another in the manner of sharing a space of reasons, what is really going on is my talking to, and perhaps merely at, you. And this problem, unlike that of the distorted agreement, cannot be fixed by making me wiser or more global and inclusive in my considerations and calculations. It requires shifting both the balance of power and our dispositions to be moved by one another.

4.4 Norms of Conversation III: Sincerity

The final norm of conversation keeps it from sliding into a third way that people talk in each other's proximity without conversing: when what they say amounts to mere words because there is not sufficient connection between what is said and those who say it. Understanding how conversations can fail in this regard leads to a norm of sincerity. That conversation requires sincerity in the sense developed in this section results from the fact that to genuinely speak with another, I have to genuinely speak for myself. Speaking for myself is a weaker requirement than even speaking to another, but it does not come free: I can utter words that fail to speak for me. Consider three characters we have met briefly before: the flighty person, the charming rogue and the principled person of prejudice. All three fail to speak for themselves and thus cannot fully engage in conversation.

Start, then, with the flighty person, captured by Jane Austen in the person of Mrs. Bennet. Mrs. Bennet's sentiments are puffed around: she cannot hold a stand against any change in prevailing attitudes or her own whims or moods. As a result, she fails to stand behind her own words, not because she does not utter them earnestly, but because there is nowhere she really stands at all. At the limit of flightiness, even the meaning of a person's words is not stable, and so it is impossible to reach sufficient referential agreement to have a conversation at all. But the limit here illustrates the general problem. Conversation takes place over time, and involves more than the mere exchange of interlocking words with another. It only amounts to this more full-blown interaction if all parties to it have sufficient stability that their shifts in position count as movement, and they are capable of being touched. The flighty person's sentiments of the moment determine her position so thoroughly that her position is more like that of the weather than a stand she takes. Though she says things, they don't amount to an articulation of who she is, what she thinks, or where she stands. And just as we cannot engage with the weather or hope to move it, but only react to it, and perhaps learn to predict its vagaries, we cannot converse with the flighty person. This failure arises from her inability to speak for herself because she does not have a stable enough self to speak for.

A charming rogue, such as Austen's Mr. Wickham, says what the conversation seems to require for its animation, without any regard for whether he can take responsibility for the position he assumes. The rogue is irresponsible because he fails to stand behind what he says: his talk is mere talk and so his invitations not genuine: they are likely to be withdrawn the moment they look like they will be accepted. He thus merely plays at conversation, and in so doing, winds up playing those with whom he speaks for fools. The rogue's charm counts as merely playing at conversation because since he takes no stand, there is no way for him to be affected by what others say: he is immune to disappointment and rejection, but also to being touched. But this means that, in the end, his attempts at conversation amount to mere stuff and nonsense, and so he turns out to be no better at conversation than the flighty self. Like the flighty self, he abjures a connection between himself and his words. The difference is that in his case, this comes from an unwillingness to forge the connection, to stand behind what he says, rather than his inability to occupy a given place at all. Although the charming rogue can speak from a given position long enough to animate the conversation, his ultimate failure as a conversation partner, the reason he can make friends easily but not keep them, is because by failing to accept that his words speak for him, he renders his words as meaningless in conversation as those of the flighty self.

The prejudiced person of principle also does not speak for herself, but for society or the moral law or God's command. In this, she resembles another figure with whom we cannot engage in genuine conversation: the conformist. The conformist is seen by philosophers as otherwise different as Emerson and Mill as not only a moral failure but a moral threat. She occupies the central position of moral danger in the view that Cavell has come to call moral perfectionism precisely because in failing to stand behind her words, she loses her grip on herself.[41] As Elizabeth Bennet says of herself upon realizing that she has misjudged the relationship between Mr. Wickham and Mr. Darcy, "I have courted prepossession and ignorance, and driven reason away, where either was concerned. Till this moment, I never knew myself."[42] Elizabeth says this on finally being truly touched by the words of another (a letter that Darcy writes to her after she has rejected his first proposal), and thus coming to realize that up until then, sure of her position and its rightness, she has not allowed herself to be so touched. The problem, we might surmise, is that like her flighty mother and the rogue she now sees for what he is, she has failed to genuinely engage in conversations because, in allowing her positions to become prejudices, she has failed to take responsibility for them.

Sincerity, in the sense the term is used here, thus refers to the relation between someone and their words, the fact that in uttering those words, they are genuinely speaking for themselves, standing behind what they say, taking responsibility for the position they articulate. Sincerity here is not merely a psychological state. It is not enough that I say my piece earnestly, that, for instance, I really believe it as I am saying it. All the characters above can speak

---

[41] The relation of moral perfectionism to conformity is one of the principal themes of the first lecture in Cavell, *Conditions Handsome and Unhandsome*. He there discusses, among other texts, Emerson's "Self-Reliance" and Mill's *On Liberty*. Notice also that speaking always in the voice of others is precisely the source of irresponsibility in idle chatter that led Heidegger to condemn certain forms of it as masking rather than disclosing our condition. Martin Heidegger, *Being and Time*, trans. John Macquarrie and Edward Robinson (Oxford: Wiley-Blackwell, 2000), §35 "Idle Talk," 211–14.

[42] *Pride and Prejudice*, vol. II, ch. XIII, 159.

earnestly. Sincerity requires further that one have a sufficiently stable and unified self for which one's words can speak as well as that it is for one's self that the words do speak. To put the point in terms more reminiscent of Cavell, speaking sincerely requires speaking in one's own voice, and that requires not only having a voice, but also having the kind of self that can have a voice of its own.[43] That the norms of casual conversation thus govern not only our words but our selves will be a main theme of Part III.

4.5 Conclusion

Through our casual conversations we construct and renovate our relationships to one another, and build and enter and find our place in shared conceptual spaces from which we can also reason together. Such conversations thus provide the background against which we reason even if they do not themselves always involve us in the more particular activities of reasoning. Since conversation is a norm-governed activity, not all communicative interaction counts as conversing. Moreover, the failure of such interaction to count as conversation may not be obvious on its face, and may require investigating the social positions of its participants and wider social norms within which the interaction is situated. When everything goes more or less right, then our conversations make and remake the ground on which our reasoning, both within casual conversation and in more directed activities, both together and alone, can function, and that ground is able to sustain the reciprocal attitudes and actions that are partly constitutive of reasoning. But as all does not always go well, it is important to be clear about the consequences of our failing to converse and also what this says about where we ought to direct some of our critical attention. If the social structure of our environment places obstacles in the way of our communicative interaction being genuine conversation, this need not be apparent to us as we go about speaking to one another. And, so, sometimes we will, through our words, find common ground and attune ourselves to one another, and thus establish the ground we need in order to reach what appear for all the world to be reasoned conclusions. But, if such

---

[43] David Owen, "Cultural Diversity and the Conversation of Justice," *Political Theory* 27, no. 5 (October 1999): 579–96.

construction does not rest on genuine conversation, but one of its more one-sided doppelgangers, then the ground will not be truly common, truly shared. As a result, the considerations we all take as counting in favor of various conclusions, while they look like they obey the norms of reciprocity and openness to criticism that would make them reasons, will, in fact, be stacked ahead of time, and thus not be reasons.[44]

Because the stacking happens prior to our interaction, it may not be easily accessible within that interaction, and so an awareness of or the ability to criticize assumptions built into our construction of the ground of reasons may not be available as a matter-of-course move in our interaction. Such criticism has a tendency to look as if it is somehow out of bounds, unreasonable, confused. And this means, in extreme and not so extreme cases, that when what we do looks for all the world like reasoning together, we are, in fact, not doing that at all, for we are not offering to speak for one another in a way that is fully reciprocal and answerable and open to all criticism. And this fact may not be apparent from our words alone. I make a proposal and you accept it, so it looks like my offer has met with the right kind of favor. But what was lacking lurked in the background, in the excluded space, well before we began talking, where your potential refusal might have found a basis and an articulation.

This suggests that we can rely neither on solely internal criteria for what is reasonable or rational, nor on any fixed and unimpeachable foundations to ensure that our interactions are reciprocal.[45] A certain background of equality and sincerity and openness to mutual influence needs to be there as well. There is thus an important and often under-appreciated role for careful investigation and upturning of sedimented attitudes, social relations, and assumptions about the means of broadcast and social propagation. It is only when we leave our reasoning and our conversations open to such radical critique and are willing to reform our practices accordingly that we can construct genuine reasons in and from our conversations and thus

---

[44] There is a parallel here with radical feminist criticisms of norms of objectivity as blinding us to the workings of patriarchal power that nevertheless need to invoke some notion of objectivity to give their criticisms sufficient force. See, for instance, MacKinnon, *Towards a Feminist Theory of the State*, and my "Radical Feminists, Reasonable Liberals: Reason, Power and Objectivity in the work of MacKinnon and Rawls," *Journal of Political Philosophy* 11, no. 2 (2003): 133–52.

[45] Again, this marks a very significant break with many in the Kantian tradition, including Korsgaard, Forst, and Habermas.

reason at all. Conversation, being norm-governed, also comes with its own virtues: of openness and trust, treating others as equals, and standing behind one's words. The picture of reasoning offered here is an ideal, which means that it is an open question whether anyone manages to live fully up to this ideal. We can now see some of the ways that we might fail, and some of the skills we would need to develop and deploy in order to succeed.

5

Reasoning as Responsive Conversation

5.1 Two Pictures: An Austenian Interlude

Mr. Collins's proposal to Elizabeth Bennet does not go well. Elizabeth, unable to register her rejection with him ends by crying, "Do not consider me now as an elegant female intending to plague you, but as a rational creature speaking the truth from her heart." Mr. Collins replies that she is "uniformly charming" and claims that he is "persuaded that when sanctioned by the express authority of both your excellent parents, my proposals will not fail of being acceptable." Austen concludes the scene by telling us that "to such perseverance in willful self-deception Elizabeth would make no reply, and immediately and in silence withdrew."[1] Sometimes more talking is not the answer.

What exactly has gone wrong? And what might be done about it? Austen offers at least three diagnoses, and despite their sources, they are all worth taking seriously. Mr. Collins thinks nothing needs to be done because nothing has gone wrong. Austen begins the next chapter with him in "silent contemplation of his successful love."[2] Now, this may merely be a result of his obtuseness and willful self-deception, but the problem cannot merely be that his proposal has been rejected this time. After all, things do not appear to stand any worse with Mr. Collins at this point than they do for Mr. Darcy after he first proposes. If anything, Darcy's initial proposal, considered as an argument meant to compel assent with the unforced force of reason is worse than Mr. Collins's: "In vain have I struggled. It will not do. My feelings will not be repressed. You must allow me to tell you how ardently I admire and love you."[3] This is followed, Austen reports, by

---

[1] Jane Austen, *Pride and Prejudice* (Oxford: Oxford University Press, 2004), vol. I, ch. XIX, 83–4.
[2] Ibid., vol. 1, ch. XX, 84.   [3] Ibid., vol. II, ch. XI, 145.

a rather passionate enumeration of all the reasons he has for *not* proposing to Elizabeth. And Elizabeth's initial response is more final than the one she tries to impress on Mr. Collins: "You could not have made me the offer of your hand in any possible way that would have tempted me to accept it . . . I had not known you a month before I felt that you were the last man in the world whom I could ever be prevailed upon to marry."[4] And, yet, this exchange, unpromising as it seems, turns out to be the beginning of a successful proposal, a model of the kind of responsiveness characteristic of reasoning as portrayed by the social picture. So it may be that Mr. Collins's mistake is not in seeing failure as success, but in prematurely judging it a success.

What about those who recognize Mr. Collins's initial failure? We have heard from Elizabeth, and will need to come back to her diagnosis. Her basic point is that Mr. Collins's failure lies in his lack of responsiveness to her rejection, which amounts to a failure to treat her like a rational creature, to reason with her. This leaves room for the possibility of a proposal that succeeds at reasoning but fails to secure acceptance. One way to respond properly to the rejection of a proposal is to withdraw it. Austen, however, gives us a third perspective on the exchange that is worth considering. For while Elizabeth and Mr. Collins were alone together in the dining room, someone was eagerly lurking by the door. As soon as Elizabeth withdraws, in rushes Mrs. Bennet, who congratulates "him and herself on the happy prospect of their nearer connection."

Mr. Collins received and returned the felicitations with equal pleasure, and then proceeded to relate the particulars of their interview, with the result of which he trusted he had every reason to be satisfied, since the refusal which his cousin has steadfastly given him would naturally flow from her bashful modesty and the genuine delicacy of her character.

This information, however, startled Mrs. Bennet;—she would have been glad to be equally satisfied that her daughter had meant to encourage him by protesting against his proposals, but she dared not to believe it, and could not help saying so.

"But depend upon it, Mr. Collins," she added, "that Lizzy shall be brought to reason. I will speak to her about it myself directly. She is a very headstrong foolish girl, and does not know her own interest; but I will *make* her know it."[5]

---

[4] Ibid.   [5] Ibid. vol. I, ch. XX, 84.

Mrs. Bennet, like her daughter, sees the attempted proposal as a failure of reasoning, but unlike her daughter, pronounces a different diagnosis of the problem. Whereas Elizabeth holds that Mr. Collins has failed to show her the responsiveness owed to a rational creature, her mother sees her failure to act in her own manifest interest as a sign of *her* irrationality. The failure to reason is hers, not his, but it is a failure she can be made to overcome: she can be "brought to reason."

Mr. Collins, confident that Elizabeth's words need not be taken seriously, is pleased with his reasons and their capacity to ultimately bring about the end he desires. Elizabeth, confident that Mr. Collins's failure to hear her words shows that he is not reasoning with her, sees a failure that can be placed squarely at his feet. And her mother, while accepting the impact of her daughter's rejection, takes them as a sign of her irrationality, and so while she takes the episode to be a failed attempt at reasoning, she places the blame for this on Elizabeth. How might we understand the impetus behind them? It might merely trace back to the personalities of the people involved: Mr. Collins is self-satisfied and obtuse, Elizabeth finds him so, and her mother wants nothing more than to marry off her daughters in a way that secures the family's financial security. But something deeper and more philosophically interesting is also at work here. These differing diagnoses derive what plausibility they have from the picture of reason they share, and so they bring out the impact that this picture has on our approach to the world and those with whom we share it.

According to the standard picture, the activity of reasoning is character-ized derivatively, in terms of reason and reasons.[6] That is, what determines whether we are reasoning on the standard picture is whether we are invoking reasons and/or being guided by reason. So, if we ask, from within this picture, whether a purported stretch of reasoning really is reasoning, we are asking not about the nature of the activity itself, but its content: is what is said really a reason? Is what is thought guided by principles of reason? I fail to engage in the activity of reasoning on this picture if the steps in my thinking process are not really reasons, but arbitrary stipulations or false-hoods or mere assertions of preferences or desires, or if I fail to connect them in a way determined by their inferential relations to one another. This kind of failure is what leads Mrs. Bennet to describe Elizabeth as headstrong and

---

[6] See Chapter 1.2.

foolish for so completely failing to attend to the obvious considerations in favor of accepting Mr. Collins. And, from this perspective, Mrs. Bennet is absolutely correct. Given the society Elizabeth lives in, her place in it, and absent the beneficent hand of an omnipotent author who is preparing a better option, she is thwarting her interests in refusing Mr. Collins's offer. These considerations, after all, lead her very sensible friend Charlotte to angle for and accept Mr. Collins's next proposal, an action she defends to Elizabeth by saying "I am not romantic you know. I never was. I ask only a comfortable home; and considering Mr. Collins's character, connections, and situation in life, I am convinced that my chance of happiness with him is as fair as most people can boast on entering the marriage state."[7]

Although particular theories will disagree about what reasons we face, all of them involve the further claim that part of what makes a consideration a reason is that it bears the appropriate authority, which, according to the standard picture, is the authority of command. That is, one way in which we might call into question whether someone's bald and unsupported assertion counts as a reason is that it has no authority to command or direct our own thoughts. Just because you say that the sky is orange or up is down or right is wrong doesn't make it so. These pronouncements cannot command my perceptions and thoughts, which is to say that they are not reasons.

The authority of command must be grounded in a backward-looking manner if it is to be legitimate. Thus, determining whether a stretch of reflection is really reasoning (as this is understood on the standard picture) requires us to look backwards, to something prior to the particular reflection itself, that might ground the authority in question. Among the kinds of things that are generally brought forth in consideration at this point are features of the world, the person purportedly reasoning, or what is being said. I can call into question whether you are reasoning by pointing out that your premises are false, or do not capture your actual beliefs and desires, but are mere fantasies or wishes, or that the considerations you are bringing forth are not suitably general to count as reasons. On the standard picture, the characteristic norms of reasoning govern these kinds of issues: they delineate the space of reasons or lay down principles of reason. They tell us directly or give us a way to determine ahead of time what reasons there are, which interests are grounds for accepting a proposal, and whether one's

---

[7] *Pride and Prejudice*, vol. I, ch. XXII, 96.

own expected happiness in companionship is one of them. From this perspective, it is not at all unreasonable for both Mr. Collins and Mr. Darcy to propose to Elizabeth in the complete confidence that she will, if she is rational, accept, and thus take any refusal on her part as a sign that she is headstrong and foolish, or not sincere in her rejection. The reasons she has for accepting either of them are plain as day, and precede anything they may say by way of making their proposals appropriately appealing. How a proposal is made or an argument presented is, on this picture, mere window-dressing, a question of manner, not substance, and certainly does not affect whether it is a reasonable one or not.

There is, however, a fourth possible interpretation of Elizabeth's rejection of Mr. Collins's proposal, one that grows out of the social picture of reasoning. It follows from some of the results of the last chapter, and, given the course of the novel, is arguably the one Austen favors. It holds that whether Mr. Collins and Elizabeth are reasoning depends on what happens going forward. The social picture begins from the activity of reasoning itself. It distinguishes reasoning from other forms of interaction such as commanding or deferring or bullying or professing. As a result, determining if a stretch of activity is really reasoning on this picture requires looking at the nature of the activity itself. It is the features of the activity that determine whether the considerations brought forth in the course of it are to count as reasons. Reasoning on this picture is an activity of inviting others to take our words as speaking for them as well and doing so in a manner that remains always open to criticism. It requires certain levels of responsiveness to our reasoning partners. On this picture, what makes something really a reason is that it figures in a stretch of reasoning. That means that reasons cannot be identified ahead of time, absent the context in which they are offered. Something might be a reason if deployed in one way, but not another. The context sensitivity here turns on how the consideration is offered, rather than, as on the standard picture, for what it is offered as a consideration. A consideration may count as a reason on this picture when offered as an invitation, but not when used to specify or bolster a command, even if in both cases, it is offered as a consideration for the same thing.

Furthermore, the kind of authority that reasoning constructs here is the authority of connection. Since the authority of connection is grounded in a forward-looking manner, the question of whether we are really reasoning will also require a forward-looking answer. That there are forward-looking considerations that serve to determine whether someone is engaged in a particular activity should not be entirely surprising. Think of the examples of playing chess from the previous chapter. There are, of course, things we can have already done or failed to do that make it the case that we are not (or no longer) playing chess despite sitting at a board and taking turns moving the pieces. These are backward-looking considerations. But, if we are to be playing chess, it must be the case that certain rules continue to be obeyed. Some of these can be cashed out in our present and past intentions, but not all of them. It is always a possibility that our criteria disappoint us, that we find that what we thought we were doing is not in fact what we were doing all along. That what we have been doing all along is not yet settled but depends on what comes in the future is what it means to say that there are forward-looking considerations that determine the nature of our activity. The point can be illustrated more vividly with cases where it is really indeterminate in the course of an activity what activity it is. Think, for instance, of a toddler taking her first steps. She gets to her feet, picks up one foot and puts it down a little further on without falling. She has taken a step. Is she walking? We don't know yet (nor does she). It will depend on what happens next.

So how might it be the case that whether we are presently reasoning is determinable in part by what happens down the road? There are of course cases we can imagine where something that starts out like a perfectly good stretch of reasoning on the standard picture disintegrates somewhere along the way. In fact, these are all too common: someone makes a cogent case for something up to a point, and then relies on a fallacious move, makes an unwarranted leap, or introduces a faulty or irrelevant piece of evidence. But in these cases, the person was reasoning until that point, or she was reasoning, but badly. The kind of forward-looking considerations that determine that we are reasoning on the social picture are somewhat different. If I offer you a consideration for believing something or doing something or picturing the world a certain way, what determines whether I am reasoning with you is whether I am issuing an invitation or attempting to command. And what determines that, in part, is both how you respond and how I respond to that, and where those responses take our interaction going forward. These are the sort of considerations that lead to Elizabeth's diagnosis of Mr. Collins's proposal as a failure of reasoning: it is not the considerations he brings forth or the facts that support them that is the problem, but his utter failure to be responsive to what she says in reply.

Note, however, that as ridiculous as his initial proposal is, we are not in a position upon hearing it to know whether he is reasoning with Elizabeth or not, at least if we are thinking of reasoning according to the social picture. The very same words could be reasons if they were the beginning of a different interaction. It is only because of the exchange of words that follows them that we can determine that they were not steps in the activity of reasoning. Until their conversation completely breaks off, it is always possible for him to retrospectively change the nature of their interaction by changing the nature of his responsiveness. This, in fact, is what happens with Mr. Darcy. And though he shows more responsiveness in the initial encounter in that he accepts her refusal for what it is, it is what happens after he leaves the room that makes his activity, taken as a whole, one of reasoning. Rather than dismissing her rejection, he asks for her reasons, and rather than taking these as signs that his ends can be more easily met with another woman, he spends the rest of the novel responding to them, both by arguing against them and by changing in response to them. Though, as Austen makes clear, he does not initially propose with the intention of reasoning with Elizabeth (either in the standard sense or the sense given by the social picture) his attachment to her makes it the case that, at least on the social picture, this is what he ends up having done. One important consequence of this fact about reasoning on the social picture is that there is a deep sense in which it is never too late to change the past: we can always change how we respond to one another in a way that will turn our interaction, including what has gone before, into reasoning. But to do so will involve not bringing each other to reason in the sense Mrs. Bennet has in mind. It will involve inviting them to reason.

5.2 The Norms of Reasoning: An Overview

Escaping the standard picture of reasoning in order to bring fully into view the activity of reasoning pictured by the social picture and thus describe an ideal of living together, requires a characterization of this activity in terms of a set of characteristic norms that distinguish reasoning from other forms of speaking, without relying on the standard picture's characterization of certain kinds of considerations as reasons. These norms would enable a diagnosis of failures of reasoning without recourse to the standard picture, and identify the skills needed to reason well. If reasoning is a form of responsive conversation, then its features and characteristic norms should carve out a subset of all conversational interactions. At the same time, following these norms should yield an activity recognizable as reasoning quite apart from the theoretical apparatus being assembled here. The considerations that get brought forth in reasoning had better share some essential features with the considerations otherwise called reasons. And, so as not to fall back into a version of the standard picture, what must give these considerations their normative status as reasons has to trace back to the norms of the activity, not something that precedes it. That is a lot to ask.

Here, roughly, is my proposal. The norms discussed below follow from the three central features of the activity of reasoning: (1) it is a form of inviting; (2) to take our words as speaking for others as well; and (3) is always open to criticism. These features each serve to narrow the category of conversation and give rise to three kinds of norms that parallel those that govern conversation more generally. They also explain why the considerations that count as reasons on this picture have features that we associate with reasons more generally: objectivity, universality, and authority.

Conversing with someone requires that what we say is intelligible to them. Reasoning with them requires, further, that what we say to them is intelligible as an invitation. That requires that what we say can be heard as an invitation, given the context. An invitation is a kind of opening up or making public, and so considerations offered as invitations must be public. Publicity then takes the place of objectivity. One consequence of thinking of reasoning as inviting is that it highlights the public or social nature of the activity of reasoning. This does not mean that we cannot reason alone, but that in reasoning, we cannot be engaging in a pattern of reflection that isolates us from others. We fail to reason then, not by being headstrong or foolish, but by isolating ourselves, even in the presence of others.

Conversing with someone requires sufficient levels of equality that we can speak with them and not merely to them. Reasoning with them requires the possibility that they accept what we say as speaking for them as well, and that requires that we are open to the possibility that they can speak for us. Reasoning is an invitation to share a certain kind of normative space, and sharing a space in this sense involves making room for each of its occupants to inhabit it as their home, not merely as a passing guest. Reasoning thus requires a level of reciprocity that makes it possible that there is a "we" for which we can both speak. Since not all invitations are offered with the hope or even desire that they be accepted, reasoning only requires this possibility, and not an actual "we."[8] Nevertheless, the need to advert to even a possible "we" makes all reasons social reasons. Though considerations that can speak for us need not be universal, they have a kind of extension beyond my individual subjectivity that secures what universality secures for reasons on the standard view. Since they have this extension only because we give it to them, the social picture also brings out clearly the responsibility we bear for the scope of our reasons.

Finally, conversing requires that we are sincere, that we stand behind our words enough that they can be taken as speaking for us. Reasoning further requires a kind of good faith which can be understood has having two components, both of which follow from reasoning being an invitation to share a particular kind of normative space: a space of reasons. First, in order to be genuinely offering an invitation, I have to be responsive to its rejection. Second, in order for the space I invite you to share with me to be a space of reasons, it has to be fully open to criticism, not only by those who inhabit it, but by anyone. This gives reasons a kind of dual structure: they are subject both to rejection by some and criticism by all. It is this openness of what we say to rejection and criticism that opens the possibility that what we say might bear the authority of connection. And so, in opening what we say to criticism, we lay the ground for our reasons to have authority. Once again, coming to understand reasoning in this way shifts what counts as a failure of reasoning. Someone who, like Mr. Collins, deploys universal, objective, authoritative considerations in pursuit of his ends, and takes himself to be justified in ignoring all opposition because he has reason on his side will turn out, on the social picture, as well as in the mind of Elizabeth Bennet, to be the one who is headstrong and foolish.[9]

---

[8] As we will see in the next chapter, those forms of reasoning which are concerned to establish or maintain an actual "we" form an important subset of the full category of reasoning.

[9] Here I am in broad agreement with Michel Foucault's distinction between polemics and "the serious play of questions and answers" aimed at "reciprocal elucidation." The activity of reasoning described by the social picture involves the serious play of questions and answers, and one of the dangers of confining our understanding of reason to the standard picture is that we lapse into polemics as we reason. See Michel Foucault, "Polemics, Politics, and Problematizations," in *The Foucault Reader*, ed. Paul Rabinow, 381–90 (London: Penguin, 1984). Thanks to David Owen for directing me to this discussion.

5.3 The Norms of Intelligibility

In order for what I say to you to be intelligible, you need to be able to understand not only the meaning of my words, but my point in saying them to you.[10] If what I say to you takes the form of an invitation, then for it to be intelligible to you as an invitation, you have to be able to understand the point of my inviting you. And that, in turn, requires that I have such a point. As was discussed in Chapter 1, there are a variety of considerations that make issuing an invitation appropriate. I may issue an invitation in complete confidence that you will accept it, but in a situation where I am nevertheless not in a position to or do not wish to command you. I may issue a genuine invitation, when I hope for your acceptance, but am unsure of it. And I may issue an invitation out of mere politeness, both confident in and hopeful that you will refuse my offer, either to show you that I have nothing to hide, or to affirm a different kind of relationship between us, one of civility or respect, though not friendship or intimacy. My point, then, in inviting you depends on which of these kinds of invitations I mean to make, and my intelligibility in making the invitation will depend on our sharing enough of a background that we can work out what kind of invitation is being made.

Similarly, there are a variety of contexts in which we might reason with one another. Perhaps we have to come to an agreement or make a decision together.[11] Perhaps we merely want to work out where each of us stands on a matter that has come up, either because it is itself important or because our conversation has turned that way. Perhaps I want to be left alone, and yet think you deserve reassurance that I have nothing to hide in so wanting. Which of these we are doing determines the kind of invitations we offer, and thus our point in offering one invitation rather than another. If we are not both sufficiently sensitive to the context in which we are reasoning and thus the kind of invitations we are offering, then our interaction threatens to degenerate into mere talking to or at each other. Think, for instance, of a case where one person is trying to lay out her position as one a reasonable person could occupy, but the person with whom she is talking thinks she is trying to convert him to her position. Whether they are talking about

---

[10] See Chapter 3.4 and 4.2.
[11] This kind of case will be the focus of Chapter 6.

matters as important as religious belief or as trivial as how to load a dishwasher, the reasons that she offers seem to him to be faulty or beside the point or question-begging, because none of them offer him an invitation he is moved to accept. As long as he does not understand what her point is in reasoning with him about this matter, he finds her invitations unintelligible as invitations.

The need for our invitations to be intelligible as invitations in order for us to be reasoning brings out three important features of reasoning on the picture being developed here. First, reasoning is essentially a social activity. It is something we not only do in the presence of others, but with others. Reasoning with others does not require their literal presence as we engage in reflection. But solitary reflection only counts as reasoning if it is answerable to others: it could be intelligibly done in their presence. Second, reasoning involves making a certain space public or reaffirming its publicity. A description of a space of reasons only counts as an invitation if the description makes that space publicly available, at least to those to whom the invitation is offered. If, in contrast, I describe some space I occupy in great but ultimately idiosyncratic detail and thus render the space unintelligible to anyone else, then I cannot be understood as inviting someone to share it with me. Third, reasoning turns out to be an activity that is highly context dependent. Not all invitations can be intelligibly offered to everyone in all situations, and so the mere fact that we cannot understand someone as offering an invitation to us or in this circumstance and she makes no attempt to render her invitation intelligible to us need not mean that she is not reasoning. It only means that she is not reasoning with us. All three claims have counterparts on a standard picture of reason, and it will be helpful in unpacking them to contrast them with these more familiar claims.

One of the central debates in philosophy in the last several decades and arguably the last several centuries has been between those who approach reasons and reasoning as natural psychological phenomena, and those who regard them as fundamentally normative.[12] Thinking of reasoning as a natural psychological phenomenon involves thinking of it as proceeding according to certain more or less causal laws, and this goes hand in hand with thinking of reasons as made up of some combination of psychological

---

[12] For a description and analysis of this divide, see Onora O'Neill, "Four Models of Practical Reasoning," in *Bounds of Justice*, 11–28 (Cambridge: Cambridge University Press, 2000).

states such as beliefs and desires and features of the world that can affect our psychological states. Thus, to take a simple example, we might think that a person has a reason to take a certain action when she has a desire for something combined with a belief that taking that action will somehow result in or bring her closer to that desired end. On such a view, reasons look like they are importantly private. Your desire for a double-cheese pizza may give you a reason to pick up the phone and order one, but it doesn't give me a reason to do so (unless of course, I have the same desire or a separate reason to act to satisfy your desires). Your desire as such does not have the same authority for me that it does for you. Reason's privacy in this sense is also a form of context dependence. What is a reason for what depends on a variety of other contingent psychological states. My belief that picking up the phone is part of a process that will eventually lead to the delivery of a pizza is only a reason for me to pick up the phone if I want a pizza.

In contrast to this, many philosophers who work downstream from Kant make a point of highlighting the normative nature of reasons, and argue that reasons cannot be understood as made up of psychological states. Reasons stand in judgment of those states. Reasons are, to use T. M. Scanlon's phrase, "considerations in favor of" forming certain attitudes. And while some psychological states might serve as such considerations, it is a mistake to think of reasons as such states.[13] Something can be a consideration in favor of forming an attitude as a result of certain inferential or causal or other relations to other things beyond our psyches. To say that reasons are normative is to say that they have a certain authority: if I have a good enough reason to believe or do something, then, barring reasons not to, I ought to believe or do it. And if this reason is a result of something other than my particular psychology, then it also looks as if its authority will have to hold more broadly. According to this line of thinking, the reason you have for ordering a pizza is not your desire, but the considerations that make that desire reasonable: the combination of the gooey cheese and the tangy sauce, the relative ease of having pizza for dinner compared to shopping for ingredients and cooking something, and so forth.[14] From here, there is an argument to show that reasoning is a

---

[13] *What We Owe to Each Other* (Cambridge, MA: Harvard University Press, 1998), 41–9.

[14] I elide here various concerns about the picture of desire that even this account of reasoning rests on. For a trenchant discussion of these problems and an attractive alternative, see Talbot Brewer, *The Retrieval of Ethics* (Oxford: Oxford University Press, 2009).

public activity. In order for something to be a reason, it must wield a certain kind of non-idiosyncratic authority. Wielding such authority requires that it applies across situations and persons, and that implies that reasons have a certain level of generality in virtue of their being reasons. That is, something that does not have this generality and thus does not have authority across some suitable range of cases is a merely idiosyncratic consideration and not a genuine reason. Since reasons must be general in this admittedly vague sense, invocations of reasons must also have a kind of generality to them. So it should be impossible to undertake a stretch of reasoning that was entirely idiosyncratic and not open to anyone else to follow. Your reasoning about the pizza does not go: I want pizza, I believe picking up the phone is a step on the route to eating one, therefore I will pick up the phone. Rather, it goes more like this: eating something cheap, easy to procure, and on the greasy side would be good given my circumstances (poor, lazy, and hard-wired to find fatty foods pleasant). A pizza is all of those things. Therefore, I have reasons to eat a pizza. Picking up the phone ... And this line of reasoning is authoritative for others. They may not be in your circumstances, and so the reasoning may not yield a reason to pick up the phone for them. But this is not because your reasons are private, but because your circumstances are special.[15] Note that this route to the publicity of reasoning involves denying a certain level of context-sensitivity of reasons, as it relies on their generality (the circumstances that make the considerations into reasons can't be too idiosyncratic). It also takes the position to be argued against to be the naturalist one, which has trouble showing why my reasons should have any bearing on you. And so it generally takes itself to be successful if it can show that reasons can be both public and authoritative.

In contrast to this position, we arrive at the publicity of reasoning on the social picture in a rather different manner. Reasoning is the activity of offering a certain kind of invitation to others. It is thus essentially public because it is directed at others. This is why it is a central activity in living together. The publicity of this activity then also has implications for the publicity of its content. If reasons are the invitations that are offered in the course of reasoning, then they also cannot be entirely idiosyncratic.

---

[15] For an example of this kind of argument, see Thomas Nagel, *The Possibility of Altruism* (Princeton, NJ: Princeton University Press, 1970).

If I attempt to offer you an invitation that is not one you can understand as meaningful, or as an invitation, then I am not actually inviting you. So, if I cite sufficiently idiosyncratic considerations in my attempt to reason with you, then you will not be able to understand my invitation as genuine. The requirement that reasons be public comes, then, not from their need to be general in order to wield the authority of command, but from their need to play a role in the activity of inviting. This means that the publicity reasons have on the social picture need not push against their context dependence. What makes reasons public is that considerations count as reasons only when invoked within a certain activity. That activity, however, is itself context dependent, and so the reasons that get invoked within it can also be context dependent. To put the contrast schematically, on the standard picture, reasons are grounded in objective features of the world. Because the grounds are objective, they can be shared, and so the considerations they invoke are public. On the social picture, the order goes in reverse: reasoning is an activity of making public, and so counts as reasoning only when it yields considerations that are shared. Among those who share these considerations, they function as objectively grounded.[16]

The differences between these approaches are further clarified by considering how each picture diagnoses failures of reasoning. Consider the case of John Nash, the Nobel-prize-winning mathematician who suffered from schizophrenia. Nash's biographer, Sylvia Nasar, opens her account of Nash's life, *A Beautiful Mind*, with a scene in a mental hospital in 1959. He is being visited by Harvard professor George Mackey, who finally asks him, "How could you, a mathematician, a man devoted to reason and logical proof... how could you believe that extraterrestrials are sending you messages? How could you believe that you are being recruited by aliens from outer space to save the world? How could you...?"

Nasar continues:

Nash looked up at last and fixed Mackey with an unblinking stare as cool and dispassionate as that of any bird or snake. "Because," Nash said slowly in his soft,

---

[16] A similar schema and argument on its behalf and for endorsing the social side of it can be found in Christine Korsgaard, "The Reasons We Can Share," in *Constructing the Kingdom of Ends*, 275–310 (Cambridge: Cambridge University Press, 1996). On this point, as on several others, Korsgaard's account of reason is in line with the social rather than the standard picture.

reasonable southern drawl, as if talking to himself, "the ideas I had about supernatural beings came to me the same way that my mathematical ideas did. So I took them seriously.[17]

The guiding thought beyond Nash's comparison of his mathematical insights and schizophrenic delusions is that in each case, he took himself to have encountered a consideration in favor of making a certain judgment. Anyone who has puzzled over a difficult problem will recognize that sense of insight when you see some feature of the problem as relevant or that some method is the right one to try here. There can be, in such cases, a clear recognition that one is on the right track, and this can even seem to be something like the way the sense descends on one that something is a consideration in favor of taking a suggestion seriously, as something that at least purports, on a view like Scanlon's, to be a reason for forming a judgment or an intention. (Scanlon describes this stage of reflection as something "seeming to be a reason".)[18] If we are both working on the problem, and I have such an insight, I might say to you, as I start madly scribbling on the board: "Hold on, I think I see it." Moreover, we might get proficient at recognizing at the moment of insight whether the flash of recognition is going to be productive or is mere grasping at straws. Nash claims that the voices he hears are, from his point of view, indistinguishable from the insights, and so they strike him as considerations in favor of forming judgments about their reality and perhaps in favor of what they urged him to do. Among other things, they weren't obviously nonsensical: they demanded that he do things for the right kinds of reasons: to bring about world peace or to protect the secrecy of what they were doing. And so even if he subjected them to the type of critical reflection Scanlon describes, it might not have changed his view of what reasons he had. Schizophrenics are, after all, notoriously rational and consistent in their thinking, even if they are disconnected from reality (a feature they share, after all, with pure mathematics).

Any account of reasoning will want to say that something has gone wrong in the course of Nash's thinking. The difference between the two pictures is not that one applauds his reasoning and the other condemns it. What differentiates them is how they diagnose the failure, and what that diagnosis

---

[17] Quoted in Sylvia Nasar, *A Beautiful Mind* (New York: Simon & Schuster, 1998), 11.
[18] *What We Owe to Each Other*, 65.

implies about other failures to reason. From within the standard picture, the problem is that what seemed to Nash to be reasons were not, in fact, reasons. The promptings of his inner voices and visions were not in fact considerations in favor of following them because they were merely the promptings of his inner voice. If he had thought about them more clearly, he would have seen that. What, in contrast, made his mathematical insights genuine insights was that they picked out genuine reasons, genuine considerations in favor of approaching a particular problem in a particular way. It may be that in either case, the only way for Nash to tell which were insights and which delusions were to follow them out to see where they led, but from our point of view, we can distinguish their goodness as reasons by pointing to their connection or lack of fit to some fact about the world beyond Nash's mind. Messages from aliens are delusions because there were no aliens sending secret messages. The thought that the embedding problem could be solved by developing methods for solving seemingly unsolvable differential equations is an insight because it led to a solution of a long-standing problem in mathematics.[19] In one case, Nash saw something that was true of the world (insofar as the world includes mathematical structures) and in the other, he only saw a figment of his imagination. His failure to reason amounted to not being able to tell the difference. Mackey's incredulity at Nash's behavior amounts to not believing (or understanding) how someone could make such a mistake.

Things look different from within the social picture. If there is a failure of reasoning here, it must be traceable not to a set of faulty reasons, but a flaw in the activity itself. Only a fuller description of his reflection can determine if it amounts to reasoning. Reasoning involves issuing invitations, and so the first question to ask is: to whom are Nash's invitations offered? What, from this perspective, differentiates the reflection that leads to mathematics from the reflection that leads to madness is that one is public while the other is private. When hit with a mathematical insight, I may not be able to transfer the sensation to your head, but the insight is only as good as the mathematics it produces, and so unless and until I can offer you a way of thinking about the problem that you can find intelligible, that insight won't have produced reasons because it won't have led me to the activity of reasoning. That is, even if I am working things out in the privacy of my own study, what I am

[19] Nasar, *A Beautiful Mind*, discusses Nash's work on and solution to the embedding problem (at 157–63).

doing is preparing an invitation to others, and the success of my attempt to reason will depend on whether anything intelligible as an invitation is forthcoming. The mark of reasoning here is precisely this making public of a space and thus the turn towards others, the setting out terms for connection. The reflections that follow Nash's schizophrenic delusions lack precisely this publicity. The spaces they created for him were not spaces that could be made public. They were not spaces from which invitations could be offered. So what marks the trains of thought that followed Nash's delusions as something other than reasoning is that they isolated him, made what he said and did in their wake unintelligible to others. In other words, what distinguishes the schizophrenic from the mathematician is not the soundness of his logic, but his isolation.

In Nash's case, it may not seem to matter which diagnosis we adopt. Both seem correct. But they do suggest different remedies, and this points to important differences in the respective pictures of reasoning. If Nash's problem is that he sometimes uses faulty logic, then the remedy is to help him correct his logic. Mackey views Nash's situation this way. Properly comfortable in and sure of his own rationality, Mackey wants to bring Nash to reason in more or less the same way that Mrs. Bennet wishes to do with her daughter. In both cases, someone has strayed from the path of reason, and needs to be brought back to their senses, made, if necessary, to see reason. That may require a stern lecture from her father (Mrs. Bennet's preferred method) or electroshock therapy (Nash's doctors' remedy of choice). Given that they have abandoned reason, they will not be brought to reason through reason itself. If, however, Nash's problem is that he is isolating himself from others, then the loss is not merely to Nash but to those from whom he is isolating himself. And the remedy may not be so much to bring him around to correct thinking, but to reach out to him, to hold out the possibility of mutual intelligibility. This strategy does not mean accepting that the voices Nash hears are anything but delusions. It may involve inviting him to see that he cannot make the reflections they prompt public, and that this is ground for being suspicious of them. This process may require cultivating the bonds of trust, so that leading him to be suspicious of his voices is not met with further withdrawal as he thereby becomes suspicious of those reaching out. This remedy involves, according to the social picture of reasoning, that we reason with Nash, that we invite him to share our space of reasons again, and be responsive to his response to those invitations (which may not mean withdrawing them). We thus have two very different diagnoses of irrationality leading to two very different remedies. On the standard picture, the remedy for irrationality will be non-rational means of bringing someone to reason. On the social picture, the remedy can be more reasoning.

This difference points to a fundamental divergence of attitudes under-lying the two pictures. The standard picture can lend a certain kind of arrogant confidence to those who are secure in the knowledge that they have reason on their side. Faced with those who disagree with them or whom they find inscrutable, their picture of reason gives them no reason to adapt or change or move from their positions. If they reach out to those whom they do not understand, it is only to bring them to reason. If, however, we are committed to reasoning as this is conceived of on the social picture, then we are committed to reaching out, to making our reflection and their grounds public, where this may require that we adjust what we think or where we stand to find common routes of communica-tion and shared spaces with others. The kinds of failures that the standard picture identifies sometimes do happen, and the remedies the standard picture suggests are sometimes appropriate. But sometimes they are not. Moreover, accepting the diagnosis and remedies offered by the social picture is not to put reason aside. Which picture is more helpful in dealing with schizophrenic delusions is a question beyond the scope of this book, but it is an interesting fact that Nash's own description of his recovery seems to follow the path laid out by the social picture.

The social picture also offers a different way to think about encounters between cultures that have very different conceptual landscapes and ways of communicating and organizing their lives. If, as on the standard picture, the publicity of reasoning is a result of the objective grounding of our reasons, then those who think or approach the world and their problems through other methods than we do will only count as reasoning if there is a way to fit their activities into ours. We are then likely to either misunderstand what they say and do in order to render it rational, or dismiss it as non-rational, possibly headstrong or foolish, possibly primitive or deluded. So, for instance, when early twentieth-century European anthropologists looked at traditional African cultures' approach to magic, they were unable to fit this worldview into a scientific one, and so they approached it as a form of religion rather than something like an alternative theoretical description of how the world works.[20] Or when settler nations looked at Indigenous law, which is often developed through sets of shared stories that include connections between a people and the land and its other inhabitants, they didn't see universal normative codes of conduct that could count as law, but stories and myths that had nothing to say on legal matters.[21] On the standard picture of reasoning, we are faced with an unappetizing choice in these cases. To dismiss African magical thinking or aboriginal storytelling as irrational practices is to prepare the way for arguments for assimilating them to our way of doing things, bringing them to reason, civilizing them. But if we reject that response, it looks like we are left accepting their claims about what the world is like as on a par with the claims of science and logic, but incommensurable nevertheless. And this conclusion leads to a kind of relativism that devalues both ways of thinking as nothing more than a set of contingent and local ways of thinking or doing things: just what we do around here. Among other problems, this blocks the thought that each society might have things to learn from the other.

We might, however, approach these divides with the diagnostic approach we generated from the social picture. In this case, a failure of publicity, of an ability to speak intelligibly across a cultural gap, is a problem, first and foremost, of isolation. Isolation, however, is a two-way street. Members of both societies lose something when they cannot share certain normative spaces. One response to such isolation is to reach out to one another, to seek ways to make intelligible invitations to one another, in part by finding ways of bridging our reasoning practices. On this view, we need not think of one group as those who reason and the other as needing to be brought to reason, but rather of two groups, each of which has practices that allow them to share normative spaces within their group, but neither of which yet has the means to reason with the other.

This process of reaching out resists a facile relativism that holds that there is no way for members of one culture to criticize the practices of another.

---

[20] Kwame Anthony Appiah, *In My Father's House* (Oxford: Oxford University Press, 1993), 107–36 discusses African practices involving magic and questions the interpretation of these as forms of religion rather than akin to science. His text provides a model of the kind of reaching across conceptual frameworks to enable reasoning together that I am advocating here.

[21] James Borrows, *Drawing Out Law* (Toronto: University of Toronto Press, 2010) offers a discussion of indigenous legal practices and reasoning and the failure of settler nations' legal systems to appreciate them as forms of law or reason. It is also a model of how to bridge that gap.

We need to distinguish cultural pluralism from cultural relativism. Cultural relativism denies that there are *any* normative standards that are not themselves grounded in culturally accepted norms. Cultural pluralism, however, is merely the claim that some of the norms within any given culture are culturally specific and that these norms can ground genuine reasons within that culture. If the scope of the "some" that cultural pluralism accepts is sufficiently narrow, it is not terribly controversial. If I am having dinner in a culture where food is eaten with one's hands and it is culturally taboo to eat with one's left hand, then those norms give me reasons to eat with my right hand even if, being left-handed, I am more likely to make a mess of things by eating this way. In contrast, in the absence of this taboo, I have no reason to eat with my right hand. Although the scope of the cultural pluralism of the picture I am sketching will be broad enough to be controversial, it is important to see that it is not so broad as to lead to cultural relativism.

With this distinction in place, we can make two further points. First, coming to recognize the practices of another group as a form of reasoning is precisely not to foreclose the possibility of criticizing them. It is to recognize the work that may need to be done in order to be able to properly articulate and formulate criticisms, as well as to simultaneously recognize the possibility that they can criticize our practices. And, second, the mere fact that any group is intelligible internally does not make it the case that they are reasoning. Although mutual intelligibility will be a necessary condition for a claim to be a reason, it is not sufficient. Although reasoning is a social activity, it is a social activity with preconditions. In order to get a fix on those preconditions, we need to turn to further features of the activity of reasoning on the social picture.

5.3 Norms of Reciprocity

Conversation involves speaking with others, and thus involves a sufficient level of equality that I can be touched by what my conversation partner says. It does not require that I hold my space of reasons open and public, and it does not require that I offer to share that space. Reasoning requires that I do both of these things. In order to genuinely offer to share a space, I have to not only be open to being affected by what my interlocutors say, but I have to be prepared to, as it were, move over within my space to make room for them. Chapter 1 argued that the invitation I make for you to take my words as speaking for you as well is, when we reason, premised on the thought that there is or could be a "we" that can be spoken for by either of us. And that implies not only that I might offer to speak for you, but that you might offer to speak for me. Sharing a space in a manner that lets either of us speak for the other requires, then, a level of reciprocity that goes beyond the kind of equality necessary for mere conversation. It is not enough that I can be touched or affected by what you say. In offering to speak for us in the manner that makes what I am doing reasoning, I must acknowledge your authority to speak for us as well, and to accept that I have only spoken for us if you accept my words as doing so.

Reasoning so conceived is not a matter of wielding the authority of command by bolstering what I say with the force of reason, but rather extending the authority of connection to you, by making my words answerable to your acceptance or rejection of them. I have to be open to the possibility that I can find my position changed in virtue of what you say even if that change involves a recognition that here I do not speak for you, that this is not a space we share. In the absence of this possibility, the mere fact that what we say to one another is mutually intelligible does not make what we are doing reasoning. And this offers a further response to the worry about cultural relativism above.

Since reasoning requires reciprocal answerability, I can only engage in this activity if there are others around me to whom I can stand in this relationship. And that may not be fully up to me to determine. That is, what establishes that we stand in a relationship in which we can reason with one another goes beyond our own attitudes towards each other. As we saw in the last chapter, background features of our society may make even the equality necessary for conversation difficult to come by. Since the requirements in order to be reasoning are even more stringent, we should expect that even more background features will need to be in place to enable this activity. If I have social power and status over you that allows me, without recourse, to decide what each of us will do and why, then even if I choose to forgo such power, my doing so is a gift to you, and we are not in the position of two people reasoning with one another, but more like a commander and a supplicant. We can further fail to be in a reciprocal relationship when the space I claim to invite you to share with me is already so firmly established by my practices and norms that though I can invite you into it, I cannot invite you to share it without radically changing my own relationship to it.[22] In such a situation, my making myself intelligible to you will not, on its own, make it the case that we are reasoning with one another.

Being fully capable of reasoning, being fully reasonable, turns out to require a kind of social achievement. Thus, we can say about some cultural practices that they prevent the possibility of being fully reasonable, because by setting up hierarchical relationships or establishing certain norms as themselves beyond the reach of challenge, they make it impossible or at least prohibitively difficult for the exchanges between people in those relationships to count as reasoning. A society need not go so far as to exclude some people from the circle of humanity to violate this requirement. It need only have in place social practices that leave some people able to decide whether they will take seriously what some others say to them. How serious a barrier such practices place in the way of their reasoning together depends on the content of those practices, the wider social context, the possible existence of countervailing practices, and, to some extent, the efforts of the individuals involved to overcome or find ways around those practices. To suggest that social practices and institutions can place barriers in the way of genuine reasoning together is not to claim that there is no point in trying to reason together before we reach a state of full justice. Our interactions can be more or less reasonable and there can be value in working to be more reasonable even where social institutions block our being fully so. And, as we have seen, that work can itself take the form of trying to reason together.

Accepting levels of reciprocity with others, like accepting the equality necessary for conversation, amounts to accepting a certain level of vulnerability. If I invite you to share my space, who knows what you will do once you are there? But it also makes possible the establishment of genuinely shared spaces: places where we can, in fact, speak for each other. To say that we can speak for each other is to say that there are considerations that count as properly authoritative for both of us, which is to say that they count as reasons for us. So the contours of the activity of reasoning as issuing a certain

---

[22] On the importance and difficulty of this kind of radical shift by members of a dominant group towards their own conceptual space as a precondition for genuine reasoning with other people in their society, see María Lugones and Elizabeth Spelman, "Have We Got a Theory for You!," in *Hypatia Reborn*, ed. Azizah al-Hibri and Margaret Simons (Bloomington: Indiana University Press, 1990).

kind of invitation further shape how the social picture will describe reasons. By starting from the activity of reasoning and then defining reasons as those things offered in the course of reasoning, a picture emerges of reasons as considerations that are, under suitable conditions, offered as invitations. When those invitations are accepted, then the considerations become reasons that are shared across the "we" for whom we accept that we can each speak. But even when the invitation is rejected, if the invitation was a genuine one, then what was offered still counts as a reason, though not for both the speaker and the one spoken to. That she could genuinely offer it to him shows that it is a reason for her. That he did not accept it shows that it is not a reason for him. Depending on the consideration in question and the context of their relationship, there will be cases where a consideration not being a reason for them undermines its claim to be a reason for her, but not every case need be like that.

What comes into view here is a point from Chapter 1: on the social picture, all reasons are social reasons or "we"-reasons, which is to say both that all reasons have a scope that extends beyond a single person (they are public and shared, they connect rather than isolate), and that this scope is not universal and not identical for all reasons.[23] Different reasons are reasons for different "we"s. The fact that something becomes a reason only when it can be a "we"-reason shows how the considerations that count as reasons on the social picture, like the considerations that count as reasons on a standard picture, are not merely subjective. This does not rule out the possibility that the "we" for which a reason is a reason is one that is not yet constituted, either because the offering of a reason is an attempt to constitute it or because one's thoughts have not yet found the audience who can properly hear them. We cannot determine that a consideration connects rather than isolates by merely counting heads, but that does not call in to question the conceptual difference.

The route that reasons take to their non-subjective status on the two pictures is rather different, and that may lead to worries. The claim that all reasons are "we"-reasons can seem implausible from two directions. Some

---

[23] See Chapter 1.3, and esp. n. 19 for references to discussions of social reasons. As should be clear from the foregoing discussion, something is a social reason not only in virtue of its scope of application but because it is what Stephen Darwall calls "second-personal": it is directed at someone (see *The Second-Person Standpoint: Morality, Respect, and Accountability* (Cambridge, MA: Harvard University Press, 2006)).

may wonder how such a view can explain the case of seemingly obvious inferences, like those made in the course of routine instrumental reasoning. If my reason for crossing the street is to get to the restaurant, it is hard to imagine that this is any kind of a "we"-reason or that in reflecting on it, either alone or by way of justifying my changing direction to cross the street to you, that I am offering to speak for you. Others will worry that since "we"-reasons are always tied to a particular "we," making all reasons "we"-reasons leaves out the category of universal reasons, whether these are moral reasons or theoretical reasons such as canons of belief formation. How is, "because I see it in good light, etc." a "we"-reason for believing what I see is there, or a goldfinch? How is "because it would be wrong" a "we"-reason? Making all reasons "we"-reasons appears to be giving up on the very thing that reason promises.

To begin to answer the first worry, note that one of our criteria for regarding someone's reasons to be genuine reasons is their intelligibility.[24] The importance of intelligibility to others arises clearly in the case of John Nash, but it is also at work in more mundane exchanges between people not suffering from mental illness. Offering as a reason for one's action or decision that "it will promote my long-term well-being," or "it is a means to my end" also depend on their intelligibility for their status as reasons. So, for instance, neither is a reason if the actions they attempt to justify are not intelligibly understood by others as justifiable in that way. It is easy to miss this point because many mundane reasons work against a vast degree of shared intelligibility. When, however, that background is thinner, as in cases that involve elements of cross-cultural communication the importance of intelligibility becomes clear. In Germany until recently, an American visitor might have found herself having the following exchange with her German host: "Why are you crossing the street?" "Because the restaurant is on the other side." "Yes, but the light is red."

---

[24] This is a recurrent theme in certain readings of Hegel as offering a social account of reason. See, in particular, Robert Pippin, *Hegel's Practical Philosophy: Rational Agency as Ethical Life* (Cambridge: Cambridge University Press, 2008) and Terry Pinkard, *Hegel's Phenomenology: The Sociality of Reason* (Cambridge: Cambridge University Press, 1996). The role of intelligibility is also stressed by Elizabeth Anscombe, *Intention*, and in J. David Velleman's work on practical reason, most recently in *How We Get Along* (Cambridge: Cambridge University Press, 2009). I return to the relation between intelligibility and reasoning in Chapter 9.

Or think of the difference between symbolic actions that are part of familiar traditions (even when these are not our own) and those that are the signs of eccentricities and mental illness. "Why do you wave your hands over the candles after you light them?" "In order to welcome Shabbat." vs. "Because that is what the voices say to do." Explanations or justifications of actions that make reference to some shared symbolic practice can serve as acceptable reasons in a way that those that only refer to idiosyncratic symbolic practices cannot. That is, though explaining that I wave my hands at the prompting of voices only I can hear may help you to understand the inner workings of my mind, it does so in a way that isolates me from you, and so is open to the objection, "But that's no reason at all." On the other hand, if I offer an explanation that makes references to shared practices that you do not share, and thus in some sense deny a connection with you, I do not do so in a manner that isolates me, but rather in a way that connects me to others. If you find what I say inscrutable, you can, as we saw above in the case of African and indigenous practices, try to reach out to me and find ways of understanding my practices that do not distort them, and I can reach out to you by trying to explain them. What separates the two cases is that the reference to a set of shared practices (even when they are not shared between speaker and listener) is capable of ultimately rendering the action intelligible whereas the references to voices, relying on idiosyncratic and private practices, is not. So the essential point is that what makes blindingly obvious reasons blindingly obvious is the thickness of the shared background of intelligibility in which they function. Since that background is shared, these reasons are "we"-reasons.[25]

To address the worry that universal reasons ought not be treated as "we"-reasons, note that a universal reason is just a "we"-reason where the "we" in question is maximally inclusive. There are two things to note about this claim. First, it treats the universality of universal reasons as a result of inclusion rather than generality. There are, in general, two methods of increasing the extension of any group or set. Increasing the inclusiveness of the set involves adding to the list of members of the set. Increasing the generality of the set, in

---

[25] Cf. Raimond Gaita's discussion of cranks, in Raimond Gaita, "Forms of the Unthinkable," in *A Common Humanity*, 171–86 (London: Routledge, 1998), esp. 161–7. What makes the crank a crank is not, according to Gaita, that he is unwilling to subject his claims to critical scrutiny, but that he does not accept a shared background against which such criticism must proceed in order to count as a form of reasoning. Thanks to David Owen for pointing me back to this discussion here.

contrast, involves thinning out the criteria of membership. Thus, I can extend outwards from the set that comprises my family by adding other families: those who live on my block, in my city, in my country, etc., or by thinning out the criteria: from people who share my family name or that of my wife and live in our house to those who share the name to those whose names start with the same letters to those who have names, and so on.

It is rather common to think of universal reasons as universal in virtue of their generality, and thus having extremely thin or no criteria for their application to a given subject. If universal reasons are universal in virtue of their generality, then there is a problem with understanding them as being reasons in virtue of their ties to any particular "we," even one whose extension is maximally wide. Armed with a consideration that is general in this sense, I can wield it in an argument that applies to you without addressing myself to you. If, moreover, generality is not just another char- acteristic of a certain class of reasons, but is criterial of being a reason at all, as some theories of reason hold, then the attempt to spell out what reasons are in terms of their being "we"-reasons will seem completely misguided.

If, however, universal reasons are maximally inclusive, not maximally general, then universal reasons can be a species of "we"-reasons. To hold that a given reason is universal is to hold that it is a "we" reason for the "we" that includes everyone. One consequence of this way of characterizing "we"-reasons is that I can extend a reason's scope to everyone without having to characterize the group "everyone" in terms of some common trait in virtue of which the reason applies to them. Universal reasons thus do not need to rely on a substantive account of our common human nature. A reason earns its universality by being addressed to everyone, and that requires being responsive to their rejection of its demands.[26]

At the same time, calling a moral reason a "we"-reason for the "we" comprised of all of humanity rather than a general reason calls attention to an important and overlooked fact about our use of moral vocabulary: it does not necessarily carry with it a universal scope of application. That is, it is perfectly possible to develop a rich moral vocabulary and moral theory that one takes to apply to all persons or all rational beings, and yet not take that category to extend to all members of the species *homo sapiens*. Treating universal reasons

---

[26] Again, it is important to stress that being responsive to the rejection of an invitation does not always require that we withdraw it in the face of rejection.

as general reasons loses sight of this fact, because it leads to the conclusion that the universal scope of our moral concepts comes from their logic or grammar. But as work by feminists, critical race theorists, and others has shown, the history of moral philosophy includes any number of examples of theories of general moral reasons combined with non-universal theories about who counts as human for the sake of the theory.[27] A commitment to the universality of our moral terms is not something we get for free from their apparent generality: it is a separate commitment that we need to make on moral grounds and thus for which we must take responsibility.[28] By deriving universality from inclusion, the social picture makes this point easier to see. The conceptualization of moral reasons as a variety of "we"-reasons then comes to look not like a theoretical shortcoming but a possible form of moral progress. Taking responsibility for the scope of our reasons is one of the ways that adopting such a picture would contribute to our enlightenment. For the maturity that Kant described as the condition brought on by Enlightenment involves the willingness to take responsibility for one's stands and positions, and not to hide behind the supposed authority of others.[29]

We can put this point in terms of another characteristic norm of reasoning: I must take responsibility for the scope of my invitations. By inviting you to share a space with me, I, implicitly or explicitly, mark out a group of people to whom the invitation applies, and in doing so, determine the scope of the reasons I offer. What the above reflections bring out is that there is not necessarily anything in the nature of the particular reason that marks its scope, and so if, for instance, I wish to try to extend its scope, to include more people in my invitation, then I have to find a way to do this. The form of the reason I offer does not do it for me. That reasons have particular domains of coverage, and that those domains may be up to us to determine, and are written into neither the reasons themselves nor the fabric of the universe marks another important difference between how reasoning is conceived on the two pictures being contrasted here.

[27] See, for illustrations, Charles Mills, *The Racial Contract* (Ithaca, NY: Cornell University Press, 1997), Richard Rorty, "Human Rights, Rationality and Sentimentality," in *On Human Rights*, ed. Stephen Shute and Susan Hurley, 111–34 (New York: Basic Books, 1993).

[28] For a related concern about the need to take responsibility for our moral stands, and not to assume that they come to us for free with our theories or our grammar, see Stanley Cavell, *The Claim of Reason* (Oxford: Oxford University Press, 1979), 215–17.

[29] Immanuel Kant, "An Answer to the Question: What is Enlightenment?," in *Kant's Political Writings*, ed. Hans Reiss, 54–60 (Cambridge: Cambridge University Press, 1991).

Finally, by describing moral reasons as "we"-reasons, our attention is directed towards the particular substantive basis each of us might offer for her moral arguments. Is the "we" that the speaker aims to be universal the "we" made up of God's children, of rational beings, of fellow inhabitants of the planet, or members of what Hume called the "party of humanity"? How we conceive of this "we" goes a long way to shaping our moral ideals and commitments and the reasons that structure them. Similar arguments could be made about other seemingly universal reasons, like the canons of belief formation.

All of which is fine and good, someone who continues to hold on to the sort of normativity that the standard picture of reason promises, but it is somewhat beside the point. The important aspect of universality that reasons must claim is not in their application but their authority, she will say. That is, there is no disagreement about the fact that some reasons apply to only some people or some situations in virtue of the particular features of their circumstances. Though we may get different interpretations of that fact, this is not where the trouble lies. The standard picture provides a clear handle on the thought that the authority of reasons is not contingent: if a consideration in favor of doing or believing something counts as a reason for someone situated as I am situated, then it is not up to me to decide whether to heed it while maintaining my rationality. Its being a reason means that it has authority over me, full stop. It looks as if this is the very aspect of the universality of reasons for which treating all reasons as "we"-reasons cannot account. A reply to this objection is to be found in the final set of norms of reasoning.

5.4 Norms of Good Faith

The final set of norms of reasoning involve refinements on the norm of sincerity that governs casual conversation more generally. They are norms of good faith. In following them, I demonstrate that my participation in the activity of reasoning is genuine, that I am participating in good faith. These norms follow from the final piece of the description of reasoning on the social picture. Reasoning is not only inviting others to share a space, but to share a space of reasons, which is to say a space the elements of which bear the authority of connection. As was argued in Chapter 2, the authority of connection is only constructed by holding the considerations that claim it always open to criticism. So I can only invite you to share such a space by holding its contents open to criticism. That, in turn, requires that I hold my invitation always open to criticism as well. Opening my invitation to criticism is a different and further requirement than issuing a genuine invitation, and thus being answerable to its rejection. The particular activity of inviting that amounts to reasoning is thus open to two forms of criticism or rejoinder. First, I have to be responsive to your rejection of my invitation for it to have been a genuine invitation. But second, for it to be an invitation to a space of reasons, it must remain always open to criticism, not only from those whom I invite to share it, but to anyone at anytime. This gives considerations that can possibly count as reasons on the social picture a kind of dual structure: they have a limited scope of authority in the sense that they are reasons only for those who are members of the "we" who can speak for each other, but at the same time, they have an open scope of challenge in order to establish that authority. And there are different consequences for rejecting a reason depending on which form of criticism or rejection is made. If I am issuing an invitation to you, among others, to take my words as speaking for all of us, you can decline my offer, and withdraw from or not join or deny the existence of the "we" I am trying to construct or reaffirm. That may leave me with a reason, but one that is not a reason for you. My response to your rejection of my invitation may be to accept that there is nothing that I can say that speaks for you as well, or at least that this is not one of the things that could be so said. All of this can be consistent with my reasoning and our reasoning, and thus with the consideration I have brought forward continuing to be a reason for me. Not all reasoning aims at agreement. Some invitations have a point even if they are rejected. Of course, whether what I am doing is reasoning depends on what I do in the wake of your rejection. What makes it the case that Mr. Collins is not and Mr. Darcy is reasoning with Elizabeth when each proposes is how they respond to her rejection, and not that one is and the other is not ultimately a successful suitor.[30]

In certain kinds of cases, there is a variant of this move that is open. In these cases, I not only try to speak for those I address, but claim to speak for others I may represent. Though these others may not be present as we reason, they should be understood as also covered by the invitation. So it is

---

[30] Though, of course, one of the things that makes Mr. Darcy ultimately successful is that he shows Elizabeth that they can reason together.

open to them to reject what I say, claiming that in saying that, I do not speak for them. This has a similar effect as when my invitation is rejected by those to whom it is explicitly offered.

In addition, looking on, others who are not even implicitly included in the scope of the invitation can criticize the considerations I bring forth in making an invitation to you, and those criticisms can call into question whether or not my invitation counts as part of reasoning. Perhaps I only appear to give you room to respond. Perhaps our relative social positions give you no grounds from which you might meaningfully reject my offer. Even if you don't see that, someone else can criticize my reasons in a way that under-mines their claims to be reasons. Such criticisms may rely on the norms of reasoning explored here. Others may rely on the grounds for the evaluation of the invitations that reasons make that will be the subject of Part III. Or someone might criticize the course of our reflection using the canons and principles of logic and reason familiar from the various theories of reason and rationality that work within the standard picture. Even when they engage in these latter forms of criticism, the import of their criticism is different from within the social picture. From the point of view of the standard picture, criticizing a course of reflection at the bar of reason shows that it is not reasoning, and thus, perhaps, that the person so reflecting is not reasonable or rational, which is to say that she might be headstrong or foolish, someone we will have to bring, perhaps kicking and screaming, to reason. From within the social picture, to criticize a course of reflection as failing to meet the canons of rationality is to point out that it isolates the speaker, not only from us onlookers but even from those with whom he purports to be reasoning. This may or may not be a matter of concern for either of us. We may or may not be mistaken to have that attitude. But the separation is a mutual affair, and so it can, in principle, be bridged from either side.

Finally, one line of criticism that is always fatal to a claim to be reasoning is that in making an offer, I have not left it open to criticism. As Kant says in the quote that organized Chapter 1, "should [reason] limit freedom of criticism by any prohibitions, it must harm itself...Reason depends on this freedom for its very existence."[31] This has important consequences for the identification and diagnosis of failures to reason.

---

[31] Immanuel Kant, *Critique of Pure Reason*, trans. Norman Kemp Smith (New York: St. Martin's Press, 1933), 593 (A738/B766).

Even if each of us wants and is in a position to reason with one another, this requirement means that the best we can hope for is a kind of provisional success, a judgment that we have not yet let our reasoning dissolve into something else. That is, there is no move within the activity governed by this norm by which we can declare that what we have said is definitively a reason, for once we do that, we have closed off further discussion, and thereby violated the norm of openness. Similarly, there is no move we can make from outside that declares once and for all that what was said counts as a reason.

Like the authority of connection that reasons bear, the activity of reasoning itself is something that can be supported as reasoning only by also looking ahead. There is no point in time at which we can definitively say that we have been reasoning. We can only, at any given moment, say that to this point, nothing we have done has undermined the possibility that we are reasoning. Reasoning, like establishing the authority of connection, is a forward-looking activity, and this further explains why it makes sense to understand it as embedded not within the goal-directed activities of concluding and deciding, but within the aimless though norm-governed confines of conversation. The social picture of reasoning does not allow us to derive reasons or principles of rationality, but merely to diagnose failures of reasoning and perhaps to suggest ways to remedy them. This chapter has considered several failures of reasoning, including Mr. Collins's proposal and John Nash's delusions. According to the social picture something similar goes wrong in each: each is closed to the possibility of criticism, and thus each involves people who isolate themselves from others, retreating into a private world of their own. Whether they are beyond reach may depend on many things, including whether they are sufficiently blind or self-satisfied to not notice or not mind their isolation. But in any case, what is needed to bring them back to the activity of reasoning is not to make them see their interests, perhaps by laying down the law or the other civilizing forces at our disposal, but to invite them back into the human fold, as people who might take what we say as speaking for them as well, and as people who might have things to say to and with and for us. In other words, the remedy for failures of reasoning will, on this picture, be more reasoning.

6

Engaged Reasoning

6.1 Engaged Conversation

Casual conversation and reasoning, as discussed in the previous chapters, are ongoing activities. As a result, we cannot derive their characteristic norms from their ends, as they have no definitive ones. But that may suggest that these activities say very little about the forms of reasoning that do have ends. Since these are the central cases of reasoning according to the standard picture, it may appear that the social picture does not merely shift our picture of reasoning but so thoroughly changes the subject as to be talking about something else altogether. That is, if the characteristic kinds of activities that count as reasoning are the sorts of episodes of decision-making, calculation, and the weighing of evidence towards the development of theories or beliefs on which the standard picture focuses, then the activities of casual conversation and open-ended inviting of others into our ways of seeing the world do not look at all like reasoning. That would suggest that even if the picture developed in the previous chapters is an attractive description of these forms of ongoing interaction, and even if these interactions seem important for human life and living together, nothing in this picture offers a new way to think of the kind of reasoning that aims at ends, whether decisions or beliefs.

This chapter develops the social picture of reasoning into the terrain on which the standard picture has definite things to say. In particular, it develops a further set of characteristic norms that cover a further specification of the activity of reasoning: a subset I call engagements. Engagements are characterized not by their ends, but by their demanding a further level of responsiveness from their participants. Among the circumstances that can give rise to an engagement, however, is the presence of certain kinds of joint ends. Thus, the norms of engagements provide a way to talk about reasoning that is directed towards an end that does not require defining its characteristic norms in terms of those ends.

If what I say or think is to count as reasoning, it must involve the making public of a space of reasons as one we could share. I make a space public in this way by inviting others to share it, to accept my proposal that they make it theirs as well. I can do this without being terribly concerned that they accept my invitation. In fact, in some cases, I can make the offer in a way that makes clear that while you are not required to accept it, your rejection will not move me to change my position, only to accept that it is not one we share. In such interactions, nothing about the conversation itself hangs on whether my invitation is accepted. In fact, many conversations are animated precisely because participants decline such invitations. Of course, to say that the success of the conversation does not hang on the acceptance of our invitations is not to say it is a matter of indifference. Much else may hang on the uptake of our invitations: they may be the building blocks of a new relationship or the cement that keeps an old one strong. But a conversation where participants offer each other reasons is no more or less successful as a conversation because the invitations the reasons constitute are accepted or not. It still helps us to work out (both in the sense of discover and construct) where we stand vis-à-vis one another, even when it reveals that we stand apart. In such conversations, we are bound by the norms governing the offering of reasons: our invitations to accept what we say as speaking for others must allow for reciprocity and must be answerable. My announcing where I stand in the manner of inviting you to join me falls well short of a command that you do so. But we are not required to find or move to or establish common ground beyond that which allows us to be mutually intelligible and thus speak with one another. When you refuse my invitation, your refusal need not, as a result of the requirements of the conversation, lead me to change my position.

There are, however, situations where my offer is not like that. In such cases, I issue an invitation as the beginning of or a step in a process that I hope will lead us to find a space we can share together. My invitation is not like an invitation to a party that you can accept or reject, but like an offer in the course of a negotiation or a suggestion in the course of an attempt to work through a common problem together. Because we are trying to find common ground, we need to be more responsive to our conversation partners than when we are reasoning with them more generally, both in the kinds of invitations we offer and how we go on if they are declined. It is this extra degree of responsiveness occasioned by the concern to find common ground that makes our conversation an engagement and the reasoning within it engaged. In particular, engaging with you in this way means that I do not merely make public where I stand, but try to find a place to stand where we can stand together. It requires me to tailor both my offers and my positions to where I think you do or could stand, and to respond to your responses to my offers in ways other than merely accepting that we stand in different places. Engaged reasoning is thus reasoning together in the most robust sense of the term. Among the circumstances that lead people to engage with one another is the presence of a joint end or goal. Thus, the norms of engagement turn out to cover forms of end-directed reasoning while nevertheless not being derived from these ends. The first half of the chapter discusses these norms. With a characterization of engagement and its norms in place, the second half of the chapter turns to a comparison between two pictures of end-directed forms of reasoning together.

6.2 Varieties of Engagement

Since the category of engagements is not a familiar one, it helps to look at a variety of examples, and bring out their common features. First, return to Elizabeth Bennet and Mr. Darcy. In the course of their idle conversation about whether or not pride is a fault in the drawing room of Netherfield, each offers the other invitations to accept what he or she said as speaking for both of them.[1] These concern such matters as whether there are people who cannot be laughed at and whether pride is a fault. It appears that nothing much hangs on whether these invitations are accepted. In fact, much of the liveliness of the exchange comes from the fact that each makes a point of declining the other's invitations, even when this requires willfully misunderstanding them, as Darcy wryly accuses Elizabeth of doing.[2] But this characterization, even of this bit of witty repartee, is perhaps too hasty. After all, even by this point in the novel, Darcy has begun to admire

---

[1] Jane Austen, *Pride and Prejudice* (Oxford: Oxford University Press, 2004), vol. I, ch. XI, 42–3. I quote and briefly discuss the relevant exchange in Chapter 3.1.

[2] Ibid.

Elizabeth, if not yet to care for her, and this gives him reasons to be more concerned about her responses to his invitations than he is, for instance, about the responses of others in the room. It is not enough that he clearly articulate his position on the matter under discussion, but also that she not reject it out of hand. As his feelings for her grow throughout the novel, he becomes more and more concerned that the reasons he offers her, the invitations to speak for her, be met with acceptance. He isn't here just looking for her approval, of him or his views, though he would be happy to have it. Rather, his admiration and care for her consists in part in the sense that her failure to share his view of the world gives him a special kind of reason to reconsider it. When, for instance, his first proposal to her is met with outright rejection, this leads him not merely to reiterate it unchanged, as Mr. Collins does, but to accept her rejection and work to change himself so that he might later be in a position from which to offer an invitation she might accept. At the same time, he does not accept all her rejections as calling for him to change. In some cases, he offers further refutations of her charges, but even here, his willingness to do so stems from his concern that they might see things in the same light, not merely to repel an unjust or false accusation. Part of what is going on here is that he comes to value her judgment, and so takes her taking of a position as evidence of its being correct. This is not all that happens, however. At least part of what moves him to be responsive to her in this heightened fashion is his growing desire to stand with her. Their encounters with one another, that is, pass, over the course of the novel, from idle chatter to engagements, on their way, of course, to an engagement. The lesson to take from this progress away from pride and prejudice towards engagement is that among the circumstances that lead us to engage with one another is some form of care or concern or admiration for one another. Such admiration can have at least two effects on the nature of our invitations in the course of our engagements. First, if I admire or care for you, then I have an independent interest in our standing together, occupying a shared space of reasons. As a result, when I offer you reasons, I both attempt to offer you reasons that I think you share, and am more responsive to your rejection of them. Since I have an interest in sharing a space of reasons with you, I have a motivation to alter my position in the space of reasons in order to find common ground. Second, my concern for you, and especially my admiration for you, may involve my taking seriously your position precisely because it is yours. If I offer you a reason and you reject it, the mere fact that you have rejected it will lead me to reconsider its wisdom. As we saw above, this need not mean that I blindly defer to your rejections. For one, if I merely fit myself to your unalterable position, then I am not working out a position we can share. But if we are engaged with one another in the sense being developed here, then I cannot brush off your rejection of my offered reason as of no consequence to my own continued attachment to it. To fix terms, call engagements brought on by our mutual concern or affection friendly engagements.

Although personal attachments to our conversation partners can lead us to engage with them, it is not the only circumstance that leads to engagement. I can also find myself engaging with strangers or those towards whom I am more indifferent if the topics we are discussing are of sufficient importance to me. This dynamic is also at work in the drawing room conversation about the vices of vanity and prejudice, perhaps more on the part of Elizabeth than Darcy. But it is a familiar enough dynamic that it can be described in the absence of Jane Austen's perceptive pen. We are at a party and having an idle conversation that wanders over a variety of relatively unimportant topics and in which we each take up our turns and say things that are appropriately responsive and sincere to count as reasons. But the conversation remains on the surface, a way to pass the time, until a topic arises about which one of us is passionate. All of a sudden, the tone changes, the invitations become more insistent and the possibility of disagreement more threatening. The conversation becomes less idle, more engaged, as we each find ourselves more concerned that what we say is not dismissed or rejected or rebutted. Faced with disagreement, we perhaps rephrase our position, perhaps amend it. We don't let what we consider to be irresponsible counter-positions stand, but subject them to criticism.

It is not the case that the conversation touches on a point about which one of us has deep but dogmatically held convictions, but rather that our attachment to the issues under discussion is sufficiently deep that we become concerned both with how what we say is received and with having something to say that others can accept. It is, we might say, the subject matter more than our positions and opinions that concern us or to which we are attached. Just as when we care about one another, caring about the subject under discussion alters the dynamics of our interaction, and gives them the characteristic features of engagement: a greater concern that our invitations are acceptable and a greater responsiveness to their rejection. Call such engagements debates.

Third, consider a kind of case that may seem wholly different from the two discussed above, but which can also lead to engagement: certain forms of goal-directed interaction. We are discussing how to spend the afternoon together, and the fact that we are trying to reach an agreement about what to do can lead us to be more attentive to the invitations we offer and more concerned that they meet with acceptance. If we are concerned not to bully each other, but to find truly shared common ground, then our need to reach agreement will have this effect. After all, we only reach an agreement when our invitations meet with acceptance. Reasoning together to reach agreements, shared decisions, and joint conclusions includes many forms of interaction that go beyond the personal engagements I have been discussing. Labor and management need to work out a contract. Members of a legislative body or a democratic public must find policies or principles to which they can all agree. States or peoples in conflict must agree on terms of peace. In these cases, one and perhaps the only reason each side needs to be responsive to the other is that they share a goal or need to find common ground or reach a decision. But the level of responsiveness needed to find common ground in these cases is similar to that in the first two categories of engagement. To see this, think about cases where two sides try to reach an agreement across differences but are not responsive in these ways. If one party continually offers proposals that it knows the other cannot accept, or refuses to be moved by the other party's rejection of a proposal, then, though we might praise them as driving a hard bargain, we are more likely to say of them that they are negotiating in bad faith, or that they are being unreasonable.

Even if the need to reach an agreement makes certain end-directed interactions into engagements, it nevertheless matters whether we approach them as engagements or as end-directed episodes of reasoning. To mark this difference, I call engagements brought on by joint goals "deliberations" and joint end-directed efforts to use reason to forge agreement "negotiations." The second half of the chapter discusses the difference between these frameworks.

Finally, many uses of theoretical reason, where we reason about the way the world is, rather than what to do, also draw us into engagements. Here, as with deliberation, what draws us to engage with our partners is nothing about our attachments, but something the interaction itself leads us to share. When we are discussing facts of the matter or trying to figure out something about the world, then the objective world is our focal point, and since that is shared among us, it leads us, as with the attempt to find a shared decision, to look for invitations that will be accepted and to be responsive to their rejection. If we are trying to figure out what happened to the last piece of pizza, explain Mr. Bingley's sudden disappearance from the neighborhood, or working out the properties of the top-quark, we each want what we have to say about the matter to be something our partners can accept, and their reasoned rejection of what we say matters to us. This gives us a different way to characterize joint exercises of theoretical reason than one that focuses on each individual aiming at the truth of his or her beliefs. It is not that in the cases above we are not trying to work out the truth, but that understanding the process of working out the truth as an engagement changes the characterization of these exercises of theoretical reasoning.

6.3 Norms of Reasonableness[3]

Although there is much that separates them, friendly engagements, debates, deliberations, and joint uses of theoretical reason all involve parties who are concerned to offer invitations that are accepted, and thus to work out what reasons they share. They represent, so conceived, a category of interaction that is narrower than, but nevertheless a form of, reasoning discussed in the previous chapter. This means that they are guided by the characteristic norms of conversation and reasoning as well as a set of new norms that are particular to engagement. Specifically, engagement places two further requirements on its participants: (1) they must offer one another considerations they in good faith take to be reasons for all of them; and (2) the rejection of an offered reason must have an impact on the future course of the engagement. If we are merely reasoning in the sense given in the last chapter, then, though I have to regard the considerations I offer as reasons

---

[3] Much of this section is adapted from my "Outline of a Theory of Reasonable Deliberation," *Canadian Journal of Philosophy* 30 (December 2000): 551–80, where the connection of these norms with the reasonable and the contrast between reasonable deliberation and rational choice is more fully developed. I have somewhat altered the formulation of the norms guiding reasonable deliberation to fit them into the larger structure developed here.

for some or other "we," I do not have to attempt to make it a "we" of which you are also a part. When I engage with you, however, I do have to offer you reasons that find support in a "we" or plural subject we share.

The second requirement also tightens the restrictions on the responsiveness required for reasoning more generally. If we are reasoning, then I have to take my invitation to be answerable to your acceptance or rejection of it, and in this sense, any reasoning requires that your rejection of my reason has an effect on what happens next. What this second requirement captures is that in an engagement we do not thereby walk away from our interaction or agree to disagree in the face of rejection, but work to respond to the rejection in a way that keeps our engagement going. Sometimes this requires that I move my position to accommodate the grounds of your rejection, and in other cases it requires me to reformulate my offer or provide it with further grounds so that you might nevertheless be moved to accept. Whereas merely conversing with someone requires a willingness to be touched by what they say, and reasoning with them requires being answerable to what they say, engagement requires a willingness to be moved by what they say. When both of these requirements are satisfied, the participants in the interaction are engaged with one another. Their interaction is an engagement. Abiding by these two norms in the course of our engagement makes our interaction reasonable in the sense this term has come to have in moral and political philosophy. The characteristic norms of engagement, then, are also norms of reasonableness.[4]

Both of these norms allow that the relationships we form with one another and the reasons those relationships support may be in flux in the course of an engagement. We form and shape and maintain our relationships in part through reasonable engagement, and yet we engage with one another in the context of those very relationships. Even in the context of a given piece of deliberation or debate, we may begin the engagement with a particular understanding of a relationship and then over the course of and as a result of the interaction, come to find ourselves with a very different understanding of our relationship. This possibility is precisely what the second norm guarantees.

---

[4] Much recent discussion of reasonableness in philosophy is prompted by John Rawls's treatment of the topic in *Political Liberalism*, paperback edn (New York: Columbia University Press, 1996).

Moreover, we sometimes engage with someone in the hopes of forming a relationship that does not yet exist.⁵ Offering reasons in reasonable engagement, no less than in casual conversation, ought not be seen on the model of taking steps in a practical deduction. Rather, even in the more restricted field of deliberation, the offering of reasons amounts to inviting (with a greater or lesser degree of confidence) one's deliberative partner to share a space of reasons. Such an invitation can be extended both to someone with whom I already share a well-defined and mutually under-stood relationship and to one with whom I do not yet share anything but the possibility of forming such a relationship. Since the course of an engagement can alter the relationship or the circumstances that prompted the engagement, it can also alter the agreement or the shared understanding that the participants eventually construct or reaffirm. The first norm of engagement is meant to get a handle on this problem without thereby reducing engagement to a less open-ended process.

Both of these norms, needless to say, require a fair amount of explication and defense. Engagement, however, like all forms of reasoning, is an activity that is forward- as well as backward-looking. As a result, understanding its norms does not lead to a theory that determines which moves in an engagement are reasonable in terms of a set of prior principles or that allows for the derivation of the reasonable outcome of an engagement from the initial positions of its participants without them actually going through the process of engaging with one another. In order to understand the first norm, that we offer each other "we"-reasons of the plural subject we take our-selves to belong to together, certain of its key terms need unpacking. The term plural subject is meant to capture something special about the first-person plural pronoun; it is a way of analyzing what is involved in our speaking or acting as a "we."⁶ People form a plural subject when they not

---

⁵ Again, peace negotiations are the most prominent example of such cases. It should, in light of the discussion so far, not be surprising that many successful peace negotiations begin by getting the parties to the same place for long enough that they have to talk to one another, about anything. Such dialogue helps create a relationship on which later deliberation can rest and build.

⁶ I borrow the term "plural subject" from Margaret Gilbert, who places it at the center of her analysis of social groups (see *On Social Facts* (Princeton, NJ: Princeton University Press, 1989), esp. ch. 4). Gilbert's analysis is aimed at determining the relationship between the intentional states of a group and those of its members, and so her account of when a group of people form a plural subject involves claims about members' intentional states. Since I am primarily concerned with questions of reasons, I define plural subjects in a manner differently than Gilbert, though I think in roughly the same spirit. Beyond Gilbert's work, there is a vast literature in the philosophy of action about the possibility and character of

only stand in some recognizable relationship to one another, but when they also share an understanding of their relationship and the reasons it authorizes. In many cases, they need not agree on the full extent of the reasons it authorizes, so long as there is significant overlap in their understanding and that overlap covers the reasons being urged in their engagement.

Because we are concerned, in engagements, to offer invitations to share a space of reasons that our partners will accept, we are led to offer reasons on the basis of presumptions about the nature of the plural subject we form, or are trying to form, with them. The hope or intent is to offer to speak for them on the basis of the authority generated by the connection forged by the presumed plural subject we form together. If, together, we do in fact constitute a plural subject (a "we") that grounds the reason in question, then it is a reason for us, and is so, we might say, inherently. That is, its authority for each of us is not a matter of chance or unrelated to our relationship to one another, but arises in virtue of that relationship. If the consideration I offer you rests on our membership in this plural subject, or on something we share in virtue of that membership, then it ought to meet with your acceptance. Thus, when, as a result of our engagement with one another, I am moved to offer you invitations that I hope or expect that you will accept, I am well advised to offer invitations that rest on what I take to be the content of the plural subject we share.

The first norm of engagement requires that each of the participants works to offer reasons to the others on the presumption that they together do or could form a plural subject, and that their engagement engages them insofar as they are members of this plural subject. For the most part, this presumption

what are often called joint or shared or "we"-intentions. See, for instance, Michael Bratman, "Shared Intentions," *Ethics* 104 (October 1993): 97–113 and "Shared Cooperative Activity," *Philosophical Review* 101, no. 2 (April 1992): 327–41, J. David Velleman, "How to Share an Intention," *Philosophy and Phenomenological Research* 57, no. 1 (March 1997): 29–50, and Abe Roth, "Practical Intersubjectivity," in *Socializing Metaphysics*, ed. Frederick Schmitt, 65–92 (Lanham, MD: Rowan & Littlefield, 2003). The crux of these discussions concerns to what degree such shared intentions are reducible to individual intentions and to what degree they are a new kind of beast. Thinking about the social in terms of shared intentions, however, can create a certain pressure to end up with an individualistic analysis, since however complicated they turn out to be, we are all pretty sure that there are such things as individual intentions, and the only question is whether we need more to understand shared ones. By shifting to the terrain of reasons and adopting a social picture, we open up the possibility of a more thoroughgoing analysis of the social that neither reduces it to collections of individual states nor introduces questionable entities like collectivities.

leads them to offer "we"-reasons of that plural subject, or at least what they take to be such reasons, and such offers and evaluations of "we"-reasons form the core of any engagement.[7] This norm offers a way of distinguishing productive vs. unproductive moves in any engagement, including deliberation, without making reference to the end of agreement. Someone who claims to be deliberating, but who merely articulates his own position without any regard for how that informs the shape of some plural subject he might form with his deliberative partners is not deliberating, but negotiating or stalling or trying to bulldoze opposition. Even someone who offers possible positions for agreement, but who makes no effort to show how they are supported by "we"-reasons, or how those reasons are in fact the "we'-reasons of this plural subject, is failing to engage with his fellow participants even if, because of the situation or the character of those he is negotiating with, taking such a hard-line strategy is the shortest path to an agreement. In the cases of friendly engagement and debate, the concern with one's partner or with the topic of conversation can lead to a concern to offer "we"-reasons. Caring about my conversation partner involves caring about what she thinks, and so wanting to align or attune myself with her, not merely to be intelligible to her, but to find common ground, form some kind of "we." If, on the other hand, I care deeply about the topic at hand, then one way that care manifests itself is a concern that my position not be idiosyncratic or otherwise private. I want to bring my conversation partners to see things as I do, and if I am not dogmatic about my position, then I may, when this fails, be moved to move towards where they are. In either case, my concern for the topic at hand leads me to search out support for that position in some shared plural subject we might belong to.

[7] This description requires a slight modification to deal with cases where the identity of the plural subject is heterogeneous, so that the identities which are relevant to the engagement are not all the same, such as deliberation between parents and children within a family, or between management and workers within a company. Such reasoning will involve each side offering not only reasons which are authoritative for all concerned as members of this family or that company, but also reasons which are meant to be authoritative for the other side: parents offer reasons which are meant to apply to children, workers reasons which are meant to apply to management. Nevertheless, the points that follow will not substantially change when the plural subject in question is heterogeneous. In particular, even in such cases, there is a difference between offering genuine "we"-reasons and merely trying to articulate one's own position. For instance, doing the former can lead the parties to reframe their relationships to one another as cooperative as well as competitive, or as fellow stakeholders in a shared endeavor. The importance of such reframing will be important when I turn to the contrast between negotiation and deliberation below.

The requirement that people engaged with one another work towards a determination of the plural subject they form and the "we"-reasons it supports does not rule out all reference to specific differences among the engaged parties. One way I can clarify our relationship to one another is by making clear to you how my own position is influenced or constrained or otherwise shaped by factors that apply to me but not to you. Sometimes, narratives of how I got to where I am, or genealogical accounts of the roots of some of my commitments, though not shared or themselves the foundations of "we"-reasons may play a role in the process of coming to understand together what sort of plural subject we do or can form. In those cases, such moves, though not, strictly speaking, involving offering presumptive "we"-reasons, contribute to our engagement.[8] But we can still say of such moves that they contribute to our deliberation only insofar as they are offered with the thought that they help us to shape or clarify the space of "we"-reasons we can come to share.[9]

The first norm of engagement describes the form of its subject matter. The second norm covers engagements' mode of proceeding. We can observe the first norm and thus offer each other "we"-reasons or considerations that help to map out our shared space of reasons while nevertheless failing to be responsive to how our invitations are taken up. In such a case, we are not centrally concerned with the acceptance of our invitations, and so not, in the sense the term has been defined here, engaging with others. I can discuss with you where we each stand, and even explore the possibility that we share some standpoints and thus form a plural subject without thereby engaging with you if I enter that discussion with the attitude that it is a matter of settled fact where we do and will stand, or am unwilling to alter my position in the face of what you say. In order to genuinely engage with you, I need a further commitment: to, at least in some cases, be willing to be moved by what you say so as to construct a plural subject or a space of shared reasons that did not previously exist. In order to be genuinely

---

[8] I will have more to say about these sorts of responses to offered reasons in Part III.

[9] I mean this to be a weak, though not an empty requirement. It should allow forms of dissent, denial, and distancing from an emerging consensus in the name of some particular aspect of a participant's positioning or history or worldview, when this rejection helps to clarify a flaw in the emerging consensus's claim to be shared or universal or neutral, and it should allow such moves to be initially inarticulate or not expressible in a dominant mode of communication, but nevertheless rule out as unreasonable such rejections when they are merely meant to reject any possibility of looking together for common ground anywhere but where the deliberator currently stands.

engaged with you, then, our conversation must leave appropriate space for the reasonable rejection of proffered "we"-reasons to affect the further course of the deliberation. Rejection of a given "we"-reason is reasonable if it rests on a warranted criticism of the presumption which sustains the original claim. Not much has been said here about what might ground such a warrant or serve as a ground of criticism of that warrant (this will be the subject of Part III), but it might rest on a rejection of the identity in virtue of which one is being presumed to be a member of the plural subject, its particular contours, or its presumed relationship to other aspects of one's position that themselves have a claim on others' recognition and respect. Thus, a wife might reject a claim made by her husband that is supported by her identity as a wife on any of these three grounds. First, she might object to their marital relationship being understood as a relationship between two unequal partners (a husband and wife rather than two co-equal human life partners). In this case, she denies that she is a member of the plural subject as he has described it. Second, she might accept this general interpretation of their relationship but contest the particular obligation he claims comes with being a wife (she might accept that it includes giving emotional support but not providing complete and constant sexual access). Here, she accepts membership in the plural subject generally, but denies that it has this shape or this extent. Finally, she might even accept the traditional subjugated sexual role of a traditional wife, and yet reject this particular entreaty on the grounds that it would conflict here and now with some other aspect of her identity which he does or is bound to respect ("Not now, honey, the children need me.").[10] Here, she accepts the "we"-reason as having authority for her, but responds by citing a countervailing "we"-reason that overrides it in this case. In all of these cases, we can understand her rejection of the reasons her husband offers to support his demands as involving a challenge to his presumption about the nature of the plural subject they form or the space of shared reasons within which it places them. Since engagement is a form of reasoning, the offer of the reason must be answerable to its refusal. Since engagement is reasoning where both parties are open to being moved by the other's words, the refusal both points up that

---

[10] Note that in the latter two cases, the relationship between husband and wife, if it is in fact reasonable, is not so traditional after all, as it gives the wife the authority to effectively reject proposals in ways which traditional marital roles do not.

they have not yet found common ground, and that there is some movement that needs to take place: in someone's position or in their understanding of the possible domain of their engagement. Such recognition and the concomitant willingness to act on it is what is captured in saying that reasonable rejection must alter the future course of the deliberation: the course is altered by some form of movement occasioned by the rejection. Of course, in many cases, it is also possible (and preferable) to disengage as a result of the considerations that are offered or the movement that is or is not on offer in response to them. Sometimes, we engage ill-advisedly and sometimes what our engagement reveals to us is that the space of reasons we can share is rather thinner than we thought. Depending on what led us into the engagement in the first place, what follows from such disengagement may differ widely. A budding friendship may dissolve or pull back to the level of mere acquaintance, or it might leave the friends realizing that there are certain topics that they need to leave alone. A heated conversation can return to safer topics. But in those cases where the engagement was joined as a result of the need to make some joint decision, as is the case in legislative debate, it may be that all sides have to accept that the best they can do is to all accept the outcome of a majority vote, not because it expresses the common ground they occupy but because it expresses a thinner common ground about how to resolve irreconcilable differences peacefully.

These norms can also be seen as norms of reasonableness. The idea of reasonableness has enjoyed a certain vogue in political philosophy in recent decades, in large part because of the work of John Rawls. Reasonableness, both in the technical confines of political philosophy and in ordinary language, is a virtue of reason that has more to do with responsiveness that with the intelligent pursuit of ends, so it should not be surprising that the norms of engagement as they emerge on a social picture of reasoning that also conceives of reasoning in terms of responsiveness should coincide with the idea of the reasonable. It nevertheless helps to situate the social picture within broader trends in political philosophy to make these connections explicit. Rawls describes as reasonable people who "are ready to propose principles and standards as fair terms of cooperation and to abide by them willingly, given the assurance that others will likewise do so."[11] Though there is a fair amount of debate about just how to unpack Rawls's

---

[11]   *Political Liberalism*, 49.

definition, it is generally thought to have some form of these two distinct elements: a readiness to propose mutually acceptable or otherwise fair terms, and a kind of responsiveness to others, both in a willingness to constrain our actions by agreed upon principles and a willingness to be responsive to the rejection of our proposals. These, however, are just the elements covered by the two norms of engagement discussed above. Offering reasons that can in good faith be taken to be "we"-reasons is tantamount to offering fair terms, terms that we can share. Being moved by your rejection of my reasons to change the course of our future engagement, shows my willingness to abide by shared terms, to not insist on my position when it is not so shared.

Moreover, the norms of engagement are norms for participating in the activity of reasoning in its fullest and most clear sense. If the activity of reasoning is the activity of interacting with others on terms of mutual respect and reciprocity, an activity of issuing invitations that our words be taken as speaking for others as well, then we most fully engage in that activity when we most fully engage others, by following the norms of engagement. In those moments, we are, it would seem, being most fully reasonable.

Engagement that is reasonable in this sense thus sustains while potentially reshaping our relationships and allows us to reach shared agreements and understandings. When I offer others a "we"-reason, I in part suggest that such a reason is supportable by our relationship (or one we might enter or develop) insofar as we form a particular plural subject. That others accept such a reason serves both to confirm that we do in fact stand in that relationship and that it does in fact support such a reason.[12] Depending on whether or not we already understand that our relationship has that feature (of supporting that reason), this process of engagement serves either to establish or reaffirm some aspect of our relationship.

The process of reasonable engagement involves, in the ideal case at least, coming to a shared understanding as to which reasons are relevant to the question at hand. If our engagement is driven by a need or desire to reach an agreement or make a decision together, then the result of deliberating reasonably can be agreement if the balance of these reasons yields a

---

[12] I assume here that the engagement is reasonable, and so the acceptance is, as it were, genuine. It is acceptance in a situation where rejection would have mattered.

determinate answer.[13] In addition, a joint commitment to reasonable deliberation means that our deliberation itself embodies a different kind of
agreement: to privilege the reasonableness of our deliberation over the
need to reach a (possibly imposed) consensus, to remain engaged with
one another even when we cannot find further common ground. Coming
to the topic of deliberation and reasoning together to reach agreement from
the side of engagement thus leads to a focus on the interaction that precedes
the decision rather than the nature of the decision reached, on the question
of whether our interaction is reasonable rather than whether our choice is
rational.

6.4 Deliberation vs. Negotiation

The significance of attending to the reasonableness of the engagement
rather than the rationality of the final agreement comes out clearly in the
case of deliberation, engagement brought about by a search for agreement
or some form of shared decision or joint conclusion. Because this form of
engagement not only has a characteristic mode of interaction (engagement)
but also a goal-directed structure or aim, many of its instances can be viewed
as a form of reasoning together on both pictures of reasoning. As a result,
thinking about what each picture reveals about these interactions is a good
way to further probe some of the differences in how each picture illuminates
or occludes certain features and possibilities of interaction.

The contrast that emerges, between deliberation and negotiation, occupies the remainder of this chapter. It is not, first and foremost, a contrast
between types of activities, but rather between interpretive frameworks for
thinking about these activities. That is, many interactions have features that
class them as both deliberations and negotiations, and so it does not always
make sense to ask of a given exchange of reasons among parties aiming to
reach an agreement if it is a negotiation or a deliberation. The value of the
contrast is that it points to two ways of understanding and interpreting what

---

[13] And even when it fails to yield a determinate answer, the fact that we generally agree on which
reasons are the relevant ones means that even decisions which we reach through voting or other non-
deliberative procedures which yield jointly accepted decisions in the absence of agreement can be
considered legitimately the decision of the plural subject we form.

goes on in such interactions and where their values, their successes and failures lie. Looking at an interaction as a deliberation reveals different features and possibilities than when it is seen as a negotiation. For instance, we evaluate its successes and failures differently. When parties involved in such an interaction see it one way rather than another, this can influence how they proceed, what they regard as helpful or appropriate moves and so forth. At the same time, however, though the categories of deliberations and negotiations overlap in this way, it is also conceivable that they do not coincide, that some interactions are properly thought of as negotiations but not deliberations or vice versa. Even, and perhaps especially, when the categories diverge, coming to see that there is another category of interaction that counts as a form of reasoning together can be helpful as we figure out both how to relate to one another and how to satisfy our various aims and ends.

Deliberation is a form of interactive reasonable engagement that is brought about by the participants' concern to reach some form of agreement, shared decision, or joint conclusion. The importance of this aim for deliberation is that it pushes the participants into an engagement, to be concerned that their invitations are accepted. The norms that govern deliberation are the norms of reasonable engagement, and the metric, as it were, for evaluating deliberation is in terms of its reasonableness: to what degree do the participants respect the norms of reasonableness. As with all forms of reasoning described by the social picture, though the parties are moved to deliberate by the aim of finding an agreement, the activity of deliberation itself does not end with a decision or agreement, but merely sets the stage for one.

A negotiation is a process whereby a number of rational individuals attempt to resolve conflicts among themselves that prevent them from each effectively pursuing their ends and satisfying their interests. What marks negotiation and distinguishes it from other forms of interaction in which rational end-pursuers participate is that it involves the exchange of reasons as the means to which each participant is committed in order to overcome the obstacles to her pursuit of her ends represented by those with whom she is negotiating. The norms governing negotiation, then, are variations on the norms that govern individual reasoning on the standard picture, and the purpose of such norms is to ensure or anyway make it more likely that all parties to the negotiation regard the final agreement as rational, backed by reasons. And the success or failure of a negotiation is, barring exceptional cases, determined by the nature of the final agreement reached and how it answers to the various particular ends and interests of the negotiators. Since negotiations are defined in terms of their ends, they must reach an agreement in order to be successful. A negotiation that continues over a lengthy period of time but in which the parties come no closer to a final agreement or compromise is, in some important sense, a failure. A deliberation, on the other hand, because it is characterized by the quality of the interaction, and not the final result, can continue indefinitely without thereby failing. It can, for instance, transform or otherwise illuminate the relationships among the parties and the spaces of reasons they inhabit.[14]

6.5   The Logic of Negotiation[15]

In most cases of negotiation, people who disagree or have divergent interests reason together in order to try to reach an agreement. Negotiated agreements in such cases are compromises among parties who have different pre-existing interests. Negotiation serves as the means by which they attempt to maximize the satisfaction of their particular ends or interests given the presence of others with different interests and the obstacle this places in their way. That is, parties involved in negotiation see each other as obstacles to the maximal satisfaction of their own interests. The point here is not that negotiating parties treat each other purely instrumentally, and negotiation as merely more cost-effective than outright domination. We

[14] Among the areas where this possibility is important is in understanding the nature of deliberative democracy. One common objection to many theories of deliberative democracy is that they turn out to be hegemonic because by emphasizing the role of democratic deliberation in forging wiser or more solid consensus, they wind up overriding certain forms of dissidence and disagreement. See, for instance, James Tully, "A New Field of Democracy and Civic Freedom," in *Public Philosophy in a New Key: Volume 1: Democracy and Civic Freedom*, 291–316 (Cambridge: Cambridge University Press, 2009), and Iris Marion Young, "Communication and the Other: Beyond Deliberative Democracy," in *Democracy and Difference*, ed. Seyla Benhabib, 120–36 (Princeton, NJ: Princeton University Press, 1996). In the terminology introduced here, we might say that they treat democratic deliberation as a form of negotiation. Part of the value of imagining deliberation as a form of engagement rather than a means to agreement is that it avoids this problem.

[15] The material in this section and the next is adapted from my "Negotiation, Deliberation and the Claims of Politics," in *Multiculturalism and Political Theory*, ed. Anthony Simon Laden and David Owen, 198–217 (Cambridge: Cambridge University Press, 2007).

can see someone as an obstacle to our plans without seeing them as less than a person. In fact, many of the ways that people can stand in our way depend on our seeing them as persons. The student who shows up to talk to me as my office hours are ending stands in the way of my going home in a very different manner than my office door does. Nevertheless, there is an important difference between seeing others as obstacles and seeing them as partners with whom we disagree. Negotiation involves seeing others as obstacles and thus the need to deal with them as an unfortunate fact. This, in turn, makes negotiation a kind of concession to the unfortunate plurality of our social world: if everyone just agreed with us, we would not have to negotiate. And that attitude, in turn, may reinforce or generate an attitude towards those with whom we find ourselves negotiating as problems for us. If I have to accept an alternative that I find less attractive in order to reach an agreement with you, then I can come to see you with resentment, as it was your presence or position that required me to compromise.

Interpreting reasoning together on the model of negotiation has several related consequences. First, negotiated agreements always require further compliance mechanisms. Distinguish between the ends I adopt and the interests they serve. Imagine that I have a set of interests that can be advanced or realized by my adopting and reaching a given end. And imagine further that I am unable to pursue this end unimpeded because you, pursuing the ends you have adopted to advance your interests, stand in my way. If we decide to negotiate our way past this situation, then we reason with one another in order to find an agreement. This agreement involves our adopting new ends that are either joint ends or at least jointly satisfiable. The agreement counts as a compromise for each of us, however, insofar as the new ends we each adopt serve to advance each of our interests less well or less fully than the ends with which we began. In other words, the agreement that negotiation aims at is an agreement in ends, not interests, and most negotiation works by leading people to adopt new ends rather than by transforming their interests.

Negotiators do not enter negotiation with the thought that it will transform their interests. Negotiation is a procedure by which the satisfaction of interests can be distributed, but it takes and leaves those interests as given. And that means that negotiated compromises generally leave some pre-existing interests unsatisfied. As a result, each side in a negotiation has a motivation to break the agreement when doing so serves their interests better than keeping the agreement. And this is why negotiated agreements always come with problems of compliance. Since nothing internal to the process of negotiation fosters trust or a sense of a shared project, even if negotiations can end or forestall open conflict, they may not lead to a true cessation of hostility. Even successful negotiations—ones that reach agreement—are always in danger of breaking down.

Second, negotiation leads each side to exaggerate its claims and thus paradoxically drives parties apart as they try to reach agreement. The less I am willing to give up, the better deal I can make, and so I have an incentive to exaggerate my interests and their importance to me. It is important to be clear about the force of this claim. It is not merely that sometimes people enter negotiation in bad faith and thus violate accepted practices to get a better deal. Clearly that happens. The point here is that the structure of negotiation itself can push even those who enter negotiation in good faith but who nevertheless view their interaction as a form of negotiation, to exaggerate their claims. Negotiation is a process of finding the geometric center among a set of conflicting interests, the place where a rational potential agreement lies. The process itself is analogous to playing tug-of-war in order to measure the relative forces exerted on the rope. The process that leads good faith negotiators to exaggerate their demands may be complex and need not involve outright intentional deception. Rather, each side may respond to resistance to their claims from the other side by, as it were, pulling harder and digging in its heels. The rejection of a claim may serve to make its satisfaction seem more important, giving it new symbolic value as a question of respect or recognition. Insofar as negotiation involves not only interaction between the groups negotiating but also the at least symbolic separation of those groups into separate sides, it may have the effect over time of solidifying intra-group ties and emphasizing inter-group differences. All of these dynamics have the effect of exaggerating the opposing claims of the negotiating groups even in the absence of bad faith and an initial intention to deceive.

Third, when negotiations fail to reach agreement, or that agreement breaks down, this can leave the conflict more intense than before. Both sides can take the failure of the negotiation as a sign that their differences really are irreconcilable, and that the only full solution to the problem must come from one side overcoming the obstacles that the other side represents. It is a striking fact about a number of recent attempts at resolving long-standing political conflicts that periods of interaction that both sides interpreted as negotiation that failed to yield final agreements were followed by periods of greater division and hostility than the period prior to the beginning of the interaction.[16] The problem here stems in part from the way that the process of negotiation generates centrifugal pressures, but also from the underlying fact that negotiation is an end-defined activity: as we saw above, the failure to achieve a negotiated agreement is seen by all sides as a sign that negotiation has failed.

One motivation for entering into negotiation is to exploit the possibility of mutual advantage afforded by some kinds of interaction.[17] That is, negotiation and bargaining are most likely to be successful means of reaching agreement when there is a kind of surplus to be had in the face of agreement, and so the question the negotiators face is how to divide up the surplus.[18] The classic form this situation takes in experimental work on bargaining and rationality involves two people who are told to split up a payoff (of $10, say). They each get their agreed share if they can reach an agreement, and nothing if not.

If the parties do not face a problem of this form (and so there is no mutual advantage to be had), negotiation may either seem like a pointless or a hopeless task. It is pointless if there is no interaction with or without an agreement. Two groups inhabiting separate islands that have no contact or

---

[16] Two clear examples are discussions in Canada about reforming the Constitution to respond to the demands of Quebec leading to the Meech Lake and Charlottetown accords, neither of which was ever ratified, and the Israeli–Palestinian negotiations in the 1990s called the Oslo process. In each case, the effect of seeing the issues under discussion as about the distribution of the satisfaction of demands and the forum where solutions were discussed as negotiations had the effect of hardening each side's demands. It also contributed to the sense on both sides that when full settlements were not reached, there was no legitimate political route out of the conflict. For further discussion of these two cases as understood through the lens of the distinction between deliberation and negotiation, see my "Negotiation, Deliberation and the Claims of Politics."

[17] John Rawls describes society as "a cooperative venture for mutual advantage" in *A Theory of Justice* (Cambridge, MA: Harvard University Press, 1971), 4, though he later abandons the idea of mutual advantage, describing in later works the fundamental idea of justice as fairness as "society as a fair system of cooperation" (*Justice as Fairness: A Restatement*, ed. Erin Kelly (Cambridge, MA: Harvard University Press, 2001), 5). David Gauthier takes up the idea of a cooperative venture for mutual advantage as essential to his own moral view in *Morals by Agreement* (Oxford: Oxford University Press, 1986). To a large degree, one can understand the differences between Gauthier and Rawls, not only in the content of their principles, but in their methods and what they take to be point of political philosophy, in terms of this difference, and the ways that focusing on mutual advantage places one within the logic of bargaining or negotiation, and the standard picture of reasons, while focusing on fair cooperation places one within the logic of deliberation and the social picture of reasoning.

[18] Of course, the surplus can come in the form of avoiding a penalty. A negotiated settlement may keep us from conflict as well as provide the basis of our cooperative interaction.

possibility of joint enterprise have no reason to negotiate with one another. It is hopeless if there is interaction but no possibility of one side benefiting from the agreement, perhaps because of their current relative inequality.

Despite these problems, viewing interaction among rational agents as negotiations has been the dominant means of interpreting them in philosophy and especially the social sciences and has tended to be the dominant interpretation given by participants to their interactions. There are clearly cases where the kind of interaction that we need to participate in is best thought of as obeying the logic of negotiation, even when our joint aim is not the divvying up of some good but making some joint decision about what to do or what to believe. One ground for engaging in negotiation or regarding our interaction as a negotiation is the importance of our reaching an agreement or shared decision. Another is that genuine deliberation requires forms of responsiveness that we might be unwilling or unwise to accept in certain circumstances. In those cases, understanding our interaction as a negotiation may, despite all of its shortcomings, be the best alternative. The point of distinguishing negotiation from deliberation is merely to highlight certain characteristics of reasoning together that, though they may appear inevitable, are really tied to the special features of negotiation. Since many of the values that we hope to realize in living together on mutually acceptable terms, such as reconciliation, recognition, respect, or connection are hard to realize through negotiation alone, any framework that treats all interactions as negotiations will occlude many of the possibilities of living together this book as a whole has been concerned to explore.

6.6 The Logic of Deliberation

Negotiation is a means to search for a compromise that balances our competing pre-existing interests. Deliberation, in contrast, involves an exchange of reasons among people who regard themselves as partners working out a shared solution to a shared problem.[19] Deliberation is, as

---

[19] For examples of deliberative democratic theory which treat the value of deliberation this way rather than as a process that yields agreement, see essays by, among others, Joshua Cohen, Henry Richardson, and Iris Marion Young in *Deliberative Democracy*, ed. James Bohman and William Rehg (Cambridge, MA: MIT Press, 1997), James Tully, *Strange Multiplicity* (Cambridge: Cambridge University Press, 1995), and my *Reasonably Radical*.

we have seen, first and foremost a form of engagement with others. Despite deliberators' concern that their invitations are accepted, they often come to deliberation with different perspectives, and thus offer reasons that may compete with one another and so not meet with shared acceptance. What is distinctive about deliberation is that despite their differences, all parties attempt to work out a set of shared reasons. They do not merely hold out for the best deal they can get, but rather try to figure out what authority to give the various offers that others make, and how they can, together, respond appropriately to the complex terrain of reasons that their competing positions generate. Part of their task in deliberation, then, is to find a way to understand their divergent claims in terms of shared reasons, for it is in doing this that they can bring others to accept their invitations, and offer, in turn, invitations that others can accept. Part of that understanding may involve seeing that the reasons they do or can come to share do not support any further agreement.

Understanding our interaction as deliberation involves understanding what we and our partners do as offering proposals to one another, and being responsive to one another's rejection and acceptance of those proposals, by allowing for the possibility that we are moved by what others say. Since the reasons we offer and those we accept depend on how we understand the plural subject we take ourselves to form together, deliberation may involve an investigation of our relationships to one another and the reasons they support. If we come to the deliberation with different understandings of just what relationship we bear to one another or what sorts of reasons that relationship authorizes, then the very process of deliberation may involve one or both of us changing our understanding of these matters and thus what reasons we have, both collectively and severally. If deliberating together moves us from an unarticulated disagreement about our relationship to a new understanding of that relationship, we may resolve our competing claims by understanding them in a new and common light. If we reach agreement in this fashion, our agreement does not have the features of a compromise that results from negotiation. Because the agreement rests on a shared understanding of the merit of the various reasons that support it, the parties to the agreement need not regard it as merely the best they can do under the circumstances, a necessary but unfortunate concession to the obstacles the others represent. Through deliberation, each party genuinely refines her understanding of herself, her relationship to others, and the reasons they authorize. If a shared understanding is reached in this manner, the original claims that go unsatisfied do not continue to exert their pull because they are seen to have insufficient authority. Any agreement that rests on this understanding expresses where each side now stands. Parties who approach their interaction as a deliberation and thus an engagement, and so are not primarily focused on the aim of reaching an agreement, sometimes put themselves in a position to arrive at agreements that can be stronger, more stable, and more lasting.

This possibility in deliberation arises from its being a form of engagement, and thus governed by the norms of reasonableness. In order to be reasonable in my engagements with others, I have to be open to being changed by the engagement itself, to being moved by what my deliberative partners say. In the absence of such openness, I cannot alter the course of our engagement in light of my partner's rejection of my offered reasons, and so I cannot adhere to the second norm of reasonableness.

My being open to being moved by what you say amounts to my giving you some say over where I stand and thus who I am. Being moved in the sense under discussion is a stronger phenomenon than being affected or touched by what others say in the way necessary for conversation. In order to converse with you and not merely speak to or at you, it must be the case that our words can affect each other. It is entirely consistent with this requirement that the effect they have is to drive us apart or to lead us to recognize that we have no way of going on speaking with one another, at least on this subject. I can be proud and stubborn and nevertheless an engaged conversationalist, letting your words affect me but not letting them change my position.

The requirement that participants in engagements and, in particular, deliberations be open to being moved by each other means that they must be capable of having their position changed as a result of the encounter. This is what the proud and stubborn conversationalist does not do. Being open to being moved does not require always moving or having no principled stands. It is important to continually recognize the possibility of taking up another's reasons and responding reasonably to them without thereby accepting them. Thus, being reasonable need not forestall the possibility of having deeply held beliefs, positions, and commitments. In such cases, though I am open to being moved by your reasons, the reasons you offer me do not in fact move me. Moreover, being open to being moved by your reasons is different than being open to being moved by anything you say or any rejection you give of my offers. It does not involve always accommodating the hard-line of one's negotiating partners. In part, this is because someone who takes a hard-line negotiating stance is not concerned to find common ground with me, and so is not engaged with me in the process of deliberation. This makes his offers and responses to my offers something other than reasons. Nevertheless, being open to being moved by another's reasons requires a certain kind of vulnerability to the influence of one's deliberative partners, and this vulnerability means that participants in deliberation must be able and willing to trust one another. This brings us back once again to the role of trust in the activity of reasoning. Insofar as discussions of reasoning together have worked within the logic of negotiation, trust and trustworthiness has not played a significant role in their analyses. To the extent trust has been discussed, the concern has been more with the possibility of deception by one or more parties and the means of uncovering it as well as the mechanisms of compliance.[20]

Whereas negotiation requires situations with the possibility of mutual advantage, deliberation requires situations of mutual intelligibility. Since deliberation involves offering to speak for others, it must, at a minimum, be already possible to speak with them. We can only deliberate with those with whom we are mutually intelligible. Situations of mutual intelligibility cut across those with the possibility of mutual advantage, and they are created where they do not already exist via different pathways than those that create the possibility of mutual advantage. The possibility of mutual advantage can be constructed by tweaking incentive structures. The possibility of mutual intelligibility is realized, in large part, through conversation and the general work of living together. So the failures of reasoning on the social picture are often remediable through more reasoning. In order to solve our collective problems deliberatively, we may need to do the hard work of learning to see

---

[20] Some exceptions to this general trend are Mark Warren, ed., *Democracy and Trust* (Cambridge: Cambridge University Press, 1999), Melissa Williams, *Voice, Trust, and Memory* (Princeton, NJ: Princeton University Press, 2000), Annette Baier, "Trust and Anti-Trust," *Ethics* 96, no. 2 (January 1986): 231–60, and Danielle Allen, *Talking to Strangers* (Chicago: University of Chicago Press, 2004). For an example of a view that relies on the standard picture and is thus led to focus not on trust but on compliance and the detection of deception, see Gauthier, *Morals by Agreement*.

each other as intelligible, and to learn to escape the various pictures embedded in our ways of thinking that can block those processes.[21]

The success of reasoning, on the social picture, depends in many instances on how we say what we say just as much as the content of what we say. Making myself intelligible by phrasing my point in a way you can understand and appreciate, and even bending my position on similar grounds, are ways of manifesting my trustworthiness and so may be important moves in a successful attempt at deliberating in good faith. Such endeavors involve a use of rhetoric, of shaping what I say in light of those who will hear it. This suggests that not all rhetoric should be dismissed as forms of manipulation designed to unreasonably change our partners' viewpoint or signs that we have no firm commitments ourselves and thus will say anything our audience wants to hear. In some cases, rhetorical devices can be seen as bringing our partners to see an aspect of a situation in a way that moves them to see reasons where they did not before, in part by showing our trustworthiness as deliberative partners. Though the social picture of reasoning both gives us the resources to recognize the reasonable role of rhetoric and to distinguish reasonable from unreasonable rhetoric, it is not a topic explored in depth here.[22]

Despite the many advantages deliberation offers over negotiation, there will be situations where straightforward engagement in deliberation is not a feasible alternative because one or both sides lack sufficient trust or trustworthiness to accept the vulnerability that good faith deliberation entails. We cannot reasonably deliberate with just anyone on any topic of disagreement. There is a large difference, however, between an analysis that concludes that deliberation is not a live option in a particular situation and one which lacks the conceptual resources to see it as a distinct alternative to begin with. If understanding our interactions as deliberations holds out attractive possibilities for reconciliation and yet circumstances (such as a lack of trust between the parties) make acting on that interpretation

[21] For examples of such work, see Kwame Anthony Appiah, *In My Father's House* (Oxford: Oxford University Press, 1993), 107–36, and James Borrows, *Drawing Out Law* (Toronto: University of Toronto Press, 2010). James Tully also provides examples of this kind of work, as well as reasons to worry that many of the habits of western political philosophy hamper it. See his *Public Philosophy in a New Key*, 2 vols. (Cambridge: Cambridge University Press, 2008).

[22] I am grateful to the ever trustworthy David Owen for bringing me to see the importance and difficulty of this question as well as the potential the social picture of reasoning offers for overcoming the traditional divide between reason and rhetoric.

impossible or unwise, then we may have reasons to think about how to change those circumstances to make true deliberation possible, and a further reason to try to implement such policies beyond whatever direct good they do. We might, as successful mediators in peace talks often do, try to get the parties together to talk about anything as a way of building up some initial trust. This means that certain forms of conversation, including but not limited to other forms of engagement, that are neither deliberations nor agreement-producing negotiations are productive nevertheless, insofar as they lay the necessary groundwork for future reasonable deliberation.[23]

Even when there is sufficient trust to engage in good faith deliberation, it can fail to reach an accord. Nothing guarantees that parties to deliberation will find sufficient common ground on which to stand together. Neverthe-less, the dynamics of deliberation can generate some level of solidarity even in the absence of a final agreement. Unlike negotiation, deliberation does not generate incentives for exaggeration. In deliberation, each party is motivated not solely or primarily by satisfying as many of its own claims as possible, but in coming to a shared set of understandings. In order for such shared understandings to be reached, each side must come to understand the demands others make, and under which they find themselves. Seeing ourselves as deliberative partners can lead us to think more about our relationships to one another, and not to dwell solely on intra-group com-monalities. Moves in a deliberation thus do not function as tugs on a rope, provoking stronger counter-tugs from the other side. Even when rejected, good faith suggestions of what the sides share draw the other side into thinking together. Thus, rather than having the effect of hardening initial differences, deliberation can bring different sides towards mutual acknowl-edgement and understanding even when it fails to bring them to embrace a fully shared decision.[24] The internal dynamic of good faith deliberation serves to increase rather than erode what trust exists. As a result, deliberation

---

[23] It also provides the beginning of an argument for the importance of public spaces where serious and engaged interaction among diverse members of a society take place, such as common schools, public forums of discussion and debate, and to a lesser degree public modes of transportation as all necessary for a deliberative democracy to thrive.

[24] Of course, the mere fact that deliberation encourages good faith participation is no insurance against the possibility that some parties will enter deliberation in bad faith. My claim is merely that the logic of deliberation does nothing itself to pervert the incentives of those who enter such deliberations in good faith, whereas the logic of negotiation can itself have the effect of pushing those who enter negotiation in good faith further apart.

that does not arrive at a final agreement is less likely to generate an even more divisive conflict.

As a result, deliberation can be ongoing without this being a sign that it has failed.[25] The very act of deliberation reflects a kind of agreement among the parties to resolve their differences cooperatively and on mutually acceptable terms, to search for and perhaps develop shared spaces of reasons that can support mutually acceptable claims. Participation in deliberation thus involves each party showing respect towards and recognition of the status of the other parties as parties whose claims matter.[26] Such respect can be a product of deliberation, but is not best thought of as one of its aims. Contrast this kind of respect with that required to engage in negotiation: recognizing the other party as an obstacle to the unimpeded pursuit of one's ends that must be dealt with, and cannot be merely ignored or overrun.[27]

In addition, since deliberation involves an attempt to determine jointly the authority of various competing reasons, it provides parties who disagree with one another a wider array of responses to the claims of others short of fully satisfying them. Thus, in the course of deliberation, it is possible for one side to acknowledge the legitimacy of the other side's offer without thereby fully accepting it. They can acknowledge that it gives rise to a reason, but urge that it is a reason that is overridden in this context. Such recognition of legitimacy can, in certain cases, go a long way towards resolving disputes without agreements, in part because it serves to (re)-establish at least some shared ground.

The continual recognition of one another as engaging together in a shared project then serves to maintain deliberators' relationships to one another as ones that can serve as the basis for further deliberation and reasoning and interaction even in the absence of a more complete lining

---

[25] Tully stresses this aspect of deliberation (though he calls it negotiation) in *Strange Multiplicity*, 135–6, and connects it to what he calls practices of freedom in "A New Field of Democracy and Freedom." See also my *Reasonably Radical*, 127.

[26] For a longer discussion of the relation between engaging in reasonable deliberation and forms of recognition, see my "Reasonable Deliberation, Constructive Power and the Struggle for Recognition," in *Recognition and Power*, ed. Bert van den Brink and David Owen, 270–89 (Cambridge: Cambridge University Press, 2007).

[27] This recognition is neither trivial nor empty as it includes the rejection of domination as a means to satisfy one's claims, whether because it is not practically feasible or not morally acceptable. Nevertheless, it is minimal compared to the recognition afforded in deliberation, and, within negotiation, it is merely considered a necessary condition for something else rather than one of the points of the activity itself.

up of interests or desires or positions. Thus deliberation, when it is reasonable, can foster a set of deep ties among people that do not rely on
agreements in their positions or their sharing full-blown, comprehensive
outlooks, whether religious or cultural or philosophical. It can thus be a
force for creating a kind of just stability in a diverse and dynamic society.[28]

Note that stability so conceived is not an end that can be pursued through
legitimate or illegitimate means, but is, rather, a by-product of pursuing
other ends legitimately. It is produced not by aiming at it, but by citizens
deliberating in good faith with one another, and recognizing this fact. What
leads citizens to feel allegiance to their shared political society is precisely the
way in which that society leaves room for them and their particular demands, and recognizes those demands even when it does not satisfy them.
Since the allegiance that generates such social stability relies on the ongoing
commitment to reasonable deliberation, any attempt to achieve it through
coercive or manipulative tactics, or by excluding certain voices in the name
of unity and agreement is bound to fail. It is precisely such tactics that
undermine the very features of the deliberation that command the allegiance, just as it is precisely the final declaration that one's position is backed
by reasons and thus beyond reproach that marks one as no longer reasoning.

Here, then, is the key difference between negotiation and deliberation.
Negotiation is an activity that aims at agreement as its end. It thus fits into a
picture of reasoning as an end-driven activity. Deliberation, on the other
hand, though it may produce agreement does so not by adopting agreement
as an end, but by constraining moves within its borders by the norms of
reasonableness. It thus fits into a social picture of reasoning.

6.7 Philosophical Engagements

The distinction between negotiation and deliberation completes the survey
of the various kinds of activities that count as reasoning on the social picture.

---

[28] John Rawls calls this "stability for the right reasons," and describes it as resting on "the deepest and
most reasonable basis of social unity available to us in a modern society" ("Reply to Habermas," repr. in
Political Liberalism, 391). Rawls says that the basis of such unity is a reasonable overlapping consensus, but
I think it is clear from the preceding passages and others parts of his work that this consensus is best
thought of not on the model of a negotiated agreement, but as the sort of joint commitment to address
differences through reasonable deliberation of the sort discussed above.

Though casual conversation does not always involve reasoning, it has rational significance insofar as it is through conversation that we attune ourselves to one another in a way that allows us to reason. Because reasoning is a form of conversation, the norms that govern conversation shape the norms that govern reasoning. These include requirements that we find agreement in the reference of our words and ways to keep our conversations going, as well as the requirement that we are open to being touched by what our partners say and that what we say to them is sufficiently sincere that we are willing to take responsibility for it. Reasoning requires being more fully responsive to our conversational partners than other forms of conversation, and this brings with it further requirements if we are to properly undertake this activity: we need to make the normative spaces public and be in a position to let those whom we offer to speak for speak for us in turn. Finally, reasoning requires a level of good faith, such that we both take our offers to be answerable to those to whom they are offered, and open to criticism from anyone and anywhere. Engaged reasoning, the subject of this chapter, involves a further level of responsiveness. Here it is not enough for me to make the normative space I invite you to share public. I must also make an effort to find a space you can in fact share. This requires that I am willing to be moved by what you say, and thus requires higher levels of trust and vulnerability than other forms of reasoning or conversation. Among the circumstances that can push us into engaged reasoning are the ends generally thought to be essential to both theoretical and practical reason, as these are understood on the standard picture. By approaching activities which have ends in terms of the requirements they place on responsiveness, the social picture offers a way to think of such end-directed activity that does not make it end-defined. None of these are activities that we must undertake, either in the ideal forms sketched here or in the somewhat degraded forms that arise in everyday life. They are not forced on us by the universe or our nature. But they bring with them certain attractive possibilities that, once clearly seen, can lead us to strive to act in these ways when we can.

Where, then, in all these activities does philosophy fit? Might philosophical reasoning be a form of engagement? Talking of philosophy as engaged will bring to mind ideas of philosophers on the barricades or taking up hard and intractable social problems rather than twiddling their thumbs in their ivory towers, and I don't want to disavow those associations. But calling philosophy a form of engagement aims to say something slightly different.

Engaged philosophy does not aim to uncover transcendental or universal truths, or to derive abstract principles, but to propose to us reasons that we might accept, and to instantiate by its very methods and tones, an intellectual space where we can decide which of these proposals to take up, which to suggest need changes, and which to reject. Engaged philosophy, so conceived, is not the province of specially trained experts who deliver unimpeachable conclusions to those who might care to heed them. Rather, it makes proposals to and enters into responsive reasoning relationships with everyone and anyone, and offers all of us ways to see our relationships and the activities that make them up, as well as the participation of philosophers in those relationships, as engagements.

When a proposal meets with acceptance, resulting in an engagement, that is often the end of the story. But what is true of romantic comedies and fairy tales is not true of democratic politics, philosophy, or human life more generally. Here, an engagement is not an end, but a beginning. And no matter how polished and well-thought out our proposals are, they must, if they are to remain reasonable, always be open to rejection and revision as we embark on the always ongoing, always unfolding, hard work of living together.

And so this book is not yet done. For after the proposal comes the response, and thus yet another moment where the standard picture of reason can hold us captive. It is this: how do we determine how to respond to the various proposals that come our way in the course of reasoning, and how do we tell whether such responses are themselves reasonable, and how to respond to them? One possible answer is that it will have to come down, even if indirectly, to whether or not it is rational for us to accept them, where this might be further cashed out in terms of whether or not they speak to our interests or desires or preferences. What other possible considerations could there be to which we would want our theories of reasons to give credence? If it turns out that there are not any others, that there is no way to picture the reasonable response to the proposals made in reasoning other than through a theory of reasons, then it looks like all this talk of a different picture of reasoning is a red herring. We are once again back to a view that starts from a characterization of reasons and evaluates bouts of reasoning in terms of them. So a complete social picture of reasoning must offer different bases for responding to the invitations that come our way in the course of reasoning. That is the subject of Part III.

PART III
Responding

At any time I may find myself isolated. A moral I derive from the *Investigations* along these lines is accordingly: I am not to give myself explanations that divide me from myself, that take sides against myself, that would exact my consent, not attract it. That would cede my voice to my isolation. Then I might never be found.

Stanley Cavell, Conditions Handsome and Unhandsome

7

Responding Reasonably

7.1 Introduction

Consider some of the proposals and claims discussed throughout the book. Mrs. Bennet at breakfast one day says that Netherfield Park has been let at last "for Mrs. Long has just been here, and she told me all about it." Mr. Darcy, in the drawing room at Netherfield, claims that "pride—where there is real superiority of mind, pride will always be under good regulation." And finally, Mr. Collins, who despite what he actually says, offers both Elizabeth and her friend Charlotte essentially the same deal: a stable and secure home with advantageous social connections, in return for having to spend one's days in the company of an obsequious, self-satisfied, tiresome fool. In each case, these proposals call for evaluation. Should Mr. Bennet take his wife's report of Mrs. Long's report as a reason to believe that Netherfield is let? Is Darcy's defense of his pride enough for Elizabeth to re-evaluate her assessment of the trait in general and of Mr. Darcy's character in particular? Is the deal that Mr. Collins offers a good one? If we are unsure how to evaluate and thus respond to such invitations to believe, value, or act, we may turn to philosophy or some other field claiming to clarify the space of reasons in order for help. And when we turn thus for help, what we presumably want is something like a theory or an algorithm that will tell us how to figure out whether this is a reason, or whether we have good reasons to accept or reject it. When does testimony count as a reason to believe? What determines whether a character trait is a flaw? On what grounds should one decide to marry? The norms of conversation, reasoning, and engagement do not directly yield answers to these questions. They are questions that arise even when all the appropriate norms of reasoning are being followed. So there must be further criteria we can use when evaluating genuine proposals, as we work out which proposals to accept and which to reject. This final part of the book works out what these might be and how they fit into the social picture of reasoning.

Doing so fills in a hole in the account presented so far. Very little has been said to this point about the grounds for our response to the invitations and offers that those who are reasoning with us make. Without such an account, however, no picture of reasoning can be truly social, or, for that matter, can be truly a picture of reasoning at all. It cannot be truly social because without an account of how the offers and invitations that constitute reasoning are met, there is only half of a social story. Part of what distinguishes the social act of commanding from that of reasoning is that reasoning requires a kind of responsiveness to how what we say is taken up that commanding does not. A picture that involves both parts of the social activity of reasoning thus needs to address the question of how to evaluate offers to speak for us. Without some substantive criteria for determining how to respond to the invitations offered when reasoning (and thus for determining how to make good faith offers in the first place), the norms developed in Part II provide a kind of formal description of reciprocal interaction rather than a picture of reasoning, per se.

Moreover, without a clear-cut account of how to evaluate each other's invitations that is itself social, the social picture risks once again collapsing into a version of the standard picture. The end of the last chapter argued that the standard picture can also describe reasoning as inviting others to take our words as speaking for them as well. What marks such a description as working within the standard picture is the further insistence that when it comes time to decide whether or not to accept such invitations, doing so is a matter of figuring out whether what we are invited to accept are *really* reasons, i.e. reasons as they are described on the standard picture. Fully escaping the seeming captivity of the standard picture, then, means working out the basic structure of a truly social account of response criteria in reasoning.

Working out such an account requires loosening the grip of yet another hold of the standard picture. Faced with a genuine proposal or an invitation to enter or reaffirm my position in a space of reasons, it looks as if what I need to figure out is whether I have reasons to accept or reject it. In other words, I appear to need an account of the reasons I have or the reasons there are for responding one way or another in order to respond reasonably. Since such an account is supposed to ground how I go on in the course of reasoning with someone, it looks like it will have to, itself, be grounded in a manner independent of the particular stretch of reasoning in which I am engaged. This line of thought not only assumes that reasons can be defined prior to the activity of reasoning, but also insists that they must be. One of the features that distinguishes the social from the standard picture of reasoning is, however, that it defines reasons in terms of reasoning and not the other way around. So the assumption and insistence that the question of what reasons there are be answered independently of how they are deployed in the course of actual stretches of reasoning lands us squarely back in the standard picture.

In fact, the hold of the standard picture here goes even deeper. An account of the reasons we face looks like it can only really help me respond to the invitations that come my way if it provides me with firm grounds for my response. If I reject someone's invitation to take her words as speaking for me, it is natural for her to ask why. And unless the reason I offer to justify my rejection is itself solidly grounded, it is also natural for her to ask why that is a reason. What distinguishes genuine reasons for rejection from unreasonable grounds for rejection seems, then, to turn on whether or not we can give final answers to these questions. The need for final answers quickly leads to a search for the unconditional grounds of our reasons, grounds that are not themselves subject to further rational questioning. And, here, philosophy provides a wealth of possible options. Instrumentalism about reasons holds that reasons must ultimately have non-rational inputs, whether in the form of mental states like desires, beliefs, or non-rationally adopted ends, or facts about the world.[1] A view like Kant's holds that there are certain fundamental rational principles that themselves ground the status of reasons, and are, by their nature, unconditional.[2] Realism about reasons, like Kant's view, grounds reasons in fundamental principles, but takes these principles to hold not in virtue of the nature of reason but in virtue of the nature of the world.[3] All of these strategies for grounding

---

[1] For a discussion of the varieties of instrumentalist views about practical reason and a discussion of what leads to them, as well as a defense of one form of instrumentalism, see Candace Vogler, *Reasonably Vicious* (Cambridge, MA: Harvard University Press, 2002).

[2] See, e.g. Christine Korsgaard, *Self-Constitution* (Oxford: Oxford University Press, 2009), but also Jürgen Habermas, "What Is Universal Pragmatics?," in *Communication and the Evolution of Society*, trans. Thomas McCarthy (Boston: Beacon Press, 1979).

[3] See, e.g., Thomas Nagel, *The Possibility of Altruism* (Princeton, NJ: Princeton University Press, 1970).

reasons work within the standard picture, because what motivates the search for the unconditioned foundations of our reasons here is the demand that they wield the authority of command and so can yield final answers that bring our reason-demanding conversations to an end.

The social picture of reasoning can serve as a truly alternative description of reasoning if it can ground an account of the criteria for the evaluation of invitations that does not itself rest on a prior account of the reasons there are. Such an account needs to be built up from the activity of reasoning itself, since what makes a consideration a reason on the social picture is that it has been offered in the course of a genuine stretch of reasoning, and what makes the rejection of an invitation reasonable is that it, too, can be made part of this activity. In other words, rather than work out what reasons we have, and then conclude that someone who invokes those considerations is acting reasonably, the social picture asks what sorts of responses might continue the activity of reasoning and what sorts of responses would mark its degeneration into other activities, such as commanding and deferring. The result is not an account of the reasons we face, but a guide to thinking through how to respond to the various invitations that come our way as we reason.

There are four basic forms that a reasonable rejection of an invitation might take. The first points, as Elizabeth Bennet does in rejecting Mr. Collins, to the ways that the invitation itself is not reasonable because not offered as part of the activity of reasoning. Perhaps it is offered insincerely or in a way that fails to make a space of reasons public. Perhaps it is offered in a way that leaves no real room for rejection of criticism. The last several chapters have discussed such grounds for rejection, and though they play some role in what follows, they are not the main concern going forward. The second type of basis for evaluation relies on the concrete contours of the space of reasons I take us to occupy. Since the contours of the spaces of reasons we occupy are themselves constructed through the various activities we engage in as we live together, they are highly context dependent. There is thus nothing much to say at the abstract level at which this book has been operating about such considerations beyond what has already been said more generally about reasoning. Nevertheless, as we go about living our lives, these are the kinds of considerations that will do the lion's share of the work as we reason together. You may have unwittingly offered me a proposal that conflicts with a well-established feature of the space of reasons we jointly occupy, and so I can reject your invitation by pointing out the looming conflict.

This is one of the things that goes on in the witty banter between Elizabeth and Mr. Darcy in the drawing room at Netherfield. Each refuses to countenance what the other is saying, pointing out how it conflicts with something the other does or should believe. The spaces of reasons we might occupy together can be extraordinarily complex, and so it is entirely possible to, as it were, innocently and thus reasonably make a proposal that can be rejected from within that space. In such cases, we can't reject the proposal on formal grounds as Elizabeth can reject the proposal of Mr. Collins. I need, instead, to point out how accepting the proposal would undermine some feature of the space of reasons I take us to share. I may have forgotten our previous commitment to be somewhere next Thursday when I suggest getting tickets for the concert, and so you can reject my proposal by reminding me of our previous engagement. Similarly, I may have a tendency to forget that Mrs. Long is a rather unreliable gossip and so when I pass along a piece of the latest news, you can reject it based on our agreed-upon evaluation of her testimony. Of course, in all of these cases, since the proposal itself is not unreasonable, there is also the possibility of reasonably accepting it, which may entail accepting that we need to remodel part of the space of reasons we inhabit. Or your invitation might not be so unwitting, but itself an invitation not only to accept what you say but to engage in the kind of remodeling of the space of reasons we inhabit together that accepting your proposal will entail. And I can turn down your proposal not as unreasonable but as an invitation to a project I see no value or point in undertaking. In these sorts of cases, what determines the reasonableness of the responses we give is both the space of reasons as it has been constructed to this point, and how it gets constructed by the exchange that follows.

The final two forms are less obvious and will be the focus of the rest of the book. The third form invokes various ways that a response to a proposal can subvert an attempt to reason together. I can fail to take up what you say as a potential reason by ignoring it. More interestingly, however, I fail to reason with you if, by failing to hold what you say open to criticism, I treat it like a command. The fourth form is less direct. I can undermine our capacity to reason together by accepting reasons that undermine my ability to treat other things offered to me as reasons going forward. Accepting certain statements as speaking for me has effects on who I am and who else I can be, and these effects may then make it the case that I can no longer reason with you and remain who I am.[4] If I am ever in such a position, then in order to keep reasoning with you, I have to reject your proposal. In doing so, I make a case for it not being a genuine reason for us because it cannot be jointly accepted in the course of our reasoning together. In what follows, I focus on two versions of this fourth form of response. First, accepting certain proposals or rejecting others amounts to giving some part of myself dictatorial authority over the rest of me. Since reason can have no dictatorial authority, someone who is so constituted cannot engage in the activity of reasoning. Second, accepting certain proposals or rejecting others can render us or what we say or do mutually unintelligible and thus not only prevent us from reasoning but also prevent us from conversing with one another. Because these moves invoke the characteristic norms of reasoning and conversation, we can draw general conclusions about them, even if we cannot derive full-blown theories of the reasons there are from them.

The second half of this chapter draws out the connection between the activity of reasoning and the identity of reasoners. In the next chapter, this connection gets deployed to develop several lines of response to the proposals that come our way as we reason. The final chapter turns to questions of intelligibility. But first, it is worth asking whether there is any advantage beyond theoretical consistency to approaching the evaluation of reasons in this manner.

7.2   The Changing Space of Reasons

Faced with a genuine proposal, and wondering whether to accept it, I go looking for guidance. I come upon an advocate of the social picture who refuses to answer my questions directly, but says instead what I must do or can do so as to continue reasoning with my interlocutor. I am likely to find such advice unsatisfactory. It does not provide me with the kind of guidance I am seeking. But if some obliging philosopher were to lay out a theory of

---

[4] As David Owen points out to me, there is also the option here of embracing becoming otherwise than who I am. Though there wouldn't then be a grounds for rejecting the proposal in that case, we might still make use of the social picture to evaluate whether such a move was reasonable by looking at how the exchange continued, and whether it continued to be reasoning.

the reasons I have or face, that theory would, just in virtue of being such a theory, have two features that should be cause for concern.

First, in setting out the reasons I face, it appears to cut off certain avenues of criticism that do not find support in those reasons. Of course, it is open to someone who does not approach the authority of reasons in terms of their openness to criticism to reject this argument as irrelevant. If a theory tells me the reasons I face, then the consequence of that theory is that considerations that do not invoke these reasons are not rational considerations, and they should not be given room to criticize the claims of others or my actions and decisions. If the theory of the reasons I face appears to have gotten the space of reasons wrong, then the fault lies with the particular theory in question, and not the general approach of working out such a theory. It may turn out, for example, that the theory wrongly tells me to accept testimony I should not. That shows the theory needs revising. But once we get our theory of reasons right, the objection continues, then any considerations that it rules out are precisely the considerations we should not take seriously. They are precisely the points from which we do not have to accept criticism. After all, at some point, we need to be able to distinguish genuine reasons from irrational considerations: no account of reasons or reasoning should give credence to schizophrenic delusions or even every bit of neighborhood gossip. So the mere fact that offering a theory of reasons draws such a line cannot be a problem.

There is, however, a further problem with starting from a theory of reasons to evaluate the proposals I receive. It is this: my actions, choices, and ongoing interactions with others can generate not only new reasons for me, but new *kinds* of reasons. For an independent theory of reasons to have the determinate content that is its great attraction, it must begin with a settled account of either the reasons we have, or the means of determining the reasons we have, what might be called the authoritative evaluative standpoints. To understand how these shifts produce new kinds of reasons, it helps to introduce the idea of an evaluative standpoint. As the name suggests, an evaluative standpoint is the position or perspective from which I evaluate the invitations I receive as I reason. In particular, it helps to distinguish individual from social evaluative standpoints. An individual agent adopts an individual evaluative standpoint when she asks whether there are reasons that apply to or are authoritative for her, considered as an individual. She takes up this standpoint, for instance, when she asks whether a course of action would be good for her. In contrast, she adopts a particular social standpoint when she asks if there are reasons that apply to or are authoritative for a particular plural subject of which she is a member, whether it would be good for that plural subject. A clear example of taking up a social standpoint is when members of a team make decisions in terms of whether a certain action, understood as part of something the team does, will be good for the team.[5] Different theories, of course, provide different accounts of what makes it the case that a course of action is "good for" either an agent or a plural subject or that certain reasons are authoritative. I am not concerned with those differences here, but rather with differences in the standpoints deemed appropriate to take up as we reason. One way to understand the emergence of new kinds of reasons is that they are grounded in new or transformed evaluative standpoints.

Once a theory has determined what the authoritative evaluative stand-points are, then it, in effect, determines once and for all the kinds of reasons that we face. This claim needs to be understood at the right level of generality. There is nothing that prevents such a theory from saying that an individual's tastes, preferences, circumstances, or whatever it is that grounds her reasons change and that these changes change the reasons she has. The more we learn of Mrs. Long's propensity to wishful thinking or her biased negative evaluation of the motivations of her neighbors, the less reason we have to trust what she says. What this kind of view must insist on, however, is that whatever aspects of an individual or of the world ground her reasons, this set must remain fixed. If, for instance, preferences are the only ultimate source of reasons for action, then it is a fixed point of the theory that preferences remain the only ultimate ground of reasons. It is, after all, precisely the point of working out a theory of what reasons there are that it can provide this prior determination of what grounds reasons.

The problem is that this fixity misdescribes how we come to have reasons. In the process of reasoning and conversation more generally, we are sometimes moved by what our partners say, not only to change our

<hr />

[5] This is sometimes called "team reasoning." See Robert Sugden, "Team Preferences," *Economics and Philosophy* 16 (2000): 175–204, Michael Bacharach, "Interactive Team Reasoning: A Contribution to the Theory of Co-operation," *Research in Economics* 53 (1999): 117–47. In team reasoning, each member of a team figures out what to do by figuring out what set of moves would jointly produce the best result for the team, and then doing her part.

beliefs or commitments or preferences but to change, in one sense, who we are and the evaluative standpoints we both occupy and which are authoritative for us. It is not only that we may take up new positions and identities and relationships in the course of living, conversing, and reasoning with others, but that we may come to understand what it is to have those positions differently. And this shift can give rise to new *kinds* of reasons.

We can also, in the course of our interactions, come to grasp new types of reasons for membership in the various plural subjects we inhabit, and this can change the nature of our belonging and thus the nature of the evaluative standpoints we occupy. Thus, even if the status of given reasons depends on our membership in various plural subjects or our occupying certain spaces of reasons, it may turn out that our reasons for being a member now are not the same as our reasons for becoming a member in the first place. This shift means that we have new kinds of reasons that are not accessible from our position outside the plural subject or our earlier position within it. Here are two examples of this kind of shift. First, take being a parent. Being a father means that I have reasons for acting one way rather than another that appeal to that role, and that I find certain actions worth undertaking because they are what fathers do, or what I think, as a father, they ought to do. It further means that I do not regard these considerations as outside impositions on my range of choices, but as expressive of who I am. Evaluating reasons grounded in this role cannot only be a matter of asking from some prior standpoint or on the basis of an independent theory what reasons I have. Instead, it involves, in part, interpreting my membership in my family and asking substantive questions about it. In particular, the shift in who I am and how I regard myself that comes from inhabiting this role means that while I can still ask, "Why be a father?" and "Should fatherhood place these claims on me?" it is a mistake to understand those questions as calling for me to take up an evaluative standpoint prior to and independent of my being a father. Part, perhaps much, of the value of being a father can only be grasped as of value by someone who is already in that role. From an external standpoint, the value of fatherhood is likely to be missed or distorted or obscured. This claim does not deny that part of what makes fatherhood a role I can affirmatively occupy is that it is, in some sense, good for me. Rather, the point is that the "me" for whom it is good cannot be properly characterized without reference to my being a father.[6] But that means that the process of becoming a father gives me new kinds of reasons, not merely new reasons.

Second, consider the European Union (EU). In the course of developing the institutions of the EU, the member states and their citizens have also transformed their understanding of what it is for. Originally conceived as a way of establishing a lasting peace in Europe in the wake of two world wars, the EU evolved into primarily an economic bloc, concerned not so much with maintaining internal peace as with competing in the global market. As it moves beyond basic economic integration, a new motivating factor for forming a European political union involves the protection of various sub-European identities (whether national or sub- or transnational). As these self-understandings change, the kinds of reasons that stem from membership in the EU change also, and with them, the relevant place of these reasons in the reasoning of particular European citizens. Again, the point is that these evolving relationships give rise not only to new reasons, but to new kinds of reasons. A Basque manufacturer, for instance, might have originally found grounds for supporting European membership in his individual interest in not fighting in a war, but come to find new reasons stemming from the advantages available to his firm, and finally the possibility of protection for Basque culture and language. Since all of these standpoints are themselves capable of being transformed by their European context, it is possible for new kinds of reasons to develop whose development cannot be explained independently of that context.

The advantage of working out what counts as a reason by asking whether it has been offered in the course of an activity that counts as reasoning is that the general contours of the space of reasons do not need to be fixed ahead of time. Starting with the norms of reasoning rather than a theory of reasons can adequately capture how our evaluation of reasons can change as a result of changes in our evaluative standpoints. It can also account for the fact that such changes can take place through our reasoning together, whether in the

---

[6] Christine Korsgaard makes a similar point about the evaluation of social reasons in terms of what might be called the plasticity of the first person perspective: "what counts as me, my incentives, my reasons, my identity, depends on, rather than precedes, the kinds of choices that I make" (*Self-Constitution* (Oxford: Oxford University Press, 2009), 199). Note that for such kinds of roles, the path to them may not be one that can be made entirely within reason. That presents a problem for the standard view, but less of one for the social picture, as what counts as reasonable can be determined in part by what follows our decisions and responses.

context of idle conversation or the more focused activities of deliberation and decision. In particular, it can properly describe cases where our continued participation in a plural subject, including deliberation within it, generate altogether new grounds for maintaining our membership in it.[7] Thus, quite apart from a desire for theoretical consistency, there are advantages to approaching the question of what reasons we face from an analysis of the activity of reasoning itself.

7.3 Flexibility or Foolishness?

The possibility that we can construct not only new reasons but new kinds of reasons leads, however, to a more deep-seated worry about this approach, and about the social picture more generally. For it may look as if the accommodation of new kinds of reasons is just a small symptom of a larger problem. The flexibility touted above might appear not as an advantage but a sign that the whole social picture is so thoroughly untethered that it cannot possibly be normative. This is perhaps the most tenacious anchor-point of the standard picture of reasons and reasoning. It manifests itself in an ambition shared by a wide variety of views within the standard picture: to provide final, theoretical, criteria for evaluating the normative status of a purported reason. That is, each theory aims to provide something like an algorithm or at least the theoretical equipment to answer, in any given situation, once and for all, the question: is that claim *really* a reason?[8] For views that descend from the work of Thomas Hobbes, which hold that all reasons for action should be evaluated from the standpoint of my individual interests, the advantage of having one fundamental evaluative standpoint is in large part that it provides this final evaluative judgment: unless a claim can find support in that standpoint, even indirectly, it just is not a reason. And no amount of discussion, reflection, or other rational activity can change

---

[7] This marks a difference with Charles Taylor's view, as I understand it. For Taylor, practical reason involves a kind of interpretational discovery rather than a kind of mutual (re)construction. See, for instance, "Explanation and Practical Reason," 36. The claim that there is a fact of the matter about what practical reasons there are that is prior to the act of reasoning together, then, is a point on which Taylor, despite his emphasis on the social elsewhere, winds up adopting the key features of the standard picture of reasons.

[8] This is as true of a Hobbesian such as David Gauthier as it is of Kantians such as Rainer Forst, Jürgen Habermas, or Christine Korsgaard.

that. Since it is not a reason, those who act as if it is, even if that includes everyone, are mistaken, irrational. But the dream of a final criterion is also one that finds articulation in work that derives from Kant, and which grounds reasons in set, formal principles. Such theories aim to establish foundations in pure reason for their principles, or argue that the principles of practical reason are constitutive and thus necessary principles of action or that there is a reason-grounding practical identity we cannot help but have as a result of what, rather than who, we are.[9] Grounding ultimate principles of reason in this way allows us to render final judgments as we reason by adverting to our theory of reasons, and this, it will seem, is the whole point of having such theories.

The social picture of reasoning does not offer such a final grounding. It maintains that all there is are the multiple evaluative standpoints that we each bring to bear in evaluating the offers of others to take what they say as speaking for us as well, and the activity of responsive, reciprocal interaction by which we attune ourselves and work out the spaces of reasons we inhabit. These, rather than some set of definitive considerations, are the resources we have for living together. What such a picture offers is not any final and positive grounding, but only a set of guidelines for engaging in the activities of reasoning and conversation, the activities by which reasons come to have the only authority they can have and the only authority that they need. These, as we have seen, include the requirement that any purported reason be always open to all lines of criticism, that invitations to speak for others be reciprocal and fully answerable, that deliberation be guided by a mutual effort to find common ground in which each is open to being moved by what the other says. These are all norms that we may cite in the course of the various activities they constitute, but none of them, taken either alone or as a group, can definitively, positively answer the question, "but is this *really* a reason?"

---

[9] This aspiration to find the unconditioned ground of reason is one that Kant thinks is part and parcel of being reason. For some, however, Kant can be understood not only as having identified this aspiration, but also how to satisfy it. See, for instance, Christine Korsgaard, *The Sources of Normativity* (Cambridge: Cambridge University Press, 1996) and *Self-Constitution*, and Rainer Forst, *The Right to Justification*, trans. Jeffrey Flynn (New York: Columbia University Press, 2011). Taking seriously the aspiration and denying that it is the type of aspiration that could ever be fully satisfied can be seen as moving one from Kant to Hegel. (This theme finds expression in Robert Pippin's work on Hegel; see *Hegel's Practical Philosophy: Rational Agency as Ethical Life* (Cambridge: Cambridge University Press, 2008), and *Hegel on Self-Consciousness* (Princeton, NJ: Princeton University Press, 2010)).

If one of the requirements of my theory of reasons is that it tells me, once and for all, that certain considerations count as reasons and others do not, then it will meet that requirement only if it draws the circle of possible reasons definitively. If there are always possibly new *kinds* of reasons turning up as we interact with one another, then no theory will be able to do this positive work. So the aspiration to finality pushes towards a view of reasons that rules out the possibility of new kinds of reasons, the kinds that, as Horatio puts it to Hamlet, "are undreamt of in your philosophy."

Those working within the standard picture can admit, even regretfully, this consequence of their theoretical aim, but reply, "what is the alternative?" If we have no way of definitively determining that a consideration really is a reason, then nothing can really have the authority of a reason, but only purport to have it and hope for the best. To some degree, the answer to this challenge is the work of this book as a whole, and the aim of the invitation it makes is to allow for a view from which things are not so bleak if we give up this aim of finality and decisive theoretical authority. But it is worth making several quick points here. First, the aim for a decisive theory finds support in the view of reasons as having the authority of command rather than the authority of connection. Definitive grounding is a requirement for the authority of command, but not, as we have seen, for the authority of connection. Second, to the extent that a consideration counts as a reason because of some final theoretical determination, then it cannot truly be invoked as a reason in the course of reasoning. If reasoning involves leaving open all considerations to any criticism, then nothing invoked within it can have such final status. Third, in the absence of such theoretical grounding, things are not as bad as they first appear. A lot of the implicit motivation for the search for theoretical grounds for reasons is a kind of vertigo, a sense that without firm and fixed criteria for positive determination of reasons, the activity of reasoning is a kind of free-for-all, or at least an exercise in the wrong sort of populism. There seems to be nothing with which to bring an entire community who is wrong about something back from the brink of collective madness and mistake. Faced with those we consider wrong or unjust or irrational, but who refuse to listen to our criticisms or hear them as carrying the force we think they carry, it looks like the absence of a theoretical grounding of our claims leaves us with nothing to say to them, no way to bring them to reason. We are thus rendered mute in the face of the world's many injustices. If everyone in a reasoning community accepts that women are not rational or not equal to men, they will all reject women's equality as a reason for anything. Not being able to point to the theoretically grounded fact that women's equality is a reason, seems to leave us with nothing to say.

These fears are mistaken on two fronts. First, engaging in genuine, open, reciprocal conversation and reasoning leads us to find all sorts of deep and wide common ground. It is easy to lose sight of all we share when we focus on persistent disagreements, but the very possibility of disagreement always rests on a much wider swath of agreement. If part of that agreement is an acceptance that reasons are always open to criticism, then it is always open for someone to raise the very criticism that those working within the standard picture want to have at their disposal. If I disagree with my reasoning partner's implicit or explicit attitudes or judgments about the status of women, I can say so, and what I say by way of argument turns, as it always does, on whether I can get them to accept my offer to take what I say as speaking for them as well. Part of what I can say is that the very activity of reasoning, insofar as it is different from, say, mutual commanding or obeying or side-by-side navigating, requires reciprocity. For them to accept my invitation is for them to be moved by what I say from their original sexist position to a new, more egalitarian one. Since it is a constitutive norm of reasoning that one is open to being so moved, if they turn out not to be so open, then we can discuss this impasse as well. If I try to reason with those whom I think are wrong or unjust it may matter whether I take myself to be engaging in the activity described by the standard or the social picture. If I am engaging in the activity of reasoning portrayed by the standard picture, then there is no reason for me to start where they are or find something in their worldview that could provide the basis of a shared set of reasons. Though doing so might be rhetorically useful, it will also appear to be a dangerous form of accommodation to the forces of injustice. On the social picture, however, searching for such common ground even with those we find unjust can be a first step in bringing them to see things differently. It is not thus a form of accommodation or mere rhetoric, but the activity of reasoning. Think, for instance, of Frederick Douglass's arguments in his July 4th address, where he points out that he need not argue that slaves are men, because the practices of the southern states assume no less, insofar as they regulate slave behavior with laws in ways very different than they treat animals. This identification of common ground is neither an accommodation to the slave-owner, nor a bit of mere rhetoric. Here, the refusal to make an argument for a proposition that no one practically doubts is not a refusal to reason but the beginning of reasoning. And Douglass is by no one's account rendered mute in the face of injustice.[10]

Second, it is mysterious just what work a theoretical grounding of reasons is supposed to do if it is not accepted as such by our reasoning partners. Bringing such a metaphysical stick to bear in actual deliberation only makes a difference if our deliberative partners find the theory convincing, which is to say, only if they accept that it speaks for them. If it does not, it may make us feel more secure in our continued insistence on our position, but it is hard to see how such security is really any different than the security of dogmatism. Armed with such a theory, I may be able to say something in the face of the world's injustices, but I am not, merely as a result of that theory, doing anything more than whistling in the wind. If we are not to rest on such dogmatism, then we have to re-enter the fray, as it were, and aim to articulate the substantive grounds we have for our position. These sorts of reasons are, after all, the ones we routinely do urge when holding our ground, and they are not really further supported by adverting to a theoretical account of what reasons there are, such that the ones we are urging are among them. Moreover, although approaching the evaluation of reasons from the side of the norms of reasoning does not give us a firm set of positive criteria for determining what reasons we have, it does not thereby give us no guidance for thinking about how to react to the offers that others make in the course of reasoning and deliberation. The rest of this chapter is devoted to the development of such criteria.

7.4 Reasoning and the Unity of the Self

If I lay out a set of considerations in favor of an action or belief and describe clearly their inferential relations to one another but take my presentation of these considerations to compel your assent, and refuse to countenance what you say in response as anything but unreasonable resistance, then, as we have seen, I am not reasoning with you according to the social picture. There is, however, another way I can fail to reason with you. In this case,

---

[10] I am grateful to David Owen for reminding me of Douglass's speech and its relevance here.

I offer my considerations as genuine proposals, ready to be responsive to your reaction to them. But now, you fail to take them up that way, instead treating them either as command-like, the final word on the matter to which you have no choice but to assent, or as having no particular force at all, either merely giving you insight into my own mindset or perhaps merely as noise I have made in response to some stimulus. Whether you treat what I say as having too much authority or too little, you fail to take up what I say as a move in the activity of reasoning, and in so doing, subvert our participation in this activity no less than I do when I try to command you. Note that such failures to take up what I say as a potential reason can be subtle and hard to diagnose in practice. So, for instance, you might take my words to speak to you, and thus not be merely noise or empty chatter, but also assume that whether or not you accept and thus authorize them depends entirely on your own judgment or interest. You do not accept, that is, that they make any kind of claim on you, but merely count as a plea backed by no sort of even provisional authority. This kind of reaction is what most easily comes to mind when we think of someone failing to take seriously what someone else says as even a potential reason.[11] For instance, here is Christine Korsgaard arguing that the failure of a husband to respect his wife's claims as reasons amounts to treating them as noise:

She says, 'My career is just as important to me as yours is to you, you know. I have ambitions too.' He says, 'It isn't the same thing for a woman.' What isn't the same? Does 'career' mean something different to her? Does 'ambition'? How about important'? Or (let's get down to brass tacks) how about 'I'? . . . She's trying to obligate him; he's trying to block it. So he tries to tell her, and he tries to tell himself, that she's just making noise.[12]

---

[11] Note here that this is a failure of reasoning on the social picture but not necessarily on the standard picture. According to some theories that rely on the standard picture, thinking through for yourself whether to grant or recognize the authority of an offered reason by solely considering its content and not who has offered it or in what context is precisely what reasoning involves.

[12] *Sources of Normativity*, 144. In the part of the argument where this passage appears, Korsgaard is also concerned to claim that we cannot actually hear the words of another in a language we know *as* mere noise. I think she may be overly optimistic in this regard, and that her optimism may result from an equivocation on the idea of noise: I can hear words as meaningful (and thus not noise) and yet not as claiming the authority of reason (and thus, in a sense, mere noise). So not being able to avoid the first need not prevent me from blocking the second. Once you accept that we can fail to treat each other's utterances as purporting to have the authority they purport to have, then there is more need to look at the variety of ways this happens.

Here, I think it is clear that the husband is being unreasonable with his wife in the sense that he is failing to treat her claims as having any provisional authority for him (this assumes that his reply is not meant as a criticism of her claim, but only a dodge of it). And it is certainly the case that reasoning with others as this activity has been depicted throughout this book requires that we do not take such an attitude to what they say to us, that we, as it were, treat what they say seriously as potentially offering us genuine reasons.

But in what follows, it is the other form of failure to respond to what someone says as offering reasons that yields guidance. Here I grant what you say the authority of command. I treat what you say as command-like rather than reason-like insofar as I do not fully open it to challenge. Recall that what differentiates reasons from commands is that reasons, having no dictatorial authority, must always be left open to challenge from all quarters. They thus have only the provisional authority that comes from being so open to challenge and, to this point, having survived those challenges. If I accept the authority of your words without holding them open to challenge, then I treat them as commands, whether or not you meant them that way. If I treat your words as commands rather than potential reasons, then we are not reasoning, and so, on this picture, neither are you, even if you were trying to do so.

Consider an example. My daughter makes all sorts of demands on me.[13] I can fail to treat those demands as possible reasons in two rather different ways, both of which make it the case that we do not reason together. First, I can fail to entertain the thought that her demands on me have any authority for me at all. I can treat them as mere noise, or as of a piece with the rest of her idle chatter only satisfying them when they happen to fortuitously coincide with my own interests. She would be right to consider such treatment unreasonable, but it is not where our attention needs to be directed at the moment.

I can also fail to treat her demands as potential reasons by treating them as commands. If I move to satisfy every demand she makes on me without further reflection, then I am also failing to reason with her. I am granting her demands dictatorial authority, not the authority of reason. She might prefer

---

[13] I first developed this example when my daughter was about 4 years old. The tone of the example, as well as one's initial reaction to it, needs to vary as we imagine its protagonist getting older. That, in itself, is an important fact about the activity of reasoning, and how it develops as we do. But it is not, unfortunately, one I have the space to explore here.

such treatment, but it also deprives her of the ability to reason with me, and thus also fails to treat her as reasonable.[14] This failure to reason can come in degrees. I can treat her words as a kind of limited command by only insulating them from some particular source of challenge. Here I treat her as not fully reasonable and treat what she says as a kind of attenuated reason. I might, for instance, allow challenges to her demands that come from my interests, but accept that her demands are immune to possible challenges from her older brothers. This gives her demands a somewhat circumscribed dictatorial authority, which in turn means that I still fail to treat them fully as potential reasons, and her as fully reasonable. In fact, one ground I might have for acting this way is my recognition that she is not fully reasonable and so unable to tolerate not having dictatorial authority over at least her older brothers. It is thoughts like this that should make it clear why treating her and what she says this way amounts to a kind of failure of respect, a failure to take what she says seriously as part of the activity of reasoning. Were someone to treat what we said to them in this way, we would find it condescending.

As this example makes clear, there is thus a requirement on the respondent that comes from the norm of reasoning that we hold open what we say to criticism. To engage in reasoning and thus to be fully reasonable, I cannot insulate the claims of others from sources of challenge. We can urge this requirement on each other insofar as we are trying to reason with them. It is a function of the social dimension of the reasonable, not something that comes from our individual psychic needs. I might be better off granting my daughter at least an attenuated dictatorial authority; it might be the easier path to household peace, for instance. And she might prefer that I do so because it is a route to the satisfaction of more of her current interests. But she can nevertheless demand of me that I not do so in order that we might, and thus she might, reason. When this demand comes from other adults with whom I interact, it can take the form of their demanding that I not treat them as children.

---

[14] That we face only these two choices with respect to infants is, according to Jean-Jacques Rousseau, at the root of our mature unreasonable desire for domination: "A child cries at birth; the first part of his childhood is spent crying. At one time we bustle about, we caress him in order to pacify him; at another, we threaten him, we strike him in order to make him keep quiet. Either we do what pleases him or we exact from him what pleases us. Either we submit to his whims or we submit him to ours. No middle ground: he must give orders or receive them" (*Émile*, trans. Allan Bloom (New York: Basic Books, 1979), 48).

In the example above, the potential challenge to my daughter's demands that I block come from a third party. But it need not. I might also insulate her claims from certain sorts of challenges that I might raise. The traditional housewife who has been trained to never treat her own dreams and ambitions as on a par with those of her husband, and so who fails to consider the possibility that a challenge to his demands might be found among those dreams and ambitions insulates his claims from a source of challenge. She therefore treats his words as command-like, rather than the offer of reasons, and so, thereby, fails to treat him as fully reasonable.[15] Though she does not challenge his authority in the way the husband challenges the wife's authority in the passage from Korsgaard above, she does end up treating him as a kind of petulant child.

There are all sorts of ways to give someone's words too much authority and thus to fail to be reasonable with her (and thereby prevent her from being reasonable with us). If I repress a certain desire or aim, pushing it into my unconscious, then it is not available to me as I consider what you say, and so not available as a source of challenge to it. In such a case, I am also prevented from fully treating what you say as a potential reason, of granting it that particular kind of authority. And so, something about my own psychic state prevents me from being fully reasonable with you and thus you from being fully reasonable with me. The requirement that I not insulate you from sources of criticism rests, again, on your demand that I be reasonable with you, not that I aid you or satisfy your desires or make you happy, and so it is a requirement that applies to and results from participation in the activity of reasoning. It is entirely possible that you prefer a world, or a relationship, where I treat your words as commands. You might prefer being happy to being reasonable. Many people do. Or we may not yet have a form of life together that is governed by reasoning, and so where the thought that we could or should be reasonable does not occur to us or intrude on our interactions at all or even to this degree. Finally, we may not be trying to engage in the activity of reasoning at all: when the sergeant issues commands to her platoon, she is not thereby being either reasonable or unreasonable, and their obedience to her commands does not

---

[15] Note that the case I have in mind here is one where the housewife both has and is aware of her ambitions and dreams, but does not see them as a possible source of criticism of her husband's claims on her. The problem is harder to diagnose in the more extreme (though arguably more common) case where her training has left her without such ambitions or aware that they are being frustrated.

amount to treating her like a child. We need not ever or always aspire to reasonableness, and we are not, as a matter of some natural fact about us, automatically or inevitably reasonable. But if we are to have such a relationship or form of life, then you have to make these demands, even if the result is that you get less of what you want. There are many attractions to participation in a form of life that includes reasoning, but those attractions merely serve to make an invitation to reasonableness more enticing, no more.

If we do manage to enter into a form of life that involves reasoning in this way, then in order to be reasonable, each of us needs the others to do their part. And that part includes not isolating potential sources of criticism of others' proposals in a way that makes them unavailable to them as we reason. Doing so violates the norms of reasoning as it treats your proposals as attenuated commands. The consequence of this requirement is that in order to reason, various parts of my psyche must remain available to one another as sources of criticisms of what others say to me. Such intra-psychic availability does not require total and constant self-transparency, but only that the various sources of my evaluation of proposals, whether these rest on my desires and preferences, interests and ends, or memberships in various plural subjects, remain available upon reflection to bear on our reasoning. It does not require that my various interests and desires each, as it were, get a turn at the reins, so that I am led pell-mell to follow one desire then another. It only requires that none of them have dictatorial authority. I achieve this when I can listen to and take seriously the claims that arise from my various parts, and think about how and whether they fit into something like my life as a whole. Even if I decide not to pursue an interest or to act in a way that will inevitably frustrate a desire, I need to be able to say something by way of an answer to it. At the very least, it requires that I do not wall off parts of my psyche. This intra-psychic availability amounts to a kind of democratic unity of the self. A self is unified in this sense when its various parts are not carved up into walled-off fragments that are unable to, as it were, talk to one another, and none has dictatorial authority. Since being reasonable with others requires not granting their demands dictatorial authority but the authority of reason, it thus requires having a unified self in this sense.[16]

---

[16] Elijah Millgram offers a similar account of psychic unity in "Incommersuarability and Practical Reason," in *Incommensurability, Incomparability and Practical Reason*, ed. Ruth Chang, 151–69 (Cambridge, MA: Harvard University Press, 1997): "Now a rough-and-ready rule of thumb for use in discussions of unity of the self at a time . . . might be this: if two thoughts belong to the same mind, then there are trains

This sense of unity plays a large role in the development of various kinds of reasonable response, so it is worth dwelling on it briefly. It is both a rather loose and a rather minimal requirement. It also runs counter to some prominent accounts of psychic unity in the philosophical literature, though it has clear affinities with the discussion of conversation in Chapters 3 and 4. It is, in essence, the intra-psychic version of the inter-psychic form of unity that is required for conversation. To be unified in this way does not require that the parts of myself display any sort of uniformity or even consistency. I can thus be unified in this way without my life being ordered according to some master value or plan.[17] Nor does it require having sets of preferences or desires that meet certain formal consistency requirements. It is looser than any of these conceptions. It is, rather, the kind of unity a family displays when its members are all on speaking terms with one another and none of them are leading double lives or preserving the veneer of civility by keeping secrets from the others. It is the kind of unity that a family loses when it shuns one of its members for violating some deeply held family principle.[18]

Nevertheless, such unity is neither empty nor unimportant. Not everyone (perhaps not anyone) manages such unity fully and all of the time. Many of us are wont to easily sacrifice this kind of unity for the more familiar forms of consistency. We deny inconvenient desires, ignore the more challenging calls of duty, silence our dreams and wilder ambitions. The unity under discussion here does not require that we always yield to such desires, calls, and dreams, but merely that we give them a fair hearing, and

of thought they could both figure in" (162)). There he argues, as I do here, that the psychic unity necessary for certain types of practical reasoning is an achievement of practical reason, not a naturally occurring precondition of it. For a somewhat related idea of the unity of selves, see Robert Brandom, *Making It Explicit* (Cambridge, MA: Harvard University Press, 1998) 559, where he describes the self as "corresponding to coresponsibility classes." In other words, the self is an entity to which the normative principle of not holding incompatible commitments applies.

[17] For a view that describes the unity of the self in something like this way, see Harry Frankfurt, "Identification and Wholeheartedness," in *The Importance of What We Care About*, 159–76 (Cambridge: Cambridge University Press, 1988). The idea of the self as being unified by a rational plan the following of which would leave one above reproach is given expression in John Rawls, *A Theory of Justice* (Cambridge, MA: Harvard University Press, 1971), 422, and criticized in, among other places, Bernard Williams, *Moral Luck* (Cambridge: Cambridge University Press, 1982), 34–5, and in Stanley Cavell, *Conditions Handsome and Unhandsome* (Chicago: University of Chicago Press, 1991), lec. 3.

[18] Note that the intra-psychic correlate to such shunning is part of the process by which agents achieve whole-heartedness on Frankfurt's view. For a critique of Frankfurt that makes basically this point, see J. David Velleman, "Identity and Identification," in *Self to Self*, 330–60 (Cambridge: Cambridge University Press, 2006).

keep them available as sources of challenges to purported reasons, whether those others offer us or those we offer ourselves.

To see what intra-psychic availability requires, consider three people who act in ways that frustrate a deep desire of theirs. The first two pursue high status professional careers as doctors or lawyers because of familial and social pressure, turning a deaf ear to their deeply held wish to be nursery school teachers. In the first case, the doctor looks at his career choices as driven by various pressures that he cannot fully identify with because they force him to forgo his wish to be a nursery school teacher. He is thus alienated: his life feels like it is controlled by forces beyond him that he does not endorse, and the result is that though he is aware of his frustrations, he does not take the frustrated desire to have sufficient authority to support reasons. In the second case, the lawyer identifies fully with her career choice, but only by fully repressing her desire to be a teacher. She is headed for neurosis. Here, her frustrated desire is walled off sufficiently to be unavailable to conscious reflection. Finally, take George Bailey, the character played by Jimmy Stewart in It's a Wonderful Life. George wants nothing more than to see the world and get out of the small town in which he has grown up. And yet every time he is about to go, something happens that keeps him at home. What is different here, however, is that in each case, George is able to evaluate the claims that are being made on him, and to decide, upon reflection, that the calls of duty (which he endorses and accepts) outweigh, in his own mind, the call of the road. This gives him the kind of psychic unity described here and it means that even if he is frustrated and at times despairing, he is neither alienated from his life, nor neurotic. He can, after all, conclude, albeit with some help from Clarence the angel, that it is wonderful. To distinguish the kind of unity we achieve through maintaining intra-psychic availability from that which essentially involves consistency, I call the former "integrity."

7.5 From Integrity to Self-Preservation

The intersubjective requirements we place on each other in order to reason together generate intrasubjective demands on each of us. I can demand of you that you not wall off parts of yourself as sources of deliberative challenge when we reason together. But what kind of demand is that, and how does it provide guidance for how to respond to proposals? The beginning of an answer is to be found in an exploration of what is required to maintain integrity. I proceed in three steps. First, the self is not naturally so integrated. Such integration is both an achievement and a fragile one, so the requirement that we maintain it is a requirement that we do something. Second, it is, at least in part, achieved by reasoning. Third, because it is a fragile achievement, it requires being sensitive to and avoiding threats to its realization.

That the self is not naturally integrated is by now a commonplace of contemporary developmental and self-psychology. The self is aptly described in some of that literature as a problem space.[19] The idea is that being an integrated self is the result of solving a set of problems, some universal and some culturally specific, problems such as continuity over time, and the reconciliation of various social roles.[20] Such problems involve threats of various kinds of dissolution. What makes a particular problem a problem of the self is that it involves forging an identification with something: an action, an interest, a desire, a wish or fantasy. Solving the problems of the self is, then, working out what is mine and what is not, which, in turn, involves working out who I am and where my boundaries lie. Understanding the self as a problem space solved by acts of identification also pushes towards a conception of the self as integrated in the sense of its parts being intra-psychically available. Taking something to be mine involves making it deliberatively available to the rest of what is mine, and in that sense integrating it with the rest of what I take to be mine or me.

The need to identify with some set of actions or interests or desires can arise in a host of different ways, and a host of different circumstances can set problems the self has to address. It is arguable that the very nature of acting or having beliefs requires continuity over time, and so continuity problems are problems for any self that acts or believes: nothing particular about one's

---

[19] See, for instance, Michael J. Chandler et al., "Personal Persistance, Identity Development, and Suicide: A Study of Native and Non-Native North American Adolescents," *Monographs of the Society of Research in Child Development* 68, no. 2 (2003): i–viii, 1–138, Michael J. Chandler et al., "Continuities of Selfhood in the Face of Radical Developmental and Cultural Change," in *Culture, Thought, and Development,* ed. Eliot Turiel et al., 65–84 (Mahwah, NJ: Lawrence Erlbaum Associates, 2000).

[20] Here, again, certain Hegelian themes about the importance of reconciliation among various social roles and institutions surface. See G. W. F. Hegel, *Elements of the Philosophy of Right,* ed. Allen Wood, trans. H. B. Nisbet (Cambridge: Cambridge University Press, 1991), Michael Hardimon, *Hegel's Social Philosophy: The Project of Reconciliation* (Cambridge: Cambridge University Press, 1994).

culture or society is necessary to set the problem of continuity for selves. Other cases depend on particular social background features. In a society where my word is my bond, I have to take responsibility for, and thus forge an identification with, my word. How to do so is a problem for selves in this society. In another society, where talk is cheap, that may be a less pressing problem. Both the fact that identification is a problem, and the fact that the particular problems we face may vary across times and places, suggest that the self is not naturally or inevitably integrated.[21]

Furthermore, there is a great deal of literature in developmental psychology suggesting that the sense of self as the locus of mental states, what is often there called a "theory of mind," is a developmental achievement, and acquires increasing richness and detail throughout childhood.[22] Thus, infants do not think of themselves as having anything like an integrated self, nor do they think of others this way. Now, it might be objected that having a sense of being an integrated self and being an integrated self are different things and the lack of the former says nothing about the lack of the latter. But that objection rests on a mistake. After all, what, exactly, does being a self consist in other than a sense that a particular set of desires and preferences and interests and actions are mine, and that their being mine places constraints on how they fit together and what might be added to or subtracted from the set? Of course, they are located in a single body, but that makes them mine only if I have a sense of this physical organism as mine, and all of it as mine. The infant who finds her hand to be the best toy she has ever seen does not seem to have that sense, and arguably part of her fascination with this toy comes from learning that it is hers in a different way than her rattle is, and part of the explanation of why it one day becomes less fascinating is that it becomes so thoroughly integrated into her sense of who she is that it recedes from the borders of her self.

The development of an integrated self is not only an achievement, but a fragile one. Integrating a self involves developing a set of tools and strategies that can allow the self's various parts to engage with one another. But having these tools does not remove the need to use them. I keep myself unified, just

---

[21] The idea of the self as a kind of achievement, and thus self-consciousness as the process of achieving such a unified self is, of course, another important theme in Hegel. See, for instance, Pippin, *Hegel's Practical Philosophy*. It can, of course, be found elsewhere in philosophy as well.

[22] John H. Flavell, "Cognitive Development: Children's Knowledge of the Mind," *Annual Review of Psychology* 50 (1999): 21–45, summarizes some of these findings and debates.

as a family does, by using these tools and strategies to keep the parts talking. Just because I have learned how to own and thus take responsibility for the deliverances of a part of my personality does not imply that I will continue to do so tomorrow. Just because we are all getting along fine today does not guarantee that, come Thanksgiving, we will not all be sitting around the table in stony silence. And while barring certain injuries or other pathologies, I am unlikely to lose my grip on my hand being part of my self, there are always other matters closer to my current boundaries that can more easily slip through my grasp.

Conversations are kept going and held together by the parties continuing to talk to one another. I also hold all of my commitments and identities and other psychic pieces together into an integrated whole by keeping them, as it were, talking to one another. What that means in practice is that I keep open the possibility that any of them can be a source of or ground for criticism of something I undertake to think or do. But, of course, keeping lines of criticism thus open is to treat my undertakings as proposals open to criticism, which is to say, as reasons. Reasoning thus turns out to be the activity of bringing various parts of my psyche, my various desires and preferences and interests and ends, my various projects and commitments and concerns, my various moods and emotions, into conversation with one another. In reasoning, I not only rely on my integrity, but bring it continually into being. Even if reasoning is not an activity that aims at decisions or aspires to decisiveness, it turns out that it is the activity of making up my mind.

Just as conversation does not have a natural end point, but achieves its attunement through being on-going, the task of self-integration that reasoning performs is not one that comes to an end. Just as nothing naturally integrates my self in the beginning, nothing naturally holds its parts in place once integrated. Integrity is an ongoing task. And that means we can fail at any time. I can shift from reasoning to issuing commands or obeying the commands of others, and I can do so internally as well, allowing one of my concerns or commitments or ends or desires to assume dictatorial authority, laying down commands that my other concerns and ends must accept and obey. When my internal conversation winds down in this way, not only do I lose my integrity, but I can also no longer treat the activities of others as reasoning, and so neither I nor they can continue to be fully reasonable.

If, in failing to maintain my integrity, I also stop reasoning with you, then this fact has two consequences for how I can reasonably respond to your proposals. First, as long as my various commitments and attachments are psychically available to me, I can address criticisms to your proposals from those quarters, even if these are not directly related to the basis of our deliberation or reasoning. This provides a rather rich and flexible and context-sensitive means of evaluating the proposals that others make to me. Second, I can also reject or criticize proposals whose acceptance would in some way threaten my ability to maintain integrity. In particular, I can resist proposals that lead to the frustration of my ends in such a way as to leave their underlying interests or desires repressed or otherwise walled off, and I can reject proposals the acceptance of which would leave me with irreconcilable commitments or projects or attachments. Whereas the first of these responses points to some commitment or end I have that acceptance of your proposal would frustrate, the second involves reference not to an end I am treating as fixed, but to something like the preservation of my self as sufficiently integrated to reason with you. It thus invokes a different kind of reason than either of the other responses. The next chapter examines these sorts of responses in detail.

8

Reasonable Responses

8.1 Evaluating Social Reasons

Responding reasonably to a proposal requires treating it prima facie as a reason. Treating a proposal as a reason requires, among other things, responding in a way that maintains or does not otherwise threaten my integrity, understood as intra-psychic availability. This chapter deploys this requirement to explore a range of reasonable responses to the invitations that come our way as we reason. First, my continued integrity allows me to reasonably respond to your offer on the basis of my memberships in various plural subjects and the kinds of reasons these authorize, even if these are not directly the basis of your offer or our connection. Second, I can decline invitations that put undue pressure on my integrity. Since part of what helps me achieve integrity is that my various projects, ends, ambitions, and desires are not frustrated without justification, considerations of integrity also serve to support a third kind of response: one that considers invitations in terms of their impact on the satisfaction of my various reasonable ends.

Reasoning involves the offer and evaluation of invitations to accept a space of reasons as one's own. When I accept a space of reasons as mine, I take myself to share something with others who also take that space of reasons as theirs: namely, an acceptance of this space of reasons, and its joint authority for us. But in so regarding myself as sharing this space with others, I also regard us as forming a plural subject, a plural subject constituted by our joint acceptance of this space of reasons as ours, not only severally but jointly. In some cases, the nature of this plural subject is rather thin: it consists only of this joint acceptance of a space of reasons. In other cases, we might be able to describe it in thicker terms, and then use that thicker description to work out in more detail the space of reasons that our plural subject shares. It might turn out in talking with you that we find that we are both impressed by the force of certain kinds of considerations for acting or thinking a certain way. In Chapter 3, I gave the example of a conversation where I complain to you about an experience with a loud cellphone user and you commiserate by telling a story about a loud TV in a restaurant. I suggested that such a conversation reveals to each of us that a place being quiet is a desideratum for choosing it, and perhaps more broadly that we will have little constructive to say to one another about day-trading. Among the things that this conversation reveals is that we form part of a plural subject of people who treat such considerations as authoritative for making certain decisions. From here, we might imagine reasonable extensions of this shared space of reasons on grounds of compatibility, as I did in moving from an interest in quiet places to a lack of interest in day-trading. But there is nothing else to go on in working out the contours of the plural subject we share than understanding the reasons we share.

In other cases, however, our relationship to one another precedes or transcends our particular exchange of reasons or conversation, and has some identifiable form: we are fellow citizens or members of the same family or club or department, we are friends or competitors, or fellow opera lovers. In these cases, there is some purchase in thinking about an invitation offered in terms of the character of the plural subject we are part of and how taking that reason to be a reason for us in virtue of that membership reveals the shape of that plural subject. These cases are easiest to identify and think about when the invitation offered or the reason given makes explicit reference to the plural subject it presumes we form, but someone might offer an invitation in the course of reasoning that has this form without such an explicit reference. Even when someone's invitation explicitly rests on the contours of a plural subject of which we are both acknowledged members, reasonably evaluating that invitation turns out to be tricky. Our relationships and their norms are not necessarily fixed, and our allegiance to them is not necessarily permanent or obligatory. Faced with an invitation that rests on a norm or feature of a plural subject of which we are a part, we must sometimes face the further question of whether that norm is justified, on what basis it can be justified, and whether, even if it is justified, our response to this fact should not be to accept the consideration as a reason for us, but to abandon the plural subject or reject the form it is in the process of taking.

In discussing engaged reasoning and deliberation in Chapter 6, I suggested a host of responses a wife might make to her husband by way of rejecting one of his proposals, all in various ways based on her situation within and vis-à-vis their plural subject as a married couple. She might, I there suggested, claim that she is not a member of the plural subject he takes her to be a member of, or that it does not have the precise form he takes it to have that would make his proposal reasonable, or that though it has this form, it does not, due to certain prevailing circumstances, support his proposal here and now as he thinks it does. In these cases, it looks as if the wife is sure about where she stands and what reasons she faces as a result of it, and how these might determine the range of reasonable responses to her husband's proposal. But things are not always so clear-cut as we reason together. Sometimes, we may be genuinely uncertain about whether to accept a description or alteration in the nature of the plural subject we form. In other cases, our reasoning together about the shape of a plural subject we form together may make it clear to me how it fits ill or well with commitments I might have as a result of other plural subjects of which I am a member, whether or not you are as well. I may not have thought much about the nature of my connections to others via our citizenship or the types of reasons it gives rise to or authorizes until someone proposes raising my taxes or I am asked to put up with fellow citizens' practices that I find morally abhorrent. It is in just such moments that I want my fellow citizens to give me good reasons, not only for accepting the policy under discussion, but also to continue to affirm my citizenship as it is now constituted. If they merely insist that we are citizens and this policy follows from that connection, they have not responded to my concerns. What I am asking is not what flows from being a citizen, or even what makes them think I am a citizen, but why should we conceive of our citizenship like that?

But things are more complicated still. Each of us is the member of many plural subjects and there is no prima facie reason to assume that all of those plural subjects place consistent demands on us. Our internal multiplicity means that the full set of social reasons each of us faces may not be easily commensurable. If my newfound unease with my citizenship arises from my religious beliefs or my concern to provide for my family, then I need to figure out what bearing the social reasons arising from those affiliations have on those that come from my being a citizen, and there may be nothing obvious or fixed about any of these memberships that makes the answer to that question straightforward.

We can distinguish three broad approaches to the evaluation of invitations we receive as we reason.[1] Consider, first, the approach taken by orthodox rational choice theory. It holds that in all cases, the only standpoint from which to evaluate any invitations is my own individual one. If, however, I always take up an individual evaluative standpoint, I am, in effect, denying that there are considerations that truly count as "we"-reasons, which is to say that I am refusing to engage in the activity of reasoning as it is described on the social picture. Someone who only reasons from the individual stand-point may find that his space of reasons coincides with those of others, and this may make it possible to coordinate their beliefs or actions, but in doing so, they will only be living side-by-side and not together. The spaces of reasons they accept as their own are never shared. A theory that takes this approach can be sophisticated and accept that an individual's well-being is affected by what happens to at least certain others, perhaps via something like sympathy. If I care about other people, then I have reasons to take their well-being into account as I reason. But that is only because their well-being in some sense contributes to my own. Even the sympathetic agent in such a theory only ever asks when evaluating a reason, is it good for me that I accept this claim?[2] Insofar as this is the question he asks when evaluating the invitations that get offered to him, then he can never truly deliberate with others, but only negotiate with them.

So, consider a second approach, taken by theories of reason that derive from Thomas Hobbes's work.[3] This approach starts from the basic insight

---

[1] The following discussion is adapted from my "Evaluating Social Reasons: Hobbes vs. Hegel," *Journal of Philosophy* 102, no. 7 (July 2005): 327–56.

[2] Note that the difference between individual and social evaluative standpoints is not the difference between whether the grounds of reasons are objective or subjective. According to some formulations of rational choice theory, reasons must find support in the satisfaction of preferences or a change in utility. Such theories will have to account for an agent's concern for others with something akin to sympathy. Amartya Sen accuses such theories of describing "rational fools" and suggests that an adequate account of rationality will have to take account of more objective sources of reasons, such as what he calls commitments. See his "Rational Fools," in *Choice, Welfare and Measurement* (Cambridge, MA: MIT Press, 1982). Sen's concern is with how broadly we conceive of individual interests, and thus with what can inform the individual evaluative standpoint. Mine, in contrast, is with how to evaluate reasons that do not appeal to that standpoint, however broadly construed. A theory can accept objective sources of individual interest without thereby abandoning its claim that all reasons must be evaluated from the individual standpoint.

[3] Thomas Hobbes, *Leviathan*, ed. Richard Tuck (Cambridge: Cambridge University Press, 1991), David Gauthier, *Morals by Agreement* (Oxford: Oxford University Press, 1986). There is a deep question of Hobbes's interpretation here that I want to bracket. Hobbes's belief in the kind of indirect reduction that lies at the heart of Gauthier's work is displayed most prominently in the argument against the Fool in

that it can be good for each of us to keep our agreements even when doing so constrains the pursuit of our short-term interests. The thought behind this claim is that by being the sort of people who can be trusted to keep agreements, we open up for ourselves a vast array of cooperative opportunities whose advantages in the long-term outweigh the short-term advantages from breaking agreements. In order to be the kind of person who can keep such agreements, I have to be willing to adopt a social evaluative perspective when such reasons are on the table. Though the Hobbesian approach begins with an individual evaluative standpoint, it moves beyond the first approach by acknowledging that sometimes we should take up a social standpoint. Imagine, to take an example from Rousseau, that we have agreed to work together to catch a deer in order to feed ourselves. I am standing at my assigned spot as we circle the deer and slowly close in. But now a rabbit hops by and I know that by abandoning my spot and chasing the rabbit, I can more easily feed myself than if I do my part in our collective endeavor. If, faced with this opportunity, I reflect on it only from my own individual standpoint, asking whether it is better for me to chase the rabbit or help hunt the deer, then I am not being faithful to our agreement. If I am always ready to defect from our agreement when doing so would be to my advantage, then no one will trust me enough to make agreements with me. So the Hobbesian argues that it is to my advantage not to always evaluate my situation from the standpoint of my advantage. I must sometimes be willing and able to take up a social standpoint.

At the same time, the Hobbesian approach maintains that the only reasons for joining a plural subject and thus taking up its standpoint must be accessible from my individual standpoint. It claims, in other words, that what ultimately grounds the rationality of my taking up a social standpoint is that it is good for me in the long run. The Hobbesian approach thus adopts the following general rule for evaluating invitations as we reason: take up a social standpoint only insofar as being a member of the plural subject that could generate such a standpoint is one I could endorse from my individual standpoint. Although social standpoints play a role, it is a subordinate one,

Leviathan. His more orthodox tendencies appear most clearly in his claims that the laws of nature do not bind in the absence of an enforcer. In calling the approach outlined in this section Hobbesian, I mean to invoke the Hobbes who argues against the Fool. The more orthodox game-theoretic work of someone such as Ken Binmore also claims to be Hobbesian, but allies itself with the other aspect of Hobbes's view (*Game Theory and the Social Contract*, 2 vols. (Cambridge, MA: MIT Press, 1994)).

and the individual standpoint continues to play a privileged, foundational role in our responses to our reasoning partners.[4]

The Hobbesian approach has the following two advantages: even though the individual standpoint plays a privileged role, it allows that my membership in a given plural subject can generate types of reasons for me that I would not otherwise have had. In addition, it may be the case that, taken on their own, some of these reasons would not meet with my endorsement from my individual standpoint. I can only be a friend if, in the evaluation of my friend's claims on me, I rely on the norms of friendship and not merely my individual interests. Since my life goes better with friends than without them, I can, from my individual standpoint, endorse taking up the standpoint of friend when evaluating the claims of particular friendships. From that perspective, I can see reasons to act in ways that do not directly benefit me as long as my general acceptance of the norm in question does so benefit me. This approach thus offers an explanation of why I should accept some reasons as authoritative when they do not appeal to my self-interest. A Hobbesian approach can recognize new kinds of considerations as reasons in virtue of their being offered in the course of certain interactions. It does not, then, run into the problems that affect an approach that begins from an account of what reasons we face independently of our participation in the activity of reasoning. It recognizes that being someone's friend gives rise to new kinds of reasons. Their force arises from the adoption of a new evaluative standpoint, not merely from the effect of the friendship on the content of our individual standpoints.

The second advantage is that although the Hobbesian approach provides the flexibility to acknowledge new kinds of reasons, it provides a determinate criteria for evaluating reasons that are rooted in various plural subjects. Not every relationship is one whose standpoint we should take up in the evaluation of the considerations it offers us. There may come a point when my friend's demands become exploitative and I conclude that I would

---

[4] It may help some readers at this point to draw a connection between this approach and Rawls's discussion of practices in his "Two Concepts of Rules," *Philosophical Review* 64, no. 1 (January 1955): 3–32, reprinted in *Collected Papers*, pp. 20–46. Some reasons derive their immediate authority from the constitutive features of a practice. The Hobbesian claims, however, that only practices that I can support from my individual evaluative standpoint can generate reasons with normative force. Thus, while the reasons within a practice need not appeal to our individual interests, the reasons that support the practice as a whole do.

rather have no friends than friends like that. The Hobbesian approach gives us a clear-cut method for identifying that point. It says that one should only take up the social evaluative standpoint of a plural subject if being a member of plural subjects like that is, all told, something I can endorse from my individual standpoint. I should, in other words, only be a member of plural subjects that are good for me.[5]

The third approach denies this central role to the individual standpoint. It claims that we can evaluate our attachment to plural subjects from individual *or* social standpoints. Not all evaluation of social reasons has to trace back to evaluation from the individual standpoint. Just as the evaluation of reasons within a plural subject can appeal to a social standpoint, the evaluation of my attachment to that plural subject can also appeal to a social standpoint. Call this approach Hegelian.[6]

The Hegelian approach rests on two claims about the relationship of an individual agent to the plural subjects to which she belongs. First, as Hegel puts the point in *The Philosophy of Right*, there are certain kinds of institutions that are special because our attachment to them is not, as he puts it, as individuals but as members (Hegel's own examples are the family, civil society, and the state).[7] That is, our participation in these institutions changes who we are rather than merely giving us a new list of rights and responsibilities. In contemporary jargon, they give us new practical identities: new senses of who we are, how we value ourselves, and what makes our actions

[5] Note that something like this structure of argument can be found with regard to political authority in the classical social contract theories of Thomas Hobbes and John Locke. Hobbes, *Leviathan*, pp. 117–18 (ch. 17, par. 2); John Locke, *Second Treatise of Government*, ed. C. B. MacPherson (Indianapolis: Hackett, 1980), 111 (§222).

[6] Something like this approach has been advocated recently by, among others, Samuel Freeman, "Reason and Agreement in Social Contract Views," *Philosophy and Public Affairs* 19, no. 2 (spring 1990): 122–57, Charles Taylor, "Exlanation and Practical Reason," and "Irreducibly Social Goods" in *Philosophical Arguments*, 34–60, 127–45 (Cambridge, MA: Harvard University Press, 1995), Onora O'Neill, "Four Models of Practical Reasoning," in *Bounds of Justice*, 11–28 (Cambridge: Cambridge University Press, 2000), and Axel Honneth, *The Struggle for Recognition*, trans. Joel Anderson (Cambridge, MA: MIT Press, 1996). Freeman calls his view Rousseauvian and O'Neill describes the view that I am here calling Hegelian "critical" and distinguishes it from a view she associates with Hegel. Note also that while the Hegelian approach draws on some resources to be found in the work of Hegel, it does not exhaust them. My reason for drawing on some but not all of the resources in Hegel is that those I draw on are less intricately connected to Hegel's full metaphysical system and thus do not tie the acceptance of what I say here to an acceptance of that whole system.

[7] G. W. F. Hegel, *Elements of the Philosophy of Right*, ed. Allen Wood, trans. H. B. Nisbet (Cambridge: Cambridge University Press, 1991), §158.

worth undertaking.[8] The examples from Chapter 7 of being a father and the changing grounds of membership in the EU rely on this connection. The thought is that some of the plural subjects we are part of change who we are in such a deep way that they not only add new standpoints from which we can evaluate reasons, but transform what the world looks like from our individual standpoint. If I want to explain the sense in which it is good for me to be a father, I may not be able to do so by pointing to benefits that would be recognizable as benefits to me prior to becoming a father.

The second shift involves changing our focus away from the relation between an agent's individual standpoint and her membership in a single plural subject towards the multiplicity of plural subjects of which any one agent is a member. Recognizing the multifaceted and multilayered nature of our affiliations further helps us to break away from the urge to reduce all reasons to individual ones. We are, for instance, not only citizens, but family members, members of various corporate entities associated with civil society, moral subjects, and rights-holders. The distinctive value of modern social life lies, according to Hegel, in its ability to allow us to occupy each of these identities at the same time and bring them into a sort of harmony.[9]

According to the Hegelian approach, the reasonableness of our responses as we reason is mischaracterized if it is presented, as the Hobbesian approach implicitly does, as a question of whether the social standpoints can be endorsed from the individual standpoint. We occupy a complicated web of social roles and the sets of considerations that can thus have a prima facie claim on us have a similarly complex geography. The effect of recognizing this complexity is that it changes the status of the individual standpoint. Sometimes evaluating the force of a given invitation involves evaluating it not from an individual standpoint, but from the standpoint of other plural subjects of which I am a member. We must thus sometimes evaluate invitations that

---

[8] The term "practical identity" comes from Christine Korsgaard, *The Sources of Normativity* (Cambridge: Cambridge University Press, 1996). She describes practical identity in basically the terms above (on p. 101).

[9] See Hegel, *Elements of the Philosophy of Right*, §32. This harmony is one of the things that makes the modern social world worthy of what Hegel calls "reconciliation." For a discussion of the importance of reconciliation to Hegel's work, and the argument that the modern social world is worthy of reconciliation, see Michael Hardimon, *Hegel's Social Philosophy: The Project of Reconciliation* (Cambridge: Cambridge University Press, 1994). Note that the project of reconciliation involves showing each member of modern society that they can comfortably occupy their various plural subjects, that these practical identities fit together, rather than showing, as the Hobbesian would aim to do, that they are each, or even all together, mutually advantageous.

appeal to one of our roles from the standpoint of a different one. Such perspectival evaluation provides standpoints that are external to any given plural subject without reducing the evaluation of all invitations to a particular privileged standpoint. When my attachment to a plural subject is transformative, my criteria for evaluating my membership in that plural subject itself can, to some extent, come from within the perspective it generates. That is, understanding the value to me of my continued membership in that plural subject is something that is best done from the perspective of that plural subject, as, for example, understanding the value of being a parent is best done from one's standpoint as a parent, and not from some neutral individual standpoint independent of one's connection to one's children. The multiplicity of my social attachments gives me a further set of standpoints from which to evaluate my membership in other plural subjects, as well as reasons for what might be called balancing or coherence so that my disparate practical identities do not give rise to what W. E. B. DuBois described as "unreconciled strivings."[10] Here, though the need to balance my various commitments involves taking up a kind of individual standpoint, it is not the same standpoint that the Hobbesian approach holds out as the basis of rationality. Rather, it is the kind of standpoint we bring into existence through establishing and maintaining our integrity, by not giving any part of ourselves dictatorial authority over the rest.

8.2 Evaluating Reasons, Hegelian Style

In evaluating the invitations and proposals that others offer us, the Hegelian approach points us towards two kinds of interrelated investigations. The first is internal to the structure of the relevant plural subject. It evaluates the reason offered in terms of the point of the plural subject in question, and our continued membership in it. Although one possible point for the continued existence of a plural subject is that it provides for the mutual advantage of the parties, this is not the only ground for forming and maintaining plural subjects. Think, for instance, about the problems of human coexistence that certain relationships, institutions, and groups help to meet and how they do

---

[10] W. E. B. DuBois, *The Souls of Black Folk* (New York: Penguin, 1989), 5.

this. That a relationship provides means for solving these problems can bolster its importance for us as we evaluate the demands that continued membership in it places on us. Such reasoning involves a great deal of interpretation, as the point of our various memberships or how these translate into reasons may not always be obvious or uncontroversial, nor are they fixed once and for all. What reasons we have in virtue of our being citizens may very well depend on how we conceive of our political relationship as citizens, and its point. Is it primarily a means of avoiding violent death at other's hands, as Hobbes believed? Then we have reason to endorse any form of regulation that secures this end. If the problem that political organization solves is that we continuously run into prisoner's dilemmas and other problems of collective action given our rationality, then we have reason to support regulation that solves coordination problems in stable and mutually beneficial ways.[11] If, finally, the problem we face is how to respect our differences and not impose our reasons on others who reasonably disagree with us, then we have reasons for adopting some form of what John Rawls calls political liberalism: a form of constitutional democracy where political decisions are made through reasonable deliberation.[12]

In addition to this internal, interpretive investigation, we can also evaluate the proposals we receive by thinking about how the claims of the plural subject that grounds a given offer fit together with our membership in other plural subjects, and the claims those make on us. If I am to evaluate the kinds of obligations and opportunities that being a member of a family places on me, I can do this not by asking how it impacts my ability to pursue my pre-existing individual interests, but also how it impacts my ability to live as a member of various other groups. I might reasonably object to the claims of family if they unduly interfere with my ability to be an active citizen or pursue a professional career, just as members of my family might reasonably object to my pursuit of my career or my political activities if they unduly interfere with my capacity to be a good father and husband. Thus, one of the grounds we may have for rejecting an offered reason and the conception of the plural subject on which it rests is that it leaves insufficient room for our other allegiances and memberships. In evaluating reasons in this way, no particular standpoint plays the fundamental role played by the individual

---

[11] This describes the project of Gauthier's *Morals by Agreement*.

[12] John Rawls, *Political Liberalism*, paperback edn (New York: Columbia University Press, 1996).

standpoint on the Hobbesian approach. Rather, we must balance and adjust, examining each membership from the standpoint of others. Does my being a citizen of a state like this make it overly burdensome to be a member of a family or a certain religion as well?[13] If so, then perhaps I need to reinterpret one of my allegiances so that they fit together more comfortably.[14] If I cannot do that, then I may have grounds for rejecting the offer whose acceptance would create such tension, or in extreme cases, my membership in the plural subject that gave rise to it. In other cases, there may be various strategies of accommodation or refashioning how my various memberships fit together into who I am. That my rejection of such offers would be reasonable then provides grounds for my fellow members to reconsider the feature of our plural subject that supported the claim in question. However we finally resolve this tension, we are led to greater clarity by reflecting, as on the first path, on the reasons each of us has for being a member of each of the plural subjects in tension. As with the Hobbesian approach, my acceptance or rejection of a proposal can be traced to my reasons for being a member of the plural subject that supports it. Unlike on the Hobbesian approach, however, my reasons for membership can be much broader.

These two forms of evaluation can intertwine. Tension between the demands of two groups or institutions of which I am a member can push me to reconsider how I conceive of them, and the demands they place on me. Reinterpreting a particular membership impacts on how that membership can co-exist with others that I, or others, might value. On the Hegelian approach, there may be no neat theoretical answers to the question of what force a given claim really has for us. Faced with a given claim, we may need to think about the point of the plural subject that supports it, and the relationships among the other plural subjects to which we belong, and each of these considerations is related to the others. In most cases, it is not

---

[13] I discuss the place of such reasons in political deliberation in *Reasonably Radical*, ch. 7.

[14] I am here allowing for more flexibility in our evaluations than Hegel does. For Hegel, the state occupies a pre-eminent place among the institutions of the modern world, and so there is an important sense in which conflicts between my allegiance to the state and other plural subjects would not, according to Hegel, be resolved by balancing, but by submission to the dictates of the state. Nevertheless, one of Hegel's justifications for giving the state such a pre-eminent place was that it did make room for its citizens to take up the various other identities he saw as essential to the realization of our freedom, so while active balancing may not fit into Hegel's account, a concern with the harmonious fit of varying identities and allegiances certainly does. I am grateful to Isaac Balbus and Stephen Engelmann for pushing me to be clearer on this point.

up to individual members to reformulate unilaterally the obligations membership in a plural subject places on them, or even the nature of their affiliation. Pressure to reinterpret a given plural subject of which I am a member can thus only lead to my making demands on others to join in such a project. Since there is no fixed set of grounds for evaluating reasons, it is impossible to develop a straightforward theory of the reasons we face. These strategies involve thinking about which responses to various proposals would continue the activity of reasoning, by, for instance, keeping in view that treating other's claims as potential reasons involves not closing off avenues of criticism, and thus making use of the need for integrity to bring to bear sources of criticisms from other plural subjects we occupy.

What does reasoning together look like if those engaged in it take a Hegelian approach to the evaluation of the proposals they receive? We weigh a variety of considerations with other people, and are attentive to the various kinds of demands our various memberships place on us and them, and the variety of reasons we have for affirming those memberships in the first place. The degree to which I let my political membership as a citizen of a given state infringe on my ability to be a practicing member of a particular religion may well depend on how I conceive of each affiliation and the grounds I have for continuing them. The evaluation of reasons thus turns out to require a search for a kind of equilibrium among not only the demands of the various plural subjects to which each of us belongs, but also the conceptions we have of those plural subjects. That is, there is no longer a neat divide between what might be called constitutional deliberation, wherein we work out the nature of our shared identity, and executive deliberation, where we work out what the content of that identity commits us to doing. Figuring out what to do is not an activity wholly separate from figuring out who I am, and neither is a question of deriving answers from a set of static premises. Because who I am is in large part determined by my membership in various plural subjects, working out who I am involves working out who others are as well. Moreover, since it is in general not up to any one of us to change the content of those plural subjects unilaterally, my reasoning with others has to aim not only at my internal equilibrium, but at the joint equilibrium of all.[15]

---

[15] It is this aspect of the Hegelian view that makes it a form of what Onora O'Neill calls a critical conception of practical reason ("Four Models of Practical Reason").

In this kind of reasoning, my integrity comes into play in two ways. First, if the various commitments and relationships that give rise to different kinds of considerations are nevertheless on speaking terms with one another and none of them has dictatorial authority, then in reasoning, I can bring various kinds of otherwise occluded considerations and criticisms to bear on any particular stretch of reasoning. This transmission can be as simple as a case where some objective consideration for or against a proposal you make is easier to see from my point of view. As we reason together, I am the one to bring it to your attention. Or it can be a more nuanced case where your framework for thinking about an issue occludes a consideration that is salient to me, because of some other commitment I have, and so I can enlighten you on its importance. In these kinds of cases, there is no particular authority given to these considerations because I have raised them. My part in their reaching your understanding is merely to communicate them to you. It is fully open to you to accept or reject them, even if this has repercussions for whether we can continue to form a plural subject together.

On the second kind of case, I do not merely transmit a criticism or consideration to you, but make the further claim that accepting the proposal you offer in its current form would threaten my integrity by asking me to take up irreconcilable positions. Since, as was argued in the last chapter, you have reason, insofar as you are reasoning with me, to demand that I maintain my integrity, my citation of a particular commitment I have beyond the plural subject we form is not merely the transmission of the conclusions of a particular viewpoint, but a wholly different kind of reason. Call these reasons of integrity. They require some further discussion of the threats to our integrity and the kinds of strategies available to meet them.

8.3 Reasons of Integrity

One feature of reasons of integrity is that, because we need to maintain this form of integrity in order to reason (and thus to reason with others), the authority of such reasons does not depend on the recognition of the values of our various commitments by our reasoning partners. Imagine that someone cites a sacred religious text as a basis for rejecting a proposal made in the course of a political deliberation among citizens. If I do not ascribe any authority to this text, then the mere fact that the text provides grounds for objecting to the proposal does not give me grounds for thinking the proposal is unreasonable. It may be that beyond the mere fact that the text grounds an objection, one can explain the values or reasoning behind the text such that, though I do not accept the mere authority of the text, I can be brought to see the sense in the objection. One might think here of Martin Luther King, Jr., who frequently cited biblical texts on his way to making an argument about justice. Though it may have been that his religious beliefs and commitments made certain forms of injustice more clearly visible to him, the ultimate reasons he gave for objecting to the injustice did not rely solely on religious teachings. Unless you can, like King, help me see the issue at hand in terms of a set of values I do endorse, your objection may not have any normative force for me.

But imagine that the critic goes on after citing the text in a different way. Rather than use the text to generate a consideration that she thinks I can directly acknowledge as a reason, she uses it to point to a commitment of hers that is irreconcilable with the commitment I am urging her to adopt via her political membership. And then she goes on to claim that adopting these irreconcilable commitments is only possible for her at the cost of her integrity. Leave aside for a moment the question of whether that claim can be made plausible and assume it can. In that case, as we saw in the last chapter, I do have reason to withdraw or alter the proposal under consideration even if I do not endorse the religious value that she does. That I have such a reason does not mean that all things considered, I ought to move to accommodate her position. Sometimes we find that we cannot occupy the same space of reasons in our current states. That may lead us to go our separate ways or find a thinner space to occupy together. But whatever the result of this interaction, citing threats to one's integrity turns out to play a different role in reasoning than do the criticisms we can raise as a result of our plural attachments being psychically available as we reason.

Understanding such responses to the proposals we make in reasoning requires further examination of threats to our integrity. What undermines intra-psychic availability is not so much merely the irreconcilability of our commitments as the assumption of dictatorial authority by some of them. When some part of me assumes dictatorial authority, this is likely to lead me into one of two basic patterns. First, I might accept this authority and alter my other commitments to be consistent with the dictatorial one. In this case, I achieve a kind of consistency in my commitments, but not one that arises through the open conversation among them, but rather from the shunning or repressing of incompatible commitments. Second, I may find myself with, as W. E. B. DuBois put it, "unreconciled strivings" or "warring ideals" that threaten to tear me asunder.[16]

Finding oneself caught between such demands can be the stuff of tragedy, whether that of Sophocles' Antigone, or Ibsen's Nora. As Ibsen's *A Doll's House* reaches a climax, Nora prepares to walk out on her upstanding husband Thorvald and their children. When he challenges her to explain herself, to give him reasons for her behavior, she is unable to offer a description of her situation that Thorvald can accept and which would account for her feeling wronged, and in her desperation and frustration remarks, "I could tear myself to pieces." Stanley Cavell remarks in his discussion of this scene that "Nora has no reasons that are acceptable," by which he does not mean that she has no grounds for her position, but only no words or language in which to offer them that could meet with Thorvald's acceptance.[17]

To understand our sense, watching the play, that her pain, her feeling, must ground something reasonable she can say to justify her leaving, we can make use of the foregoing discussion: she finds herself in a situation where she is being torn to pieces, which is to say that she finds that different parts of her ground considerations that cannot enter the same conversation. This inability means that she cannot offer considerations grounded in part of who she is to Thorvald that he can, in his present state, accept. As a result, she cannot reason with Thorvald directly (he, after all, accuses her of "speaking like a child"). Faced with these difficulties, she has for a long time purchased both a kind of psychic consistency and household peace by giving her identity as a respectable wife dictatorial authority. What she realizes at the end of the play is that she can no longer do this. But this recognition need not be thought of as a merely selfish demand to pursue different projects, which is how Thorvald appears to see it. She might also recognize that her previous response achieved unity at the expense of integrity and thus her ability to truly live with Thorvald, to be in a position to reason with him.

---

[16] *Souls of Black Folk*, 5.
[17] *Conditions Handsome and Unhandsome* (Chicago: University of Chicago Press, 1990), 108–15.

Not giving dictatorial authority to her identity as a wife and mother means giving a hearing to her other commitments, a hearing to precisely those commitments and concerns that he cannot hear as reasons. This means that there is a path forward for Thorvald, should he be able to see it. If we imagine that he wishes to be able to live with, be truly married to, Nora, he must be able to reason with her. And thus he must take this threat to her integrity as a reason, even though it does not speak in the dominant idiom of respectability where he resides, and in which she has, as Cavell says, no acceptable reasons. On the other hand, he need not share her newfound commitment to be treated as more than a doll as his own. He only needs to recognize it as a commitment of hers that she must not silence. That is, all he needs to recognize is that her need for integrity is not only a reason for her to respond to threats to that integrity, but also a reason for him.

The tragic form that gives rise to this kind of reason of integrity involves having two conflicting commitments that, as they stand, cannot be reconciled without giving one of them dictatorial authority. So understood, it is a form that also arises in more run-of-the-mill cases, where it is sometimes easier to see what goes on and how we might respond, in part because there may be a common language in which to articulate the competing demands. If I have commitments to my department to attend department meetings, and commitments to my family to pick my kids up from school, then these place me under competing demands if my department schedules a meeting at a time I must pick up my kids. How do reasons of structural integrity play a role in my reasoning in such a case? And how can it possibly be the case that my failure to raise the question of integrity or another's failure to heed it means that any of us is failing to reason?

I am trying to decide whether to go to my department meeting, or, more likely, how I need to arrange my day to make it possible. If I entertain the thought of just going to the meeting as if it did not conflict with other commitments, then the part of me that is committed to picking up my kids can raise an objection that so doing would be to abandon that commitment. Ignoring or silencing that concern is to give dictatorial authority to my commitment to the meeting. But it is also the case that merely skipping the meeting to pick up the kids is to give dictatorial authority to my commitments as a parent. Reasoning about how to go to the meeting must steer a path between these, allowing all of my various parts to have a say in what I decide to do.

What, then, might reasoning look like if we pay explicit attention to reasons of integrity? Consider two kinds of illustration. First, there are strategies we use on a regular basis to organize our individual lives to make space for otherwise incompatible commitments without giving them dictatorial authority. I can accord various aspects of my identity priority in different areas of my life, as when I take my identity as a citizen to override other identities in democratic politics, but to take a back seat in deliberations within my family about where to go on vacation or how to divide up household responsibilities. This arrangement establishes areas where some parts of myself have commanding authority, but not because they command that authority, but because it lies within a certain domain. What prevents this commanding authority from being dictatorial authority is that the bounds of that domain are open for discussion and adjustment. In other cases, I divide these domains temporally, by allowing for a greater devotion to a particular project or end now by limiting the duration of its hold on me, as when I throw myself into a project or a game because I know it will only last for a few hours or weeks. Finally, I can reconceive one or more otherwise conflicting commitments so that they fit more easily together, as when I rein in my professional ambitions to make room for my ambitions for a fulfilling family life. These strategies help me to achieve the integrity needed to reason, because they involve paying heed to the demands of all my various parts, not jettisoning them in the face of difficulties or unilaterally subordinating some to others. But they also help me achieve integrity in a more literal sense: in deploying these strategies, I hold myself together. That is, I make of my various parts something whole, some one thing: me.

It should not be surprising if it turns out that a requirement of reasoning is not something we achieve alone. This is no less true with the demand to achieve and maintain integrity. The primary threats to our integrity come from other people and our relationships with them. Adding other people into the description of the threats to our integrity brings out the fact that not only must we preserve our integrity for their sakes, but that doing so is an activity that requires their cooperation. We cannot hold ourselves together all alone.

Return to the conflict between making the meeting and picking up my kids from school. In the case of each of the conflicting demands on me, I stand under these demands because of how I have arranged to structure relationships with others. The meeting I need to go to has been scheduled according to whatever the department's rules are for scheduling meetings. It is not a result of immutable facts about the universe or human psychology. Similarly, my duty to pick up my kids from school is a result of having structured a whole set of relationships, with my wife, with my kids, with their school, in a particular way. It is thus false to the situation I find myself in to present it merely as a conflict I must navigate alone. It helps, then, to back up a couple of frames and ask how the possibility of this conflict arising might have shaped the deliberations that led to it.

Think, for instance about the deliberation among my colleagues about when to schedule this meeting. Someone makes a proposal for a meeting time that conflicts with when I normally pick up my kids. So I object, saying it places me under a conflict between my duties as department member and my duties as a parent. What kind of conflict is this, exactly, and why should it ground an objection I can make to my colleagues? In line with the discussion above, it is not that my particular parental responsibilities should matter, in and of themselves, to my colleagues. When I speak as a parent of my children, I do not take myself to be speaking for them or even trying to. At the same time, we all think that this conflict is a relevant fact to bring up in the discussion. How, then, should we understand this interaction as reasoning given what has been said so far?

It is possible to interpret the discussion of the department meeting as a kind of negotiation in which each of us has a previously determined set of ends and desires. Under this description, I want to schedule the meeting at a time that is most convenient for me, given my other projects and plans. I have a standing commitment to pick up my kids on certain days at certain times and so I will be more successful at my various life projects if I don't also have a meeting then, since such a meeting requires me to sacrifice one or the other. But, so understood, this is no different than any number of other things I might want to get done that day. Maybe I also was hoping to catch a film screening, meet with a graduate student, or go for a long bike ride along the lake. My colleagues also each have their own wishes and desires. One does not want to make a special trip into the department, another has a set of other meetings to attend, and a third strongly prefers meetings in the morning. Each of us brings these preferences to bear as we work out a time that maximally satisfies them. In the most sparse form of this picture, we each maneuver to get as much as we can, and we end up with some compromise that may be dependent on who is stubborn, who is skilled at presenting his case, and who has the most pressing additional commitments. On a softer picture, we are all collegial and so are each committed to fair negotiations. We are all thus jointly further committed to find a meeting time that distributes the burdens to each person's individual projects fairly. In either case, however, our individual desires, interests, ends, and commitments serve as the building blocks of individual reasons and these are then used to find a kind of center of gravity among the various pulls as we find a time to meet. On such a picture, the activity of reasoning as such seems to play no special role. We might have put all our various plans and projects and commitments into a scheduling program and let it spit out the optimal time to meet. Furthermore, when I accept that I need to arrange for someone else to pick up my kids because the meeting has in the end been scheduled at the proposed time, it is not because I have accepted other people's reasons, only their immovability as obstacles I must navigate.

But there is another way to conceive of this situation, and it is the one I have been inviting you to consider throughout this book. Here, the discussion gets interpreted as a piece of reasonable deliberation among a group of people who form a plural subject as members of a department. In the course of the deliberation, we offer one another reasons in the form of offers to take what we say as speaking for the department. When one of us suggests a meeting time, the question it raises is, is that a time that we can support? Because, as we saw in the previous section, each of us is also a member of any number of other plural subjects, part of how we each evaluate this question is from the perspective of these other memberships. So, for instance, if the proposed meeting time conflicts with my standing commitment to pick up my kids, then I can ask whether or not the burdens of departmental membership are compatible with the burdens of fatherhood. My rejection of the meeting time on the grounds that it conflicts with my need to pick up my kids is then a way of asking my colleagues to change the burdens of department life to keep them compatible with the other aspects of my identity.

The way such a claim comes to have authority in our deliberations is not that my identity as a parent has authority for the others, but because of the ways that this part of who I am impacts the other parts of who I am, and thus, the kind of other commitments I can honor. I am not merely a member of the department and a father, but me (a member of the department), and as such, also at the same time me (a father). As a result, something that is a reason for me (qua department member) must also be a reason for me (qua father), and thus compatible with the reasons I have that are grounded in my being a father, because part of my being me is that I am both a member of the department and a father. (Of course, this goes the other way, too: my being a father must sometimes come to terms with my being a department member. Neither, if I am to be reasonable, can have dictatorial authority.)

When I say to my colleague (perhaps overstating my case in the process) that by continually scheduling meetings at times when I have parental responsibilities, she is pulling me apart, this is a different kind of reason than one that merely cites those parental responsibilities. My parental responsibilities may be, on their own, no concern of hers, and give her no reasons to do anything, but my maintaining my integrity is a source of reasons for her, and it is these reasons I press in pointing out the difficulty of maintaining my integrity given the pressure under which she places me.

There are, thus, two avenues to maintaining my integrity in the face of threats to it: the sort of individual strategies mentioned above, wherein I try to fit the pieces of my life together into a sufficiently coherent whole, and reasonable people around me who respond to my difficulties in achieving such integrity as giving them reasons to reduce the centrifugal pressures on my life. The social picture of reasoning takes integrity to be both a condition and a product of reasoning. Since reasoning is something we do with others, other people are not only the primary obstacles to our integrity, but also the primary contributors to it. Each of us is an individual self, but we only get and stay that way with the help of others.

8.4 Other Threats to Integrity: The Frustration of Ends

Not all threats to our integrity are structural, and so not all of the circumstances that can undermine our capacity to reason with others involve the pressures that threaten to tear us apart. My ability to reason is also threatened from more direct threats to my self. Since human selves need to be embodied, threats to the survival of the self include threats to the survival of the body. Insofar as something threatens my life, then, this threat also grounds reasonable responses to it. That threats to my life give me reasons one way or another may seem so obvious as to not need saying. But the reasons I am pointing to here are the reasons that come about through the social picture, which means that they are considerations we can appropriately raise while reasoning with one another, invitations to take what we say as speaking for others as well. Saying that threats to my life count as reasons is to say not only that they give me justification for avoiding them, but that they also give reasons to others to avoid or prevent them. At the same time, since these considerations are tied to my ability to continue to reason, they do not support avoiding any and all threats to my life no matter what it takes. I have reason, on this view, to take all reasonable precautions, but not unreasonable ones.

Moving into more subtle ground, one source of psychic disintegration comes when I can only hold part of myself together by repressing or otherwise silencing other parts. Some traumas lead us to wall off certain memories or desires or plans, to, in psychoanalytic terms, repress them. Concerns about integrity thus give us reason to avoid such traumas, and to find ways to cope with them that do not yield such repression.[18] As with threats to our lives, they give others reasons to help us in this.

Another source of disintegration can come from the continual frustration of certain ends. If I have an end to which I am committed, and I am routinely frustrated in my pursuit of it, then I am likely to give up on it. Contrast two scenarios in which this happens. In the first, the forces that resist me are reasonable, and offer me challenges to the claims that my pursuit of this end generates. I accept the force of these challenges, and it is this acceptance that leads me to change or forgo my end. In this case, though my end is frustrated, my self remains intact. This scenario describes many of the episodes in George Bailey's wonderful life. In the second, however, the forces that frustrate me are not reasonable. They block my way without offering challenges I can accept. Though I give up my end in frustration, I do so by more or less walling it off from the rest of myself, turning a deaf ear to the interests that generated the end in the first place. This scenario

---

[18] For a powerful account of how trauma can unmake the self and what sorts of activities may be required to remake it, see Susan Brison, *Aftermath: Violence and the Remaking of the Self* (Princeton, NJ: Princeton University Press, 2001).

describes the professional pushed into her career by family pressure. In this case, my self loses its integrity and I lose my ability to reason with others. But that just means that I have reasons to prevent such frustrations, to pursue my ends when they are reasonable, and work to clear away any unreasonable barriers to my ability to do so.

There are two advantages of deriving the rational importance of my ends and interests from concerns of integrity. First, it gives rational weight to my interests when they are reasonable, when they do not meet with valid challenges to the claims they generate. Considerations of integrity on a social picture of reasons thus have a certain kind of weight, insofar as they are requirements for reasoning, but not a kind of weight that requires overcoming or outweighing by the demands of others. Reasons of integrity have authority insofar as they are reasonable, not because of any prior claim of the importance of each person to himself.

Second, I have such reasons not only to pursue those interests that are reasonable, but also to challenge social structures and attitudes that unreasonably stand in the way of such pursuits. Reasons of integrity, when they are generated through reasoning together need not presume a given social structure as fixed. They can tell us to do more than merely navigate its treacherous shoals as best we can. Instead, they can point us back to the social, showing that the threat to our integrity lies beyond our individual psyche. When my circumstances, including the larger structures of my society, pull me apart, I have, and thus we have, reason to change our circumstances if we wish to be reasonable. Our being reasonable is a collective achievement, and one that may require more than our goodwill.

This final point also highlights the fact that what counts as a threat to the self may very well depend on all sorts of cultural and historical factors, even if there are also some universal forms of unity any self must achieve. As I said in Chapter 7, the problem space that makes up the self need not be derivable from purely universal considerations, whether metaphysical or biological. Moreover, the resources I have available to solve the various problems involved in constituting myself as a self may depend on my culture. Preserving the kind of integrity that I require to reason thus may require something different in different times and places. This variation means that threats to the self take different forms, as do the available means of self-preservation. In a study of differential rates of suicide among Native and non-Native Canadian teenagers, a group of developmental psychologists argue that the members of each group have different resources available with which to solve the problems of self-continuity. Native Canadian societies rely much more heavily on cultural continuity to generate continuity of the self. Non-Native societies, on the other hand, rely on resources more familiar to contemporary philosophers of mind: bodily or psychological continuity. As a result, disruptions in the cultural continuity of both Native and Non-native societies have differing impact on the two groups, raising a much more severe threat to the integrity of the Native teenagers, a threat that leads to a much higher suicide rate in those communities.[19] My culture may leave me without the resources I need, or set me a set of ultimately inconsistent problems to solve, or set us problems that we cannot all successfully solve. The limits of my culture may be the limits of my world, but that need not mean that they provide a good home for me. These brief remarks are meant to suggest that the fact that I have adopted a particular end can play a role in reasoning on the social picture, even if it is not the role it plays on the standard one. Though ends do not automatically ground our reasons, they can be the source of reasonable responses to the proposals others make to us. I can reject your proposal that we walk to the store together because I was planning to spend the afternoon reading on the porch, and I can reject your offer of marriage because, as Elizabeth Bennet says to Mr. Collins, "you could not make *me* happy."[20]

---

[19] Chandler et al., "Personal Persistance, Identity Development, and Suicide."
[20] Jane Austen, *Pride and Prejudice* (Oxford: Oxford University Press, 2004), vol. I, ch. XIX, 82.

9

Intelligible Responses

9.1 Intelligibility Revisited

The last two chapters argued that the norms of the activity of reasoning require that in reasoning with each other, we maintain our integrity, so as to be able to subject the proposals we make to one another to criticism. Doing so denies these proposals dictatorial authority, and thus makes it possible for them to establish the authority of connection, and so to count as reasons. On the basis of this requirement, we can make reference to our ends and commitments and our need to maintain integrity in our responses to the proposals others make to us, and this explains, from within the social picture, how these kinds of considerations play a role in reasoning. But there are two classes of reasons that we have not yet found a basis for in the social picture: instrumental reasons and reasons that rely on the basic inferential schemas of theoretical reason. These kinds of reasons are so basic to our understanding of what reasons we face and what reasoning is, that no picture of reasoning could plausibly be considered a picture of *reasoning* if it did not include reference to such considerations as legitimate moves in the activity of reasoning. Completing the social picture requires finding a place within it for responses to proposals which advert to the relation of means to ends and to such inferential patterns as those of deductive logic, induction, and inference to the best explanation.[1]

The activity of reasoning as described on the social picture involves the interactive process of inviting others to take what we say as speaking for them as well in a way that is fully open to their criticism, reciprocal, and

---

[1] In listing all of these forms of inference as of a piece, I do not mean to make any substantive claim about whether they are all equally valid forms of inference. I mean only to suggest that these are the types of patterns that we rely on in theoretical reasoning, and so the kinds of patterns that we should have some way of investigating and grounding in the social picture.

responsive. So a place for instrumental reasons within the social picture would make clear why pointing to something like the relation between means and ends is a legitimate move in this interactive process. It would make clear why someone who is wary of an invitation to share a space of reasons or endorse a conclusion that is claimed to follow from that space should be reassured by our pointing out how it fits into a means–ends pattern, or how it is an example of inference to the best explanation or supported by deductive principles. And it should make clear why a criticism of an invitation that points to its violation of such principles should carry weight. As with the reasonable responses investigated in the last chapter, the necessary grounds are to be found within the norms of reasoning that support these kinds of responses, that show them to be reasonable.

These principles support reasonable responses because failure to follow them would render what we say and do unintelligible. Recall that mutual intelligibility is not merely a requirement of reasoning, but of the broader category of conversation. Rooting these kinds of moves in the broader category gives us a way of understanding the widespread sense that these principles are more firmly rooted than those that appeal to particular ends or prudential or moral considerations. In order to engage in genuine conversation, we need to agree on a number of points, not always and without fail, but generally and widely enough to make communication possible. We have to agree on the references of our words, and more generally on a wider shared background or form of life that allows us to project words meaningfully into new uses and to understand the point of our saying what we say to one another. These requirements are gathered together under the norms of mutual intelligibility. Mutual intelligibility is an admittedly loose notion, as befits a norm of an activity as loose as conversation. But despite its looseness, it does generate certain requirements, among which are those that support reference to means–end relationships and schemas of theoretical reasoning.

If what I say to you is unintelligible to you that means that you cannot interpret what I say as bearing meaning, that, at least to you, it is nonsense. When we think of nonsensical utterances, we are likely, at first, to think of examples like "all mimsy were the borogoves," from Lewis Carroll's "Jabberwocky." What makes this sentence meaningless is that two of its words are not English words, and so are not themselves capable of bearing meaning in an English sentence. This kind of example pushes us towards a view that holds that individual words are the fundamental bearers of meaning, and that understanding a sentence is a matter of understanding each of its words. But in the discussion of casual conversation in Chapter 3 it was argued that I can understand each of the words you utter and yet not understand what you are saying in uttering them. One way to understand that idea is that the fundamental bearer of meaning in language is not the word but the sentence. On such a view, individual words get their meaning from their place within a sentence and not the other way around. What gives a sentence meaning is not only that all of its parts are capable of bearing meaning, but that the arrangement of its parts follows a set of grammatical rules that make it a well-formed sentence.[2] In fact, the claims from Chapter 3 extend this idea further, beyond the mere arrangement of the parts of a sentence to include the context of its utterance. To say that I cannot understand what you are saying without understanding your point in saying it, here and now, to me, is to say that the meaning of what you say is not entirely determined by the arrangement of the words you utter into sentences. So, the requirement of intelligibility with regard to what we say amounts to requiring that we follow sets of rules that govern the form of what we say, the relation of its parts to one another, and their context.

Part of the context of our utterances is both our beliefs and our actions and how these relate to various facts about the world, and to various practices, assumptions, and commitments that shape what I call, following Wittgenstein, our form of life. This context means that I can fail to be intelligible to you while uttering an otherwise meaningful sentence if that sentence does not bear the proper relationship to these things beyond it. If I believe that the sky is blue, and the evidence for its being blue is, as it were, as plain as day, then if I say to you, "The sky is really orange," my statement is properly regarded as nonsense. Though you can clearly understand not only each of the words but how they arrange themselves here into a thought, you cannot, as it stands, have any way of making sense of the thought it expresses as meaningful against the backdrop of a pure blue sky. Though the content of what I say is also false, you would be remiss in your response to me if you merely said, "No it isn't. It's blue," unless various

---

[2] For discussion of this claim and defense of a strong form of it that denies that the parts of a sentence can bear meaning independently and traces this idea to Frege and Wittgenstein, see Cora Diamond, "What Nonsense Might Be," *Philosophy* 56, no. 215 (January 1981): 5–22, and James Conant, "Wittgenstein on Meaning and Use," *Philosophical Investigations* 21, no. 3 (July 1998): 222–50.

special circumstances obtained. Perhaps you know that I am color blind, or am still learning my English color words. In such cases, telling me that the sky is blue is not so much registering a contrary proposition about the color of the sky, but correcting my use of certain terms. But barring circumstances like these, a proper reply to such a statement would be to ask, "What do you mean, the sky is orange?" In this case, the failure of intelligibility lies in the relationship between my words and my beliefs, and perhaps the evidence for them. But a similar problem can arise before I say anything. If my beliefs do not properly cohere, then there is nothing I can say that bears the proper relationship to them to be a bearer of meaning. If I believe that all men are mortal, Socrates is a man, and Socrates is immortal, then nothing I say that invokes these concepts can bear the proper relationship to all three of these beliefs. So the requirement that I speak intelligibly extends beyond my words not only to the individual beliefs I have, but to my system of beliefs.

Talk of meaning gets a clear purchase in the case of sentences and even the relation of sentences to beliefs and the evidence for those beliefs. But it may seem as if this language will not be helpful for thinking about actions, and reasoning about actions. There are, however, analogues in the sphere of action to the various forms of nonsense discussed above. There are a whole repertoire of bodily movements that we describe as essentially meaningless, such as jerks and twitches. What makes a movement a twitch, for instance, is not that it is small or quick, or even that it is not under our conscious control, but that it is, in a sense, meaningless. If I ask why you moved your arm as you just did, and you tell me, "it was a twitch" what you are saying is that there was no point in it, it was not the sort of movement that could be made sense of. Twitches, then, are like nonsense words.[3] I can also fail to act intelligibly if the arrangement of the parts of my action do not follow certain formal guidelines. In particular, it looks like what I do cannot be made sense of as an action if it aims at no end or aims at an end to which it is not a means. To borrow an example of Elizabeth Anscombe's, if I continue to pump the handle of a water pump in order to fill a bucket, knowing that there is a hole in the pipe that prevents the pump from working, then you

---

[3] It is, I think, the recognition of something like this point that leads Elizabeth Anscombe to characterize intentional actions as "actions to which a certain sense of the question 'Why?' is given application," which is to say at the very least actions that can bear a certain kind of meaning or intelligibility because they exhibit a certain pattern of coherence. G. E. M. Anscombe, *Intention* (Oxford: Basil Blackwell, 1957), 9.

might say to me, "I don't understand what you are doing." In a case like this one, it is not only that my action cannot bear the analogue of meaning, cannot be a sensible action, but that there is no way for me to talk meaningfully about this action, considered not only as the physical movement of the pump handle, but the performance of this movement in order to fill the bucket. There is no intelligible response to my implied challenge that does not disavow the behavior or its end.

Christine Korsgaard nicely brings out the parallels between the arrangement of our beliefs and the arrangement of our behavior and our ends in our ability to be intelligible in the following passage:

> trying to persuade someone who actually doubted the instrumental principle that she should act on it would be like trying to persuade someone who actually doubted the principle of non-contradiction that he should believe it. It would be *exactly* like that. When Aristotle said that trying to persuade someone of the principle of non-contradiction is like trying to argue with a vegetable, he was not just being abusive. A person who denies the principle of non-contradiction asserts that anything may follow from anything, and that therefore he is committed to nothing . . . [Such a person] does not reject a particular restriction on his beliefs, he rejects the very project of having beliefs. And parallel points can be made about someone who denies the instrumental principle.[4]

There are many deep and controversial questions in these waters that occupy philosophers of action and philosophers of language, and, while I do not engage them here, I do not mean to deny their difficulty. My aim so far has been merely to render plausible the thought that the requirement of mutual intelligibility found among the norms of conversation might reach beyond our choices of words into the arrangement of our beliefs and actions. This provides a way for the requirement of intelligibility to ground our reference to principles of instrumental reason or the schemas of theoretical reason as we reason.

When what I say or what I do appears unintelligible to you, you might challenge me to explain myself. "What, precisely, do you think you are

---

[4] Christine Korsgaard, "The Normativity of Instrumental Reason," in *The Constitution of Agency* 27–68 (Oxford: Oxford University Press, 1998), 61. Korsgaard goes on to say that someone who rejected the instrumental principle would be rejecting "self-conscious action itself." I ultimately want to draw a slightly different conclusion: that it amounts to a rejection of meaningful action itself. Whether all self-conscious action must be meaningful or all meaningful action self-conscious are questions that I leave aside.

doing?" "What, exactly, do you mean?" And one way to understand the requirement of intelligibility in conversation is that such questions are always admissible when asked sincerely. Moreover, they require the kind of response that can render one's words or actions intelligible. If I can point to a feature of what I have said or done that renders it intelligible to you, then I have given you an adequate response to this challenge, and if you do not understand what I have said or done, then you can legitimately challenge its intelligibility within our conversation. So, the requirement of mutual intelligibility on conversation authorizes our reference to features of an action or utterance that determines its intelligibility.

The rest of the chapter argues that among these features are conformity to principles of instrumental reason and the basic schemas of theoretical reasoning. Reference to these principles, then, count as legitimate moves in the social activity of reasoning. This case does not rest on a particular view about the nature of action or even intentional action, or about language or belief beyond the basic point above about sense inhering in the arrangement of parts into a whole.[5] But it does go beyond merely claiming that violation of these principles makes us unintelligible. According to the social picture of reasoning, it is the intelligibility brought out by our citation of these principles that make them principles of reason and not the other way around. Merely showing that reference to a certain pattern or relation is sufficient to render some utterance or action intelligible is enough to show why it can function as a reason in the course of our reasoning. No further grounding in the nature of action or the world would be necessary. In addition, reference to these further grounds does not function as a reason in cases where they do not also render the action or utterance intelligible.

9.2 The Intelligibility of Means–Ends Relations

Explanations of action that invoke instrumental relations are, barring special circumstances, not only generally intelligible, but often work by rendering intelligible the action they aim to explain. As I put on my coat and head for the door, I call out that I am headed to the local sandwich shop. "Why?"

---

[5] Though I am sympathetic to the fuller Fregean/Wittgensteinian claim that the meaning of parts is only graspable via the meaning of the whole, I do not, as far as I can see, rely on it in the arguments here.

you ask. "In order to get some lunch," I reply. Here, I connect my behavior (walking to the local sandwich shop) to an end (getting some lunch) to which it is a clear means. In doing so, I show you that my behavior and my end form a coherent whole of the sort that can bear the practical analogue of meaning. In fact, we can understand both your question and my response as turning on the precise specification of my action. That is, instead of asking "why are you doing that?" you might have asked, "What, precisely, are you doing?" Offering you the end I have in view is a way of saying that I am going to the sandwich shop in order to get some lunch rather than, say, to get some exercise, or repay some money I borrowed from my friend who works there. In more fully specifying the action I am undertaking, I make certain other aspects of what I am doing intelligible and accept other constraints on how I carry out the action in question. If I am going to get some lunch, then I will need to give a further explanation of what I am doing if I have just eaten or you know that I have no way of actually paying for my lunch. Neither of these is important if I am going to get some exercise, although in this case the fact that the sandwich shop is at the corner renders this answer subject to further challenge. Adverting to means–end relations is thus a way of making it clear what the point of my doing one thing rather than another is, and thus treating my behavior as if it could be the bearer of meaning. In doing so, I situate it in a space of reasons, by making certain kinds of questions and challenges intelligible and others not. That we can render our behavior intelligible by pointing to our ends in undertaking it has led many philosophers to suggest that the proper relation of ends and means is somehow deeply built into the structure of action.[6]

Whether or not that suggestion is correct, the relation of an action to its end is part of its logical or grammatical structure, part of, as Wittgenstein or Brandom might say, the language game of giving and asking for reasons.[7] It is this fact about grammatical structure that is the salient one from the perspective of the social picture. In other words, what explains why pointing out the end of my action can serve as a legitimate move in a stretch of reasoning is not that I have pointed to some underlying fact about the structure of action (even if I have), but that I have made what I am doing or saying about it

---

[6] See, for instance, Christine Korsgaard, *Self-Constitution* (Oxford: Oxford University Press, 2009). Candace Vogler, *Reasonably Vicious* (Cambridge, MA: Harvard University Press, 2002).

[7] Ludwig Wittgenstein, *Philosophical Investigations*, trans. G. E. M. Anscombe (Oxford: Wiley-Blackwell, 1991). Robert Brandom, *Making It Explicit* (Cambridge, MA: Harvard University Press, 1998).

intelligible. To see that it is the rendering intelligible that is doing the work in legitimating this move in reasoning, note that relating my action to its ends will not always work. Return, for instance, to the example of the conversation about crossing the street in Germany: "Why are you crossing the street?" "Because the restaurant is over there." "Yes, but the light is red."

Here, in the context of a set of social norms about not crossing the street on a red light, the mere fact that crossing the street is a means to getting to the restaurant does not serve as an appropriate reason for crossing the street. By pointing to the end of my action when what was confusing about it was its violation of a norm I do not render what I am doing intelligible. As a result, pointing out my end does not carry the normative force it did in the sandwich case, not because I have failed to sufficiently describe the structure of my action, but because I have not cleared up the feature of the action that was not fully intelligible to my host.

In such a case, the problem of lack of mutual intelligibility has to do as much with the questions being asked as with the structure of the action. When my host asks "why did you cross the street?" it turns out that we do not share enough of a common background for me to understand what he is saying, because I have not yet grasped his point in asking me. I have understood him to mean, "what is your end?" and he has meant to ask, "what is your justification for violating a norm?" So it seems as if the adequacy of certain references to the causal chains that make up means—end relationships, or the conceptual ones that make up part—whole relationships, depend in part on further background agreement. Not every such chain answers the what or why demand others make of us. Such relationships do the work we want of them when they are intelligible to our interlocutor as answers to his questions and not when not. Of course, faced with such failures of communication, we can respond by looking for a clearer understanding.

Moreover, there are plenty of cases where adverting to features of my action that do not locate it in a casual stream of means and ends nevertheless renders what I am doing intelligible. In these cases, we take such references to be reasonable responses to our queries. The clearest such cases involve symbolic actions, actions that are somehow supposed to represent or express something without thereby bringing something else about or being constitutive of it. Here, the arrangement of parts that gives an action meaning is not that of means and ends, but of action and expression. In some religions, worshippers kneel to pray, while in others they stand. To the question, "Why are you kneeling to pray?" one might respond that it shows respect for God or humility in offering a prayer. Such a response does not point to a means–end relationship: kneeling is not a way of bringing about respect, as if the posture had internal physiological effects that brought on the attitude, and it is not exactly part of showing respect: I can show respect without kneeling, and kneel in the process of denying respect. It is, according to a certain set of understandings and social practices, a sign of respect, just as according to other practices, standing is. The mention of respect serves as an adequate response to the why question by rendering the action intelligible, by giving its meaning, and it does that by connecting it to something like a form of life, rather than a causal relationship. Furthermore, the criterion of intelligibility also gives us a way to distinguish symbolic meaning or rituals that we think can ground reasons from idiosyncratic and neurotic or psychotic beliefs that cannot. This is just to reiterate the point about the publicity of reasons from Chapter 5. What went wrong with John Nash's responses to the voices he heard was not that some suggested casually efficacious actions and others did not. We can imagine that both those that proposed solutions to mathematical problems and those that sent him on secret missions for the CIA arguably told him to take appropriate means to ends he had. It was, rather, that only the former could eventually be made intelligible to others, could be the basis of genuine conversations.[8] Similarly, the response about kneeling to show respect relies on a background under-standing that kneeling can signify respect and is not, for instance, only a means of lowering one's head so as to more easily read something written close to the ground.

9.3 The Intelligibility of Inferential Schema

The terrain of discussion about the basic principles of theoretical reason is more vast and more filled with disagreement than that about principles of practical reason. While there is the kind of general agreement about the

---

[8] Sylvia Nasar, *A Beautiful Mind* (New York: Simon & Schuster, 1998). For a Freudian discussion of the difference between private and public interpretations of one's actions, see Jonathan Lear, *Open Minded: Working Out the Logic of the Soul* (Cambridge, MA: Harvard University Press, 1998), esp. the chapter entitled, "Restlessness, Phantasy, and the Concept of Mind."

principle of non-contradiction that there is about the principle of instrumental reason, beyond that things become more complicated. There are
debates about the status, beyond the principle of non-contradiction, of the
other axioms of first order logic, the truths of mathematics, the basic laws of
physics and the special sciences, and various forms of inference such as
inference to the best explanation. Working through these debates with an
eye to fitting some of the positions taken there into the social picture would
require a whole other book. Rather than try to cram even a précis of such a
book into these final pages, I offer a more general outline of an approach
that would tie such schemas to a requirement on intelligibility. Such an
approach would put whichever such schema we find central to making our
assertions intelligible at the disposal of those who are engaged in the activity
of reasoning described by the social picture.

As we saw above, the principle of instrumental reason requires that
certain patterns of coherence hold among our ends and our actions in
order for those actions to be intelligible, the possible bearers of the practical
analogue of meaning. We can similarly think of the basic schema of
theoretical reasoning as requiring patterns of coherence among our beliefs,
the world, and our assertions that make it possible for our assertions to be
meaningful. What threatens to render my assertion that the sky is orange not
just false but nonsensical is that there is not a way to understand the
constellation of my beliefs, the evidence available to me, and perhaps
other things I have asserted as exhibiting the necessary pattern of coherence.
So if you challenge my assertion by claiming that you find it unintelligible,
I have to respond to that challenge by exhibiting such a pattern.

Robert Brandom's account of how assertions both bear meaning and
involve us in the game of giving and asking for reasons provides a handy
language in which to develop this idea.[9] Brandom describes the patterns of
coherence above as patterns of inferential commitments. The idea is that in
making an assertion, I commit myself not only to the truth of its content,
but also a whole host of other claims that follow from it. So, for instance, in
asserting that the sky is orange, I commit myself to it not being blue, to it
being colored, and so forth. It also entitles you to ascribe these further beliefs
to me. I must accept these commitments in making assertions if my assertions are to be intelligible, to be possible bearers of meaning. One of the

---

[9] *Making It Explicit.*

ways that my claim that the sky is orange can fail to be intelligible is if I do not thereby license you to ascribe to me the belief that the sky is not blue. Just as with the case of violations of the instrumental principle, in the face of failures to exhibit the required patterns of inferential commitment, you can ask what I mean by a given assertion. If I assert that the sky is orange, but refuse to deny that it is blue, you can intelligibly ask what I am saying. And answering your request that I start making sense involves interpreting my assertion in a way that shows that I can in fact exhibit the necessary coherence. A similar argument could be deployed about principles guiding our reliance on evidence or our calculation of probabilities or the avoidance of certain basic fallacies. In each case, someone who violates such principles fails to exhibit a kind of coherence in their inferential commitments that makes interpreting their assertions as intelligible difficult. And citing these principles in our challenges can be understood as inviting others to show us how their pattern of commitments is in fact sufficiently coherent to allow for meaning, or changing their commitments if they cannot. I take it that something like this is the work that Frederick Douglass hopes his refusal to argue that the slave is a man will play in his argument against slavery. By pointing out to the slave-owner that he is committed by his action to already accepting the proposition that the slave is a man, Douglass challenges the slave-owner to show how his commitment to this proposition can be squared with acceptance of the institution of slavery, and to change if he cannot.

This shows, then, that the requirement of mutual intelligibility on conversation makes references to such principles and criticisms of assertions that violate them acceptable moves within conversation and within reasoning. If we are to be intelligible to one another, we have to accept the same requirements on the coherence of our patterns of inferential commitments. This does not mean that we have to agree in our judgments about what those commitments commit us to. We can intelligibly disagree about whether pride is a virtue or a vice or whether there is sufficient evidence to conclude that the butler did it. But in order to have that disagreement, we have to agree in our commitment to maintaining certain patterns of coherence. Or as Wittgenstein says, we have to agree in forms of life.[10]

---

[10] Wittgenstein, *Philosophical Investigations*, §§241–2.

Of course, as with reliance on the instrumental principle, the question now arises whether these references are intelligible because of the independent truth of the principles in question, or whether it is their role in rendering us intelligible to one another that grants them the authority they have as we reason. To see that their authority might rest only on their capacity to render us intelligible, it helps, as with the instrumental principle, to consider cases where intelligibility and the exhibition of certain patterns of coherence come apart. Consider, first, a case where someone says something that I challenge because, taken as an assertion, it leaves her failing to exhibit the necessary pattern of coherence among what she says, what she believes, and her available evidence. She might respond by explaining that she didn't mean to make an assertion of fact, but was speaking poetically or merely making a joke. There are all sorts of things we can do with our words beyond making assertions, and in the context of forms of life where they are licensed under certain contexts, we can make ourselves intelligible as doing these things without thereby demonstrating a pattern of coherence that includes what we have said taken as an assertion. Such a response renders what someone says sufficiently intelligible to meet the demands of conversation, even if what was said, taken as an assertion, violates whatever principles of theoretical reason we accept.

The fact that we can do all sorts of things by uttering sentences can also make reference to the principles of theoretical reason an insufficient answer to a charge of unintelligibility. Living together involves more than debates about our entitlement to make assertions and one can fail to be intelligible in any number of circumstances without violating the principles of theoretical reason. I might find it hard to understand what you are doing or saying because it violates more particular norms of our interaction, or our roles within some more particular practice, even though nothing you say is meaningless in a more general sense. Take, for instance, Mrs. Bennet, who complains to her husband who is continually making eminently sensible, if sarcastic, remarks that exhibit a clear sense of inferential coherence that "you take delight in vexing me. You have no compassion on my poor nerves."[11] She is, in essence, saying that she does not understand what he is playing at, that he is not following what she understands to be his role as her husband: to coddle her wishful thinking and not stand in the way of

---

[11] Jane Austen, *Pride and Prejudice* (Oxford: Oxford University Press, 2004), vol. I, ch. I, 2.

her effort to get their daughters married. Her failure to understand him is not because his words violate a schema of theoretical reason. In response to such a complaint, it is not be enough for him to show her that he is entitled by his beliefs and evidence and former statements to say what he has said, or that he is further willing to accept the inferential commitments his assertions establish. His unintelligibility to her does not lie there, and so adverting to it is not a proper response to her challenge. Nevertheless, her failure to understand her husband does mean that they are not really conversing with one another, that they are talking past one another (or at least, that he is talking past her). Her challenge then, is a legitimate one, even if it does not turn on the violation of principles of theoretical reason.

9.4 A Reason to Reason

The foregoing discussions aimed to make plausible the idea that we can approach the question of the importance and normativity of instrumental reasons and various basic patterns of inference not directly or only through their connection to the causal order of things and the way that structures or rationalizes our thoughts and behavior, but through their place within our conversations and their capacity to render what we say and do intelligible to one another. This need not imply that everything there is to say about these forms of reasoning can be rendered in the idiom of intelligibility. But it does provide grounds for thinking that there are well-established spaces within the social picture for responding to one another's proposals by citing these basic principles of reason and adverting to the connections they support.

What these discussions do not establish is that the underlying structure of these grounds bottoms out in intelligibility and not something like the causal structure of the world. Everything said above could hold and yet it still be true that what renders reference to the end of an action intelligible is nothing about the criteria of intelligibility themselves, but the fact that I am pointing to a genuinely relevant fact. It turns out, however, that the question of what explains what at this level is irrelevant to working out the range of reasonable responses we can make while reasoning. In sketching a social picture of reasoning, I am working out the details of a particular activity we might engage in. If we can understand what engaging in this activity requires and see the point in doing so, it does not matter to what degree the rules of this activity find further support in something beyond it. Intelligibility within this activity may very well track features of the world beyond this activity. It would be surprising for such an activity to persist in the absence of such connections. But it is not these connections that determine the legitimacy of moves within the activity. These must be determined by the rules of the activity itself. To take a close analogy: it would be surprising to find a human society communicating in a language that had no resources for accurately describing the world in a way that allowed its speakers to fruitfully and reliably interact with their environment. But constructing a meaningful sentence in any particular language depends on the rules of that language, not the way it picks out objects in the world or whether its way of doing that can withstand critical scrutiny. For one thing, it may be possible to express ideas in that language that have no corresponding basis in the real world. Similarly, the question of why reference to a given pattern of inference or familiar principle of reason is a legitimate move as we reason together must be answered by appeal to the norms of that activity, and such an answer will be complete. Answering such questions, however, does not tell us whether this is an activity we want to engage in, just as figuring out whether a sentence is well formed in a given language does not tell us if that language is one we want to speak, or what its strengths and weaknesses as a language are. This book has tried to answer these questions about the activity of reasoning by exhibiting some of the attractions of the form of living together reasoning makes possible. It is worth briefly recalling one of them. If our criterion for the appropriateness of certain responses as we converse and reason is that they maintain or help to foster mutual intelligibility, then we are led to a certain set of attitudes and practices in the face of failures to reason together. Mutual intelligibility is, after all, a relational property, and being mutually unintelligible may require movement and explanation and efforts at greater understanding on my part as much as yours. If I see our problem as one of a lack of mutual intelligibility rather than your being irrational, then the kinds of responses I am likely to be moved to make are very different. If I regard your claims or actions as irrational, in violation of a set of theoretically and finally grounded principles, then I approach our failure to engage with one another as lying with you, and if I want to overcome this failure, I look for ways to bring you to reason, perhaps by trying to persuade or convince you of my position, perhaps by non-rational forms of manipulation and coercion (seeing as you are clearly not fully rational). If, however, I diagnose our failure as a lack of mutual intelligibility, then it is as likely to result from my failure to understand you as it is to be a result of your failure to conform to my framework for understanding. Faced with a breakdown of communication, I can ask you to explain what you have said or done, not in the way that a parent scolds a wayward child, but in the way a student asks a teacher, to help me past my failure to understand you. Your response can then further elucidate what you have said, or exhibit a background commitment or understanding that you take to explain the breakdown, or it can lead you to rethink whether you want to continue to stand behind what you have said or done. Understanding each other does not require that we agree with one another, and so being reasonable does not demand that we should or even can always adjust our position in a search for accommodation. But overcoming failures of intelligibility by seeking mutual understanding, as the social picture suggests we need to do in order to reason, is itself a process of inviting others to find words that we can in turn hear as invitations. Doing so is not a matter of bringing them to reason but rather of reasoning with them.

9.5 Conclusion: Proposals and Invitations

I began this book by casting Jane Austen's Elizabeth Bennet as an archetypal rational creature in order to suggest that our standard ways of thinking about reasons and reasoning are not fit to offer such a creature the proposals she warrants. When we rely on our standard pictures of reasoning, we too often come off sounding like Mr. Collins. And, so, it is only natural, now that we have at our disposal an alternative social picture of reasoning, to ask whether it does any better. Are we, equipped with the work of this book, in any better position to offer proposals to rational creatures?

In the course of *Pride and Prejudice*, Elizabeth Bennet receives three proposals of marriage: one from Mr. Collins and two from Mr. Darcy. She rejects two and accepts one. And while the ground for her acceptance of the final proposal is well prepared by the novel as a whole, when it finally comes, it is, on its own, hardly remarkable:

After a short pause, her companion added, "You are too generous to trifle with me. If your feelings are still what they were last April, tell me so at once. *My* affections and wishes are unchanged, but one word from you will silence me on this subject for ever."

Elizabeth feeling all the more than common awkwardness and anxiety of his situation, now forced herself to speak; and immediately, though not very fluently, gave him to understand, that her sentiments had undergone so material a change, since the period to which he alluded, as to make her receive with gratitude and pleasure, his present assurances.[12]

What, then, distinguishes this proposal from the others? Mr. Collins, as we have seen, offers her a long-winded set of reasons for his proposal, reasons that profess without inviting and thus which fail to take her seriously as a rational creature. Now it is easy to think that much of Mr. Collins's problem lays in the particular reasons he gives. After all, given that this is a proposal of marriage, one might not fault Elizabeth for expecting more in the way of passion and feelings or concerns for her happiness and less in the way of the kind of general reasons that Mr. Collins offers. But recall that Elizabeth's rejection not only of him as a suitor but his manner of proposing is not based on his lack of feeling, but his failure to treat her as a rational creature. If feeling was what was essential to a proposal, then she could hardly have done better than Mr. Darcy's first attempt: "in vain have I struggled. It will not do. My feelings will not be repressed. You must allow me to tell you how ardently I admire and love you."[13]

Though Elizabeth's rejection of this proposal is rather overdetermined at the moment when it is offered, Mr. Darcy's first proposal has something in common with the proposal from Mr. Collins, something to which our tour through the social picture of reasoning has taught us to be attentive: neither Mr. Collins nor Mr. Darcy in his first proposal, issues an invitation. Both speak in the idiom of command. As we have seen, in commanding or using its idiom, in leaving no room for those with whom we speak to reply or reject what we have said, we are not reasoning with them in the sense I have been developing and thus not offering proposals to rational creatures. Seen in this light, Austen's way of setting up Mr. Darcy's second, successful proposal, warrants more attention. For it is not only that Mr. Darcy has now become a sought after suitor, but that in broaching the topic at hand,

---

[12] Vol. III, ch. XVI, 280.   [13] Ibid. vol. II, ch. XI, 146.

he begins by opening up space for Elizabeth's refusal and signals that it will have an effect on him. By doing so, he makes clear that his words are invitations and not commands, that he wishes to propose without commanding, that he has understood the values of reasoning in the wider activity of living together.

Among those values are the relationships the activity of reasoning makes possible, relationships in which we can offer one another invitations to take our words as speaking for them as well. In order to realize such value, however, we must know when to stop professing and start proposing, to stop talking and writing and start listening. And so while it is tempting to end this book as it began, with the wit and wisdom of Jane Austen, I will try to apply her lessons rather than cite them, and conclude with the traditional device used to mark an invitation as an invitation: the plea for a response. *Répondez s'il vous plaît.*

Bibliography

Alcoff, Linda. "The Problem of Speaking for Others." *Cultural Critique* (winter 1991–2): 5–32.

Allen, Danielle. *Talking to Strangers*. Chicago: University of Chicago Press, 2004.

Anscombe, G. E. M. *Intention*. Oxford: Basil Blackwell, 1957.

Appiah, Kwame Anthony. *In My Father's House*. Oxford: Oxford University Press, 1993.

Arendt, Hannah. *The Human Condition*. Chicago: University of Chicago Press, 1958.

—— "What Is Authority?" In *Between Past and Present*, by Hannah Arendt, 91–142. New York: Penguin, 1961.

—— "On Violence." In *Crises of the Republic*, 103–98. New York: Harcourt Brace, 1972.

Austen, Jane. *Pride and Prejudice*. Oxford: Oxford University Press, 2004.

Austin, J. L. *How to Do Things with Words*. 2nd edn, Cambridge, MA: Harvard University Press, 1975.

Bacharach, Michael. "Interactive Team Reasoning: A Contribution to the Theory of Co-operation." *Research in Economics* 53 (1999): 117–47.

Baier, Annette. "Trust and Anti-Trust." *Ethics* 96, no. 2 (January 1986): 231–60.

Bartky, Sandra. "Foucault, Femininity and the Modernization of Patriarchal Power," in *Femininity and Domination*, by Sandra Bartky, 63–82. New York: Routledge, 1990.

—— "On Psychological Oppression," in *Femininity and Domination*, by Sandra Bartky, 22–32. New York: Routledge, 1990.

Baz, Avner. "On When Words Are Called for: Cavell, McDowell, and the Wording of the World." *Inquiry* 46 (2003): 473–500.

Binmore, Ken. *Game Theory and the Social Contract*. 2 vols. Cambridge, MA: MIT Press, 1994.

Bohman, James, and William Rehg. *Deliberative Democracy*. Cambridge, MA: MIT Press, 1997.

Borrows, James. *Drawing Out Law*. Toronto: University of Toronto Press, 2010.

Brandom, Robert. *Making It Explicit*. Cambridge, MA: Harvard University Press, 1998.

—— *Reason in Philosophy: Animating Ideas*. Cambridge, MA: Harvard University Press, 2009.

Bratman, Michael. "Shared Cooperative Activity." *Philosophical Review* 101, no. 2 (April 1992): 327–41.

—— "Shared Intentions." *Ethics* 104 (October 1993): 97–113.

Brewer, Talbot. *The Retrieval of Ethics*. Oxford: Oxford University Press, 2009.

Brison, Susan. *Aftermath: Violence and the Remaking of the Self*. Princeton, NJ: Princeton University Press, 2001.

Cavell, Stanley. "The Availability of Wittgenstein's Later Philosophy," in *Must We Mean What We Say?*, by Stanley Cavell. New York: Charles Scribner's Sons, 1969.

—— *The Claim of Reason*. Oxford: Oxford University Press, 1979.

—— *Conditions Handsome and Unhandsome*. Chicago: University of Chicago Press, 1991.

—— "Passionate and Performative Utterance," in *Contending with Stanley Cavell*, ed. Russell Goodman, 177–98. Oxford: Oxford University Press, 2005.

Chandler, Michael J., Christopher Lalonde, and Bryan Sokol. "Continuities of Selfhood in the Face of Radical Developmental and Cultural Change," in *Culture, Thought, and Development*, ed. Eliot Turiel, Larry Nucci and Geoffrey Saxe, 65–84. Mahwah, NJ: Lawrence Erlbaum Associates, 2000.

——, Christopher E. Lalonde, Bryan Sokol, Darcy Hallett and James E. Marcia. "Personal Persistence, Identity Development, and Suicide: A Study of Native and Non-Native North American Adolescents." Monographs of the Society of Research in Child Development 68, no. 2 (2003): i–viii, 1–138.

Clark, Herbert, and Susan Brennan. "Conceptual Pacts and Lexical Choice in Conversation." *Journal of Experimental Psychology* 22, no. 6 (1996): 1482–93.

Conant, James. "Wittgenstein on Meaning and Use." *Philosophical Investigations* 21, no. 3 (July 1998): 222–50.

Dancy, Jonathan. *Ethics without Principles*. Oxford: Oxford University Press, 2004.

Darwall, Stephen. *The Second-Person Standpoint: Morality, Respect, and Accountability*. Cambridge, MA: Harvard University Press, 2006.

Deleuze, Gilles and Michel Foucault. "Intellectuals and Power," in *Language, Counter-Memory, Practice*, ed. Donald Bouchard, trans. Donald Bouchard and Sherry Simon. Ithaca, NY: Cornell University Press, 1977.

Diamond, Cora. "What Nonsense Might Be." *Philosophy* 56, no. 215 (January 1981): 5–22.

—— "Anything But Argument." *Philosophical Investigations* 5, no. 1 (January 1982): 23–41.

Dickinson, Amy. *The Mighty Queens of Freeville*. New York: Hyperion, 2009.

DuBois, W. E. B. *The Souls of Black Folk*. New York: Penguin, 1989.

Dunbar, Robin. *Gossip, Grooming and the Origin of Language*. Cambridge, MA: Harvard University Press, 1997.

Eggins, Suzanne and Diana Slade. *Analysing Casual Conversation*. London: Continuum, 1997.

Flavell, John H. "Cognitive Development: Children's Knowledge of the Mind." *Annual Review of Psychology* 50 (1999): 21–45.

Forst, Rainer. *The Right to Justification,* trans. Jeffrey Flynn. New York: Columbia University Press, 2011.

Foucault, Michel. *Discipline and Punish*. New York: Random House, 1975.

—— "Polemics, Politics, and Problematizations," in *The Foucault Reader*, by Michel Foucault, ed. Paul Rabinow, 381–90. London: Penguin, 1984.

—— "What Is Enlightenment?," in *The Foucault Reader*, by Michel Foucault, ed. Paul Rabinow, 32–50. New York: Pantheon, 1984.

Frankfurt, Harry. "Identification and Wholeheartedness," in *The Importance of What We Care About*, by Harry Frankfurt, 159–76. Cambridge: Cambridge University Press, 1988.

Freeman, Samuel. "Reason and Agreement in Social Contract Views." *Philosophy and Public Affairs* 19, no. 2 (spring 1990): 122–57.

Gaita, Raimond. "Forms of the Unthinkable," in *A Common Humanity*, by Raimond Gaita, 171–86. London: Routledge, 1998.

Gauthier, David. *Morals by Agreement*. Oxford: Oxford University Press, 1986.

Gilbert, Margaret. *On Social Facts*. Princeton, NJ: Princeton University Press, 1989.

Goffman, Erving. "Alienation from Interaction," in *Interaction Ritual: Essays on Face-to-Face Behavior*, by Erving Goffman, 113–36. New York: Pantheon, 1982.

Habermas, Jürgen. "What Is Universal Pragmatics?," in *Communication and the Evolution of Society*, trans. Thomas McCarthy. Boston: Beacon Press, 1979.

—— *The Theory of Communicative Action*, trans. Thomas McCarthy. 2 vols. Boston: Beacon Press, 1984.

—— "Discourse Ethics: Notes on a Program of Philosophical Justification," in *Moral Consciousness and Communicative Action*, trans. Christian Lenhart and Shierry Weber Nicholsen. Cambridge, MA: MIT Press, 1990.

—— "From Kant to Hegel: On Robert Brandom's Pragmatic Philosophy of Language," in *Truth and Justification*, ed. and trans. Barbara Fultner. Cambridge, MA: MIT Press, 2003.

Hampton, Jean. *The Authority of Reason*. Cambridge: Cambridge University Press, 1996.

Hardimon, Michael. *Hegel's Social Philosophy: The Project of Reconciliation*. Cambridge: Cambridge University Press, 1994.

Hegel, G. W. F. *Elements of the Philosophy of Right,* ed. Allen Wood, trans. H. B. Nisbet. Cambridge: Cambridge University Press, 1991.

Heidegger, Martin. *Being and Time,* trans. John Macquarrie and Edward Robinson. Oxford: Wiley-Blackwell, 2000.

Hobbes, Thomas. *Leviathan,* ed. Richard Tuck. Cambridge: Cambridge University Press, 1991.

Honig, Bonnie. *Political Theory and the Displacement of Politics.* Ithaca, NY: Cornell University Press, 1993.

Honneth, Axel. *The Struggle for Recognition,* trans. Joel Anderson. Cambridge, MA: MIT Press, 1996.

Kant, Immanuel. *Critique of Pure Reason,* trans. Norman Kemp Smith. New York: St. Martin's Press, 1933.

—— "An Answer to the Question: What Is Enlightenment?," in *Kant's Political Writings*, by Immanuel Kant, ed. Hans Reiss, 54–60. Cambridge: Cambridge University Press, 1991.

—— *Groundwork of the Metaphysics of Morals,* ed. and trans. Mary Gregor. Cambridge: Cambridge University Press, 1998.

Kelly, Erin. "Human Rights as Foreign Policy Imperatives," in *The Ethics of Assistance: Morality and the Distant Needy*, ed. D. Chatterjee. Cambridge: Cambridge University Press, 2004.

Korsgaard, Christine. "The Reasons We Can Share," in *Creating the Kingdom of Ends*, by Christine Korsgaard, 275–310. Cambridge: Cambridge University Press, 1996.

—— "Skepticism about Practical Reason," in *Constructing the Kingdom of Ends*, by Christine Korsgaard, 311–34. Cambridge: Cambridge University Press, 1996.

—— *The Sources of Normativity.* Cambridge: Cambridge University Press, 1996.

—— "Autonomy and the Second Person Within." *Ethics* (University of Chicago Press) 118 (October 2007): 8–23.

—— "The Normativity of Instrumental Reasons," in *The Constitution of Agency*, by Christine Korsgaard, 27–68. Oxford: Oxford University Press, 2008.

—— *Self-Constitution.* Oxford: Oxford University Press, 2009.

Laden, Anthony Simon. "Outline of a Theory of Reasonable Deliberation." *Canadian Journal of Philosophy* 30 (December 2000): 551–80.

—— *Reasonably Radical: Deliberative Liberalism and the Politics of Identity.* Ithaca, NY: Cornell University Press, 2001.

—— "Democratic Legitimacy and the 2000 Election." *Law and Philosophy* 21 (2002): 197–220.

—— "Radical Feminists, Reasonable Liberals: Reason, Power and Objectivity in the work of MacKinnon and Rawls." *Journal of Political Philosophy* 11, no. 2 (2003): 133–52.

—— "Evaluating Social Reasons: Hobbes vs. Hegel." *Journal of Philosophy* 102, no. 7 (July 2005): 327–56.

—— "Negotiation, Deliberation and the Claims of Politics," in *Multiculturalism and Political Theory*, ed. Anthony Simon Laden and David Owen, 198–217. Cambridge: Cambridge University Press, 2007.

——— "Reasonable Deliberation, Constructive Power and the Struggle for Recognition," in *Recognition and Power*, ed. Bert van den Brink and David Owen, 270–89. Cambridge: Cambridge University Press, 2007.

——— "The Trouble with Prudence." *Philosophical Explorations* 12, no. 1 (2009): 19–40.

——— "The Justice of Justification," in *Habermas and Rawls: Disputing the Political*. New York: Routledge, 2010.

——— "Learning to be Equal: Just Schools and Schools of Justice," in *Education, Justice and Democracy*, by Danielle Allen and Rob Reich. Chicago: University of Chicago Press, 2012.

Lear, Jonathan. *Open Minded: Working Out the Logic of the Soul*. Cambridge, MA: Harvard University Press, 1998.

Locke, John. *Second Treatise of Government,* ed. C. B. Macpherson. Indianapolis: Hackett, 1980.

Lugones, María, and Elizabeth Spelman. "Have We Got a Theory for You!," in *Hypatia Reborn*, ed. Azizah al-Hibri and Margaret Simons. Bloomington: Indiana University Press, 1990.

Lureau, Annette. *Unequal Childhoods: Class, Race and Family Life*. Berkeley: University of California Press, 2003.

McDowell, John. "Virtue and Reason." *Monist* 62, no. 3 (July 1979): 331–50.

MacKinnon, Catharine. "Difference and Dominance: On Sex Discrimination," in *Feminism Unmodified*, by Catharine MacKinnon, 32–44. Cambridge, MA: Harvard University Press, 1987.

——— *Towards a Feminist Theory of the State*. Cambridge, MA: Harvard University Press, 1989.

Markell, Patchen. "The Rule of the People: Arendt, Archê, and Democracy." *American Political Science Review* 100, no. 1 (February 2006): 1–14.

Millgram, Elijah. "Incommensurability and Practical Reason," in *Incommensurability, Incomparability and Practical Reason*, ed. Ruth Chang, 151–69. Cambridge, MA: Harvard University Press, 1997.

——— *Practical Induction*. Cambridge, MA: Harvard University Press, 1997.

Mills, Charles. *The Racial Contract*. Ithaca, NY: Cornell University Press, 1997.

Morreal, John. "Gossip and Humor," in *Good Gossip*, ed. Robert Goodman and Aaron Ben-Ze'ev, 56–64. Lawrence, KS: University of Kansas Press, 1994.

Nagel, Thomas. *The Possibility of Altruism*. Princeton, NJ: Princeton University Press, 1970.

Nasar, Sylvia. *A Beautiful Mind*. New York: Simon & Schuster, 1998.

Nietzsche, Friedrich. *On the Genealogy of Morals,* ed. and trans. Walter Kaufmann. New York: Random House, 1967.

Nozick, Robert. *Philosophical Explanations*. Cambridge, MA: Harvard University Press, 1981.

O'Neill, Onora. "Reason and Politics in the Kantian Enterprise," in *Constructions of Reason*, by Onora O'Neill, 3–27. Cambridge: Cambridge University Press, 1989.

—— "Justice, Gender, and International Boundaries," in *The Quality of Life*, ed. Martha Nussbaum and Amartya Sen, 303–23. Oxford: Oxford University Press, 1993.

—— *Towards Justice and Virtue*. Cambridge: Cambridge University Press, 1996.

—— "Four Models of Practical Reasoning," in *Bounds of Justice*, by Onora O'Neill, 11–28. Cambridge: Cambridge University Press, 2000.

Owen, David. "Cultural Diversity and the Conversation of Justice." *Political Theory* 27, no. 5 (October 1999): 579–96.

Pettit, Philip. *Republicanism: A Theory of Freedom and Government*. Oxford: Oxford University Press, 1999.

Pinkard, Terry. *Hegel's Phenomenology: The Sociality of Reason*. Cambridge: Cambridge University Press, 1996.

Pippin, Robert. *Hegel on Self-Consciousness*. Princeton, NJ: Princeton University Press, 2010.

—— *Hegel's Practical Philosophy: Rational Agency as Ethical Life*. Cambridge: Cambridge University Press, 2008.

Rawls, John. "Two Concepts of Rules." *Philosophical Review* 64, no. 1 (January 1955): 3–32.

—— *A Theory of Justice*. Cambridge, MA: Harvard University Press, 1971.

—— *Political Liberalism*. Paperback edn. New York: Columbia University Press, 1996.

—— "The Idea of Public Reason Revisited," in *Collected Papers*, by John Rawls, ed. Samuel Freeman, 573–613. Cambridge, MA: Harvard University Press, 1999.

—— *Lectures on the History of Moral Philosophy,* ed. Barbara Herman. Cambridge, MA: Harvard University Press, 2000.

—— *Justice as Fairness: A Restatement,* ed. Erin Kelly. Cambridge, MA: Harvard University Press, 2001.

Reath, Andrews. "Legislating the Moral Law." *Noûs* 28, no. 4 (December 1994): 435–64.

Rorty, Richard. "Human Rights, Rationality and Sentimentality," in *On Human Rights*, ed. Stephen Shute and Susan Hurley, 111–34. New York: Basic Books, 1993.

Roth, Abe. "Practical Intersubjectivity," in *Socializing Metaphysics*, ed. Frederick Schmitt, 65–92. Lanham, MD: Rowan & Littlefield, 2003.

Rousseau, Jean-Jacques. *Politics and the Arts: Letter to M. d'Alembert on the Theatre,* ed. and trans. Allan Bloom. Glencoe, IL: Free Press, 1960.

—— *Émile,* trans. Allan Bloom. New York: Basic books, 1979.

—— *Reveries of a Solitary Walker,* trans. Peter France. New York: Penguin, 1979.

—— "Discourse on the Origin of Inequality," in *"The Discourses" and Other Early Political Writings*, by Jean-Jacques Rousseau, ed. and trans. Victor Gourevitch. Cambridge: Cambridge University Press, 1997.

—— "The Social Contract," in *The Social Contract and Other Later Political Writings*, by Jean-Jacques Rousseau, ed. and trans. Victor Gourevitch. Cambridge: Cambridge University Press, 1997.

Scanlon, T. M. *What We Owe to Each Other.* Cambridge, MA: Harvard University Press, 1998.

Schapiro, Tamar. "Compliance, Complicity and the Nature of Nonideal Conditions." *Journal of Philosophy* 100, no. 7 (July 2003): 329–55.

Sellars, Wilfrid. *In the Space of Reasons,* ed. Kevin Sharp and Robert Brandom. Cambridge, MA: Harvard University Press, 2007.

Sen, Amartya. "Rational Fools," in *Choice, Welfare and Measurement*, by Amartya Sen. Cambridge, MA: MIT Press, 1982.

Sugden, Robert. "Team Preferences." *Economics and Philosophy* 16 (2000): 175–204.

Tannen, Deborah. *You Just Don't Understand: Women and Men In Conversation.* New York: William Morrow and Co., 1990.

Taylor, Charles. "Explanation and Practical Reason," in *Philosophical Arguments*, by Charles Taylor, 34–60. Cambridge, MA: Harvard University Press, 1995.

—— "To Follow a Rule," in *Philosophical Arguments*, by Charles Taylor, 165–80. Cambridge, MA: Harvard University Press, 1995.

—— "Irreducibly Social Goods," in *Philosophical Arguments*, by Charles Taylor, 127–45. Cambridge, MA: Harvard University Press, 1995.

Tully, James. *Strange Multiplicity.* Cambridge: Cambridge University Press, 1995.

—— *Public Philosophy in a New Key.* 2 vols. Cambridge: Cambridge University Press, 2008.

—— "A New Field of Democracy and Civic Freedom," in *Public Philosophy in a New Key: Volume 1: Democracy and Civic Freedom*, by James Tully, 291–316. Cambridge: Cambridge University Press, 2008.

—— "To Think and Act Differently: Comparing Critical Ethos and Critical Theory." Vol. 1, in *Public Philosophy in a New Key*, by James Tully, 71–132. Cambridge: Cambridge University Press, 2009.

Velleman, David. "Identity and Identification," in *Self to Self*, by J. David Velleman, 330–360. Cambridge: Cambridge University Press, 2006.

—— *Self to Self.* Cambridge: Cambridge University Press, 2006.

—— *How We Get Along.* Cambridge: Cambridge University Press, 2009.

Vogler, Candace. *Reasonably Vicious.* Cambridge, MA: Harvard University Press, 2002.

Warren, Mark, ed. *Democracy and Trust.* Cambridge: Cambridge University Press, 1999.

Williams, Bernard. "Internal and External Reasons," in *Moral Luck*, by Bernard Williams, 101–113. Cambridge: Cambridge University Press, 1982.

—— *Moral Luck*. Cambridge: Cambridge University Press, 1982.

Williams, Melissa. *Voice, Trust, and Memory.* Princeton, NJ: Princeton University Press, 2000.

Wittgenstein, Ludwig. *Philosophical Investigations,* trans. G. E. M. Anscombe. Oxford: Wiley-Blackwell, 1991.

Young, Iris Marion. *Justice and the Politics of Difference.* Princeton, NJ: Princeton University Press, 1990.

—— "Communication and the Other: Beyond Deliberative Democracy," in *Democracy and Difference*, ed. Seyla Benhabib, 120–36. Princeton, NJ: Princeton University Press, 1996.

Index

Lightning Source UK Ltd.
Milton Keynes UK
UKOW04f0032250414

230554UK00002B/2/P